Engines of Change

Engines of Change

Party Factions in American Politics, 1868–2010

DANIEL DISALVO

OXFORD
UNIVERSITY PRESS

OXFORD
UNIVERSITY PRESS

Oxford University Press, Inc., publishes works that further
Oxford University's objective of excellence
in research, scholarship, and education.

Oxford   New York
Auckland   Cape Town   Dar es Salaam   Hong Kong   Karachi
Kuala Lumpur   Madrid   Melbourne   Mexico City   Nairobi
New Delhi   Shanghai   Taipei   Toronto

With offices in
Argentina   Austria   Brazil   Chile   Czech Republic   France   Greece
Guatemala   Hungary   Italy   Japan   Poland   Portugal   Singapore
South Korea   Switzerland   Thailand   Turkey   Ukraine   Vietnam

Published by Oxford University Press, Inc.
198 Madison Avenue, New York, New York 10016

www.oup.com

Oxford is a registered trademark of Oxford University Press

Library of Congress Cataloging-in-Publication Data
DiSalvo, Daniel.
Engines of change : party factions in American politics, 1868–2010 / Daniel DiSalvo.
    p.   cm.—(Oxford studies in postwar American political development)
Includes bibliographical references and index.
ISBN 978-0-19-989170-2 (acid-free paper)
1. Political parties—United States—History. I. Title.
JK2261.D57   2012
324.27309′04—dc23   2011036775

9 8 7 6 5 4 3 2 1

Printed in the United States of America
on acid-free paper

To my parents, with love and appreciation

TABLE OF CONTENTS

ACKNOWLEDGMENTS

Without much support from many quarters this book would never have been written. Its origins lie in my doctoral dissertation at the University of Virginia. My biggest intellectual and personal debt is to my adviser James W. Ceaser. He combines one of the sharpest minds in the academy with one of the most affable personalities. His deep knowledge of American political thought and history greatly influenced me, as will be evident to readers familiar with his work. At the same time, his wit, keen intelligence, and personal generosity sustained me over the course of writing my dissertation and then revising it into this book.

I'm also very grateful to Eric Patashnik, my other dissertation supervisor, for all the guidance he provided on this project. Eric contributed greatly to improving the analytic rigor of what remains a vast and sprawling undertaking. In addition, he helped me see how my view of factions fits within and speaks to the existing scholarship on political parties.

I'd also like to express my thanks to other people who read the manuscript, or parts of it, at various stages in its long gestation period, including Sidney Milkis and Brian Balogh (who both graciously served on my dissertation committee), Paula Baker, Don Critchlow, David Mayhew, Dan Galvin, Byron Shafer, Steve Thomas, Marty Levin, Robert Saldin, Patrick Roberts, Josh Dunn, and Vince Boudreau. Their comments and counsel benefited me a great deal.

My editors at Oxford, David McBride and Steven Teles, did a fine job in shepherding my manuscript. I appreciate their finding two thoughtful and demanding reviewers, whose comments forced me to greatly improve my text. The Mellon Foundation and the Committee on the American Founding at Amherst College provided me with a post-doc that afforded me the time to covert a dissertation filled with graduate student prose into a publishable manuscript. Any errors that remain in the text are solely my responsibility.

Finally, I'd like to thank my parents, to whom this book is dedicated, for their unconditional love and support.

PREFACE

Factions and Parties in America

The 1950s were a turbulent time for the Democratic Party. On the heels of World War II, the party found itself deeply divided. Northerners were locked in fierce combat with Southerners for control of the party. Hailing from the urban and industrial areas of the Northeast and Great Lakes littoral, a network of Democrats emerged with the belief that the party needed to move left if it wanted to regain the White House, solidify its congressional majorities, and promote the public interest. Working through the Americans for Democratic Action, AFL-CIO, and civil rights organizations, this coalition reformulated liberalism. Theologian Reinhold Niebuhr, historian Arthur Schlesinger, Jr., United Auto Workers President Walter Reuther, and Senator Hubert Humphrey, drew its ideological contours. It sought to use the national government to increase the standard of living for working-class Americans, combat segregation, and undermine the institutional advantages of their Southern rivals.

This Liberal-Labor alliance sought to make their agenda the Democratic Party's agenda. By injecting itself into congressional politics and the Democratic Party's presidential selection process, it prepared the ground for major federal legislation. It managed to restructure national political institutions, in particular the House Rules Committee, to promote civil rights for African-Americans, medical insurance for the elderly, and federal aid for elementary and secondary schools. To a substantial extent, this alliance was responsible for the party's ideological flavor and programmatic commitments from 1958 to 1968. Born in crisis and tainted by segregation, the alliance transformed the public image of the national Democratic Party to one centered on a commitment to programmatic reform.[1]

All this is familiar history. Yet, it raises an important issue: To properly understand American political parties one must look beneath their labels. Beneath those labels are *factions* that have goals, incentives, and resources that conflict with the larger party in which they reside. These factions are loosely organized networks made up of members of Congress, party activists, pressure groups, policy entrepreneurs, and intellectuals. Factions are engines of political change that develop new ideas, refine them into workable policies, and promote them in government. Because America's big-tent parties are cumbersome instruments, the study of factions helps account for changes in public policy, modes of electoral mobilization, and the parties' ideological positions. Factions are a fruitful way to see how different elements within a party—elements too often studied in isolation—interact and mobilize. My development of the concept of faction is a way of bringing some order to the contentious conflicts that arise within large, diffuse parties.

The argument advanced in this book is that the concept of faction is a useful one with which to undertake a more systematic treatment of what occurs within American parties. The study of factions illuminates how parties shape national institutions. Rather than look at party change as the result of larger forces at work in the polity, factions reveal how parties themselves can be agents of change. A central claim is that factions are often more important than the parties as wholes in setting the government's agenda and determining outcomes in a variety of institutional venues. As we shall see, this claim differs significantly from the arguments made by the great scholars of political parties of the last century.

For political scientists the political party has served as the Holy Grail. According to one scholar, parties are "the indispensable instrument that [bring] cohesion and unity, and hence effectiveness, to the government as a whole by linking the executive and legislative branches in a bond of common interest."[2] Woodrow Wilson believed: "You cannot compound a successful government out of antagonisms."[3] Without unified party control of government "deadlock" and "stalemate" would result. Only vigorous political parties could render America's fragmented governmental system coherent.

Over the past century, political scientists have looked to political parties as instruments for coordinating and directing American government only to come up, for the most part, empty-handed. Unlike parties elsewhere, decentralization, vague ideological appeals, permeability, undisciplined legislative groups, and variable local organization characterized America's parties. Reformers sought to make America's parties more "responsible," which meant making them more national, programmatic, and cohesive. Such parties would, they held, facilitate policy making by reducing the constitutional separation between the executive and legislative branches.[4] Many hoped American parties would more closely resemble their British counterparts.[5] Except on rare occasions, however, the parties-as-wholes did not seem to be the agents of cohesion in American politics. By the 1980s, party scholarship stressed the decline of parties. For alternatives, analysts in the 1990s turned to interest groups, social movements, policy entrepreneurs, or individual legislators as the central actors in the political system.[6]

Yet, factions—which exist somewhere between the unitary ideal of a "responsible" party and the diversity of smaller units—have been largely ignored. Indeed, they have many of the properties usually ascribed to parties and perform many of the same functions, albeit in a slightly different way. *Engines of Change* identifies and examines these factions in the United States from the 1870s to the present. This book is at once a synthesis, drawing on a large number of scholarly works in political science and history, and an original piece of research. The central argument is that factions often tie together smaller party subunits and infuse America's large, diffuse parties with purpose. To paraphrase Lord Bryce, life is to an organism what factions are to parties.[7] Unlike many other works on parties, which explore a single area—such as parties in Congress or election campaigns—this study makes its case by examining party factions in a variety of settings, including Congress, presidential nominations, electoral bases, and presidential-congressional relations.

American political parties have been said to resist the modernizing trends of rationalization and bureaucratization.[8] Yet factions reveal the parties to be more vibrant and less diffuse than they are often depicted. If parties occasionally lack purpose, factions often provide one. They are instruments that coordinate party activists, elected officials, interest groups, and intellectuals in efforts to rationalize the public agenda and the policy process. They put new ideas on the table and take concerted action to promote their adoption. It is often the case that when commentators speak of one of the parties taking action, what they really mean is that a faction has done so.

The conception of parties as driven by factions differs substantially from the dominant theories of American political parties (discussed in Chapter 2). In the work of V.O. Key, E.E. Schattschneider, and Anthony Downs, parties are envisaged as competing leadership teams.[9] Competition between at least two such teams sustains democracy by offering citizens a choice between them. Interparty competition is decisive. The parties adjust, adapt, and adopt new techniques in their efforts to win votes. As Schattschneider once put it: "Democracy is not to be found *in* the parties but *between* the parties."[10] The premise here, on the other hand, is that a systematic treatment of what happens *within* American parties shows us something important about them and about how they impact other institutions of government. Rather than the benefits of parties deriving solely from interparty competition, I argue that many of those benefits derive from intraparty competition among factions or between a faction and the rest of the party. Attention to factions illuminates the internal challenges parties face in seeking to win elections.

John Aldrich, a leading scholar of American parties, has defined them as "the creature of the politicians, the ambitious office seeker and officeholder."[11] He places politicians at the center of American parties. Partly in response to Aldrich, Marty Cohen, Hans Noel, David Karol, and John Zaller have written the most recent theoretical statement on parties in their book *The Party Decides*.[12] They argue that parties should be defined as "coalitions of intense policy demanders" rather than competing teams of ambitious of office seekers. While their book makes a strong case for this new definition of parties—one with many resonances to the conception of parties as driven by factions—it sets up a misleading choice about whether politicians or groups are at the center of the party. Indeed, Aldrich himself carved out an important role for activists within the party.

The study of factions shows that this choice is secondary to tracing how the relationship between them operates in actual politics. Furthermore, Cohen and his colleagues don't fully draw out the implications of their new definition regarding how the parties affect change in American politics.[13] In contrast, this study offers a theoretical definition of intraparty factions and traces the affects of twelve factions on the course of American political development.

Examining factions highlights, once again, the permeability and capaciousness of American political parties. The United States is one of the largest and most diverse countries in the world. Therefore, every faction must bring groups into political alliance. While harmony of interest holds together any faction, it is often necessary to apply the glue of bargains and patronage promises as well. Factions' activity shows the importance of bringing in ideologues, fund-raisers, think tanks, and interest groups to properly understand American political parties. The faction perspective also emphasizes the importance of policy preferences within the parties. It is because factions are motivated by a set of ideological convictions that they are engines of change. As we shall see, altering the definition of parties—by looking at them through the lens of faction—has significant implications for how they are evaluated.

The claim that factions drive change is particularly relevant today when the idea of party realignments, once a dominant mode of conceptualizing political change, is highly contested in political science. The classic definition of a realignment is a major electoral shift in the relative strength of the political parties that endures for roughly thirty years, accompanied by an alteration in the political ideas setting the government's agenda, followed by major changes in public policy. Some scholars argue that the idea of party realignments should be retired altogether. David Mayhew found the theory wanting in almost every respect. He invites analysts of American politics to turn their sights to other sources of change. Others hold that stripped of some assumptions, the concept remains helpful.[14]

Taking Mayhew's suggestion, this book documents how factions structure political linkages to shape the development of political conflict and public policy. Consonant with much scholarship in the field of American political development, I stress how political elites are goal-oriented. Based on that assumption, I then analyze how their goals are shaped, modified, and frustrated by historical context. The theoretical perspective that unites the treatment of a number of institutional milieus is the emphasis on the interaction between interests—the items that factions pursue through the means at their disposal—and institutions—the organizations in which authoritative decisions are made. Institutional arrangements shape the way factions pursue their interests, and factions' pursuit of their interests can conversely shape institutions in unforeseen ways. It is a reciprocal and dynamic process that occurs in political time. By linking interests and institutions, factions help explain the distinctiveness of American democratic politics.

I do not attempt to offer a parsimonious theory of political change, since such a theory is likely to remain elusive. The factors driving political change are multiple, complex, and often hinge on "accident and force" rather than "reflection and choice" as Publius put it in *The Federalist*. My aim is rather to offer a set of mid-range theories between abstract theories (which can lead to reductionism) and empirical studies (which can undermine any efforts to generalize). For the most part, the theories and patterns I discover emerge inductively from the historical analysis rather than deductively from an a priori model.

To make my case, I trace the actions of twelve factions, producing descriptive inferences about factions' political actions in different institutional arenas in order to achieve their goals.[15] I try to capitalize on the broad scope—in terms of time and place—that this study covers. While this approach may miss things explored in greater detail by experts in a given area, there is virtue in today's specialized academy to taking a step back to look for broader patterns of political development. By treating groupings not hitherto conceptualized as factions, I develop a synthetic arrangement of the agents clamoring to transform the parties and make their mark on American democracy. Contrary to Wilson and a battalion of political scientists since his time, this book shows that American government has managed reasonably well with antagonisms channeled by party factions.

Engines of Change

CHAPTER 1

Four Questions About American Party Factions

In order to properly take the measure of factions in American politics, we must address four questions: What is a faction? What do factions do? Who are the factions in America? What are the causes of factions? With answers to these questions in hand, we can better distinguish factions from other groupings within the parties and analyze the strategies, behavior, and effects of factions. This book offers an historical treatment of the roles factions have played in shaping party ideologies, presidential nominations, the distribution of power in Congress, presidential governance, and the development of the American state. The results, I hope, shed some light on many of the central puzzles that have occupied students of American political parties and national institutions.

What Are Factions?

One goal of this study is to define and identify factions more rigorously, in order to allow for comparison and generalization. The job of conceptual clarification is especially important in this instance because the term *faction* has so many connotations that lead the analyst astray. Well-defined concepts, consistently used, are the foundations of political science.[1] Without them every researcher would, like Sisyphus, have to begin each inquiry anew. Political science needs such general categories to highlight important items in different times and places. Only in this way can the analyst avoid getting lost in the trees before finding the forest. Alexis de Tocqueville aptly characterized the trade-off inherent in conceptual development as follows:

> General ideas do not attest to the strength of human intelligence, but rather to its insufficiency, because there are no beings in nature exactly alike: no identical facts, no rules indiscriminately applicable in the same

manner to several objects at once. General ideas are admirable in that they permit the human mind to bring rapid judgments to a great number of objects at one time; but on the other hand, they never provide it with anything but incomplete notions, and they make it lose in exactness what they give it in extent.[2]

Therefore, the approach to factions taken here starts from historical particulars and builds to provisional generalizations, following Max Weber's dictum that "the final and definitive concept cannot stand at the beginning of an investigation, but must come at the end."[3] Even if there is some dissent from the conceptualization of faction advanced here, we will at least have an explicit definition from which to take our bearings and a definite set of cases to investigate and study. Those constitute significant advances.

The existing literature on American intraparty factions at the national level is small and largely unsystematic. Historians, on whom this work draws widely, regularly refer to factions in their narrative accounts of different periods. But they use the term colloquially. Most work by political scientists treats state rather than the national parties.[4] Unlike many analysts of European parties who take an interest in competition *within* parties, students of American parties have been more interested in competition *between* parties.[5] John Gerring has even written that "factionalism does *not* appear to be a salient characteristic of the American party system."[6] Therefore, we know much less than we should about factional activity over the course of American political development.

If factions are vital, why have scholars largely overlooked them? First, many analysts focus on studying institutions with clear and distinct rules, norms, and processes of organizations. This has led to neglect of the more diffuse networks that comprise factions—where the rules, norms, and processes are harder to distinguish. Second, many scholars have been wedded to a definition of parties that puts elected officials at the center of their conception of parties. Until recently, there was a tendency to dismiss actors outside the formal party structures as not really part of the parties at all. Third, factions have not received extensive treatment because of the negative qualities associated with them. According to David Hume, "factions subvert government, render laws impotent, and beget the fiercest animosities among men of the same nation."[7] The *Federalist* famously called for institutions with teeth in them to "break and control the violence of faction."[8] Factions are often said to wreak havoc in states where parties have not yet developed or to be destructive forces where stable parties exist.[9] The view that they inspire fear and loathing and are things to be avoided or overcome has endured.[10]

In spite of the conceptual baggage, *faction* is the best term to indicate the phenomenon of interest here. Other analysts have employed different words to designate party subunits, such as "cliques," "blocs," "movements," "wings," "currents," or "tendencies." But all of these terms slightly miss the target. Clique and bloc suggest small tightly bound groups that are short-lived. Movement, wing, current, and tendency, imply broad, highly diffuse entities of uncertain temporal duration.[11] As we shall see, factions can also be distinguished from the galaxy of caucuses, coalitions, pressure groups, clubs, and alliances that may exist inside American parties.

The conception of faction employed here holds any negative connotations in abeyance. Factions exist inside established parties, where, whether motivated by ideology or interest, their dangerous character is tempered. As we shall see, they can even produce some positive results. A faction, as defined here, is a party subunit that has (1) the ideological consistency, (2) the organizational capacity, and (3) the temporal durability to (4) undertake significant actions to shift a party's agenda priorities and reputation along the Left-Right spectrum. Factions exist when some party members share a common identity, are conscious of differences that separate them from other party members, and cooperate on a range of issues. Factions acquire names, create organizations, and articulate positions that are different from the mainstream of their party.[12] The battle between factions and the larger party might be characterized as the struggle for the "soul" of the party.

American party factions vary in type and character on each of the four elements that define them. Some factions are motivated more by their purposes. For these factions, the ideological aspect is front and center. Other factions lack such ideological consistency but are better organized. For them, the material resources secured by factional organization are the sustaining element. While there can be significant variation in the mode of factional organization, factions blur the lines between pressure groups, policy entrepreneurs, and social movements. They are agents of political linkage. Focus on the formal party institutions or interest groups overlooks partisan networks that draw on resources from a variety of auxiliary associations. Factional analysis reveals the cross-pollination of formal partisan organizations and informal networks, as adherents frequently serve in both interest groups and official party capacities. Consequently, factions are not ephemera that exist for an election cycle but rather are entities that endure for a while.

Factions exist inside larger parties. A party is best described in a two-fold sense: as a team and as an institution. Analyzing parties at any one time requires keeping both parts in mind. As Anthony Downs has written, a party is a "team seeking to control the governing apparatus by gaining office in a duly constituted election."[13] John Aldrich writes: "Political parties can be seen as coalitions of elites to capture and use political office. . . . [Yet] a political party is . . . [also] an institutionalized coalition, one that has adopted rules, norms, and procedures."[14] The players on these teams include officeholders, staffers, titular leaders, party

officials, pollsters, consultants, and volunteers. Parties seek electoral authorization to run governing institutions. Those involved in elections will present programs in their effort to win office. Once elected, legislators draw on allies to fulfill
promises made on the stump. Not only do all these activities require teamwork,
they also require institutions. Parties have consequently crafted organizations
with rules and regulations, such as nominating conventions, national and state
party committees, and congressional caucuses.

Yet, the strength of the party institution, its center of gravity, and rules of
operation are sufficiently plastic to have changed substantially over time.
James A. Schlesinger has written that, for American parties, "the formal structure is obviously not the real organization."[15] In addition to the formal apparatus, then, the institutional component also consists of a larger informal
network that varies in character according to the historical period. This network is usually comprised of individuals drawn from interest groups, labor
unions, private associations, the press corps, and think tanks. These outside
groups have not always been considered part of the party. They should be.
While there is often a great deal of overlap, it is nonetheless the case that at
certain points the energy of the party is found more within the informal network than within the formal institutions of the party. This is why John Aldrich,
a leading scholar of political parties, oscillates between treating the party as
run by and for politicians and something driven by broader "coalitions."

Since parties are not simply aggregations of voter preferences or demographic groups, they are occasionally driven by "parties within parties" or factions. Defining parties simply as teams downplays the idea that they have their
own policy preferences. Parties, in that view, make promises on the campaign
trail and then once in office seek to enact whatever policies increase their
chances of winning future elections. But more is really at stake in electoral
victory than winning itself because factions can inject parties with policy preferences independent of electoral considerations. It is these ideas that often go
on to have the biggest effects on American political development.

Ultimately, factions are players on the party team; although, when they
emerge, they are not part of the starting line-up. Their aim is to become the
starting line-up, or at least to call the plays. In the most critical cases, they seek
to spark a clubhouse revolt, fire the coach, and take over the franchise. As one
group of scholars recently put it, "The various factions that make up a political
party are active in politics precisely because they have intense preferences on
certain issues, and it is a notable feature of a strong party that party factions are
well-positioned to defend their preferences."[16] Therefore, when a sufficient
number of party elites form a faction, their goal is to change (or prevent the
change) of the values, norms, ideas, expectations, and rules of the political
game. In this sense, factions seek to pour new wine into old bottles.

What Do Factions Do?

At key moments in American history, factions try to move their party along the Left-Right political spectrum—toward or away from the political center. For some, this means pulling their party further to the left, for others to the right. The aim is to change the party's reputation. How factions impel this movement depends on the type of faction, the resources at its disposal, and where it exerts itself in the political system. As we shall see, factions operate in different institutional venues to accomplish this goal. Rather than being institutions that are reactive to exogenous forces—which is the usual implication of American parties—parties driven by factions are powerful agents of change that can redraw the lines of political contestation.

Consequently, intraparty conflict generated by factions has major implications for interparty competition because factional activity has consequences for the opportunities, incentives, and constraints of the other party. The changes effected by factions cause the opposing party to react. How the American two-party system operates thus depends on the existence and power of factions, which complicates the classic center-seeking model of two-party competition. The temperature of party competition cannot, therefore, be taken by only looking at what happens between the two parties. One must also account for what happens within them.

Attention to factions challenges the classic model of two-party competition. In that model, the two parties compete in elections to capture the median voter. As center-seeking entities, the parties tend to resemble each other. The competition between them supposedly produces moderate policies because politicians are responsive to median preferences.[17] However, the center-seeking view of parties rests on the assumption that the electorate is well informed about candidates and public policy. The last half century of political science research suggests that that assumption is highly questionable.[18] Larry Bartels has written, "The political ignorance of the American voter is one of the best documented features of contemporary politics."[19] Therefore, even if "voters are not fools" and function as the "rational god of vengeance and reward," as V.O. Key colorfully put it, the fact that they aren't paying much attention relaxes the two party-system's center-seeking incentives.[20] "Whatever elections may be doing," Bartels concludes a recent study, "they are *not* forcing elected officials to cater to the policy preferences of the 'median voter.'"[21] Consequently, a number of political scientists have found that the Democratic and Republican parties regularly nominate candidates to the left or right of the ideological center.[22]

Given the public's limited political knowledge, factions retain a good deal of room to maneuver in order to shape their party's brand and convert their views into public policy, even if factions' views are well to the left or right of centrist voters.[23] Parties thus walk a tight rope. Factions often determine how they balance the electoral cost of moving farther from the center with the boost in enthusiasm they get from appealing to their principal supporters. The calculation for factions and parties is whether the costs for moving too far to the right or left will be offset by soliciting greater resources from core constituencies.[24] Even when factions seek to move their party closer to the political center—doing the same thing as the center-seeking parties—the cause of the shift is not responsiveness to voters but factions.

Therefore, factions complicate the Downsian picture in ways that are not fully captured by other analysts because of how factions condition the behavior of partisan actors with their unique sets of norms, rules, and customs. Factions shape behavior, in part, due to their members' desire for recognition: the acknowledgement of their status and worth. That demand in turn requires us to treat ideas as sources of why different factions behave as they do. Shared ideas are essential for the collective action that facilitates or impedes parties seeking or fleeing the political center.

In sum, factions exploit voters' attention deficit disorder in order to move their party closer to their preferences. The purpose of examining 140 years of party history in the following pages is to show that the parties have been vehicles through which factions attempt to shape the party's overall reputation and change government policies in ways they desire. In the broadest terms, then, the claim that factions drive parties is also a claim about how American democracy functions.

However, exploiting public ignorance to push policies in line with a faction's preferences is not always an option. Indeed, such initiatives are only likely to be adopted in circumstances where the public does not have strong preferences or their preferences are contradictory. When the public has widely held and clear positions, party leaders are more likely to adopt policies close to those positions. Yet, even in those instances, factions may try to exploit the obscure features of policy design. For example, the public can have a meaningful debate and express a preference for whether the government should provide health care for all citizens or whether it should expand immigration. However, once a decision has been made at this level, *how* the government tries to do these things quickly becomes so detailed that the public is no longer able to participate effectively. The technical complexity of real policy extends far beyond the average citizen's political knowledge.[25] In such instances, policy initiatives can be framed such that the broad thrust appeals to median voters, while factions that pay closer attention can shape specific parts of the policy. Put differently, the median voter on any given policy is different from the median voter in the general electorate. Factions are attentive to playing off those differences and try to position the party accordingly.

Related to the Left-Right internal dynamics of the parties, factions have also been the vehicles for insurgent challenges to the establishment. Since the Civil War, American politics has been divided by efforts to harmonize a strong national state with traditional notions of individualism and democracy.[26] The result has been persistent conflicts over the extent and desirability of concentrated power and centralized authority. One could argue that the central question dividing the parties for much of the last 150 years has been the proper size and role of the state in the economy and society. Some factions have attacked power in big business, centralized government, and the cultural and professional elite. Others have sought to defend traditional conceptions of individual freedom and self-reliance against the rise of the corporation and the state. And still other factions have sought to empower the modern state against what they viewed as a romantic Jeffersonianism.[27]

How have factions tried to move the parties along the Left-Right political spectrum and recalibrate the balance between the establishment and the people? Factions seek to make their mark on the party and the polity by pressing their case in the areas where parties' programs, reputations, and images are forged. National institutions are implicated in factional conflict because they are the sites where politicians try to embed certain ideas and images in the public mind. Presidential politics and the Congress are the two central arenas where factions try to secure symbolic and substantive outcomes that will define the party's reputation. It is policymakers' public actions that create the "causal chains" that define the party and that can be used against legislators in future campaigns.[28] Some factions direct most or all of their efforts to redefine the party into presidential politics, others work primarily in Congress, while still others operate in both areas.

There are five roles factions have played in American politics, which are the subjects of the chapters that follow. First, they have been conveyor belts of ideas. They inject new ideas into the party and refashion old ones to fit their preferences. By linking politicians to outside groups, such as think tanks, factions help shape a party's public philosophy. The parties may stand for a few broad things, but factions are the devils in the details. The effort to modify or defend the programmatic character of the party means that factions must develop an alternative public philosophy or ideology.[29] A faction will espouse a different ideological recipe, challenging the dominant view or potential rivals within the party. Chapter 3 details the ideological views of each of the factions included in this study.

Second, factions are key actors in the quadrennial drama of presidential nominations. Chapter 4 documents how they have sought to block rival candidates, promote their own, and catalyze changes in candidate selection procedures. During the nomination struggle, factions provide affiliated candidates with organizational resources, including campaign operatives, financial contributors, media outlets, and policy analysts. At times, candidates' connections (or opposition) to existing factions help distinguish them among the attentive publics from which are drawn delegates to the national conventions and voters in primary elections. Positioning vis-à-vis factions can help a candidate find the lane he or she intends to run in.

Third, factions shift the distribution of power in Congress, even sometimes going so far as to change the institution's rules. Sometimes factions centralize power; other times they decentralize it. Most often this happens informally under the existing procedural rules, which a faction is positioned to take advantage of. Occasionally, however, factions resort to the formal alteration of procedure to defeat their rivals and advance their agenda. In either scenario, factions are instrumental in determining the power of the party leadership, committees, subcommittees, and outside groups in the legislative process. They thus powerfully shape the sort of public policies that make it onto the congressional agenda and are enacted into law. This is the subject of Chapter 6.

Fourth, factions shape presidents' governing strategies. Although presidents and some members of Congress run for office under the same party label, that doesn't mean that they see eye to eye. Electoral debts to or distance from a faction are a central part of the political landscape presidents confront. Factions affiliated with a president can help him promote his agenda in the media, on Capitol Hill, and at the grassroots level. Yet they can also become a burr in the president's side, especially if the faction deems him insufficiently committed to its cause. In contrast, factions opposed to a president from their party can mobilize opposition to him and frustrate his goals. They can use parliamentary procedure and media exposure to raise the costs of action, forcing a president to spend valuable political capital. Attuned to these realities, a central presidential task is the management of factions. Chapter 7 analyzes how factions are often key pieces in a president's political puzzle.

Fifth, factions have shaped the development of the American state. They have been at the center of disputes over its size, shape, and character. Those disputes and their consequences are the subject of Chapter 8. Despite constitutional barriers to the creation of a large national state, America has done it. This process of state building is one in which new governing institutions are created, existing institutions are expanded or strengthened, or the relationship between government and society is altered. Some factions have sought to recalibrate the distribution of power between the political parties and the bureaucracy. Others have sought to keep power lodged in institutions such as the political parties, the federal courts, and congressional committees. The trajectory of state building since the Civil War, therefore, has been as much the result of factional struggles within the major parties as the result of conflict between the two parties.

On the basis of their activity, factions can be roughly divided into two types: those that seek preservation and those that seek change. Change factions, typically driven by ideology, often begin outside of government and work their way in. These factions have three strategic options: attempt to take over the party, decide to cooperate with it, or splinter into a third party. Status quo factions are usually insiders that tend to differentiate themselves on pragmatic or strategic grounds. These factions are forced to choose among four tactics: act as a veto power, cooperate, align with the opposition party, or take public stands to raise the costs of action. As a general rule, status quo factions tend toward the congressional strategy. Change factions are inclined to try to redefine the party from the top down, beginning with the presidency. Whether factions are promoters of change or defenders of the status quo, when they battle over agenda priorities, they are contesting the meaning of party membership.[30] They are either defenders of the old faith or harbingers of a new creed.

Who Are the American Factions?

According to the definition above, there have been at least twelve national intraparty factions from end of the Civil War to the present. The study begins in 1868 because that is when the two-party system dominated by Republicans and Democrats fully took hold. Since no "dataset" on American factions exists, something approximating one had to be created. To identify these factions, I created a checklist of faction properties (Appendix) and then used it like a colander to sift through American political history. By checking off the different qualities on the list, a party subunit eventually met the criteria of ideological distinctiveness, temporal durability, and organizational capacity that define a faction. Thus, what remained in the colander, so to speak, were the factions included in the study (Table 1.1). Some groupings within the parties that have been colloquially referred to as factions—such as the Gold Bug Democrats or the Henry Wallace Progressives—were excluded from the study because they did not meet certain thresholds and are better described as other kinds of entities that can exist within parties, such as cliques, blocs, movements, wings, currents, or tendencies. My method brought the qualities that factions share across time into focus, while being attentive to historical differences. When possible, I retained the names faction members used or were called by others at the time. Only when there were a number of competing names or the faction did not explicitly adopt one did I intervene to select or modify the label for the sake of clarity.

The list of twelve factions that emerged from my historical canvass indicates that factions have been a fairly constant phenomenon in American politics.

Table 1.1 **List of Intraparty Factions***

1.	Stalwart Republicans (1868–1888)
2.	Liberal/Mugwump Republicans (1868–1888)
3.	Half-Breed Republicans (1872–1888)
4.	Old Guard—Conservative Republicans (1896–1916)
5.	Progressives Republicans (1904–1928)
6.	Populist Democrats (1896–1924)
7.	Southern Democrats (1938–1976)
8.	Liberal Republicans (1938–1968)
9.	Liberal-Labor Democrats (1958–1976)
10.	New Politics Democrats (1966–1980)
11.	New Right Republicans (1964–1996)
12.	New Democrats (1986–2007)

*The years when these factions are said to "end" are obviously not hard and fast. Rather, they are approximations, meant to indicate when the faction lost much of its power.

At least one faction has been present within one of the two major parties between 1870–1920 and 1936–2005. Only during the 1920s was there an absence of coherent factions within either party. The factions are also reasonably evenly distributed within the parties—seven in the Republican Party and five in the Democratic Party. Generally speaking, as Samuel Lubell once contended, factions were more likely to emerge within a period's dominant party.[31] The GOP was the dominant party of the Gilded Age (with three factions to none for the Democrats) and Democrats the dominant party after the New Deal (with three factions to one for the Republicans). Yet, the list also shows that factions—and some of the most consequential among them—can and do emerge from within the minority party.

The change factions that worked almost exclusively in presidential politics are the Liberal Republicans (later called Mugwumps) of the Gilded Age, Populist Democrats of the Progressive Era, and the New Democrats of the late twentieth century. Consistent with the behavior of change factions, the latter three all sought to take over their respective parties, while the Liberals employed a splinter strategy to move the GOP closer to their preferences.

- Liberal Republicans—at various times also called "Independents," "Reformers," and "Mugwumps"—sought to make the GOP stand for free markets, efficient government, and rule by a well-bred Northeastern Protestant elite. They emerged in the late 1860s to oppose the Grant Administration and the continuation of the military occupation of the South. In 1872, they broke party ranks to nominate Horace Greeley for president. Four years later, they backed Rutherford B. Hayes, the eventual GOP nominee. In 1884, they endorsed and voted for Democrat Grover Cleveland. They played a balance of power politics to recast the GOP. The reason for this was largely a function of size and geography. Compared to other factions, the Liberal faction was small and geographically concentrated. Unable to take over the party without a larger social and electoral base, they sought to use their numbers in swing states to force Republican presidential aspirants to pay them heed.[32]

- Led by the towering figure of William Jennings Bryan, Populist Democrats filled the Democratic Party's programmatic void in the first two decades of the twentieth century. As Elizabeth Sanders has written, "the post-1896 Democratic party was an overwhelmingly agrarian vehicle that carried the legacy of populism." Hailing from the agricultural Midwest and the South and voicing a distinct response to industrialization, they wrested the party from the hands of Northern hard-money men and Southern states-rights conservatives. Populists sought to increase the power of the federal government to check corporate excesses and readjust sectional imbalances. Their means to this end was to expand "the statutory state," rather than grant administrative agencies discretionary powers. Populists repeatedly forced conservative Democrats to assent to their solutions in areas such as railroad regulation, banking, and antitrust. They made their agenda the party agenda by securing the presidential nomination for Bryan three times and making themselves indispensable to the passage of President Wilson's New Freedom.[33]

- After Walter Mondale's presidential defeat in 1984, New Democrats emerged within the Democratic Party. Initially, they were largely from the suburban South and West rather than the urban Northeast or Midwest. It was the Democratic Party's failure to win presidential elections that sparked the faction's formation. Between 1968 and 1984 Democrats lost four of five presidential elections—two by huge margins. Carter's lonely victory in 1976 was viewed as the result of exceptional circumstances created by Watergate. New Democrats argued that only a move to the political center could revive the party's prospects, which had been badly damaged by the takeover of the party by left-wing activists and interest groups. As one of the faction's founders, Senator Sam Nunn (D-GA) put it: "The perception is that the party has moved away from mainstream America." They held that only a novel and "centrist" policy agenda could recapture the White House and set the party on a solid foundation for the future. Bill Clinton ran successfully as a New Democrat but failed to govern consistently on their agenda. New Democrats failed to take over the Democratic Party.[34]

The "Old Guard" Republicans and the Southern Democrats are America's two twentieth-century status quo factions. Both operated primarily in congressional politics. Both informally shifted the balance of power within the legislature. And both succeeded by oscillating between cooperating and blocking their rivals.

- The "Old Guard" held sway within the Republican Party at the dawn of the twentieth century. Led by Nelson Aldrich (R-RI) and the other members of the "Senate Four"—William Allison (R-IA), Orville Platt (R-CT), and John Spooner (R-WI)—the faction was comprised primarily of legislators from the Northeast and their allies in big business. According to one description, "The average Old Guard leader . . . was an urban, upper-middle-class, college educated, native-born, Protestant who came from economically and socially well-established Anglo-Saxon stock. He was either a businessman, a newspaperman, or a politician, who at fifty-four was a lifelong Republican with many years of political experience."[35] They effectively vetoed Theodore Roosevelt's progressive policies, especially during his last two years in office. By aligning themselves with President William H. Taft, they aimed to encourage economic development and use their power in Congress to block inflationary policy measures. Old Guard conservatives firmly committed the GOP to the protective tariff and internal improvements.[36]
- The New Deal awakened the Calhounite fear of a powerful federal government bent on transforming Dixie, which turned Southern support into opposition. In 1938, Southern Democrats began to cooperate with conservative congressional Republicans. Their intention was to use their dominant position inside the Democratic congressional majority to defend "states rights" and the "southern way of life."[37] In practice, this meant protecting segregation, preventing labor union penetration, and promoting state-aided economic growth in the region. They employed all three status quo faction strategies: vetoing measures with which they disagreed, forging an alliance with Republicans, and cooperating with Northern Democrats to achieve their goals. Democratic presidents from Franklin Roosevelt to Lyndon Johnson would be forced to adjust their policies, strategies, and rhetoric to deal with the Southern faction.[38]

There is only one status quo faction that operated in both presidential and congressional politics: the Stalwart Republicans.

- Stalwarts Republicans defended state-aided economic development, the imperatives of party organization and regularity, and concern for the fate of African-Americans in the South. They were machine politicians, strongest in the industrial states and the South, who coalesced in the 1870s to defend the patronage system that developed during Reconstruction. They sought to control Republican presidential nominations from 1868 to 1888, direct presidents' patronage policies, and exercise power in Congress by developing a more disciplined party network.[39]

There are four change factions that took their case into both arenas of the nation's national electoral politics: Progressive Republicans, Liberal-Labor Democrats, New Politics Democrats, and New Right Republicans. With varying degrees of success, all of them aimed to take over their respective party.

- Progressive Republicans emerged from the Midwest and West to challenge Old Guard dominance in the early twentieth century. The most powerful strain of Progressivism on the national stage was not the Northeastern, urban, and nationalistic one, but rather the rural and egalitarian Midwestern "fear of bigness, of concentration and control." Most of the major figures in the Progressive faction arrived in Congress in 1906. Almost all of them hailed from agricultural states. Most were lawyers who attended public universities in their home states. Many had won their seats by running against their states' regular Republican organization. These Progressives sought to bring more policy areas under the thumb of administrative experts. Hostile to the "state of courts and parties" they aimed to weaken state parties and the corrupt legislatures they dominated. Applying their expertise, administrators would circumscribe the issues that required politicians' attention. Their policy aims were to reduce tariffs, provide more extensive railroad regulation, and break up the trusts.[40]
- Liberal-Labor Democrats reached their apogee during the late 1950s and early 1960s. A predominant element in this faction was labor movement elites, especially the American Federation of Labor (AFL), Congress of Industrial Organizations (CIO), and the United Auto Workers (UAW), union lobbyists, and the Committee on Political Education's (COPE) political operatives. They combined with the leadership of powerful liberal associations to form a truly effective national intraparty faction. Often called the "liberal lobby," some of the most prominent organizations in this formation were the National Association for the Advancement of Colored People (NAACP), American Civil Liberties Union (ACLU), and the Americans for Democratic Action (ADA). Labor and the liberal associations wove together an interlocking directorate of affiliated members of Congress (and their staffs), especially members of the Democratic Study Group in the House and a bloc of roughly twenty Senators. The faction's party takeover strategy emerged in the development of a thorough policy agenda in Congress that presidents Kennedy and Johnson would later adopt.[41]

- In the late 1960s, New Politics Democrats brought a host of new ideas, issues, lifestyles, and tastes to national attention. They arose out of the middle-class suburbs, were formed on university campuses, and cut their teeth in opposition to the Vietnam War. New Politics Democrats were highly skeptical about American beneficence in foreign affairs. On the domestic front, this faction was deeply concerned about the behavior of politicians, minority rights, environmentalism, and consumer protection. Most spectacularly, they redesigned the Democratic Party's presidential selection procedures to ensure the nomination for one of their own: George McGovern in 1972. Yet, it was by securing seats in Congress, posts on important committee and subcommittee staffs, and heading up "public interest" groups that New Politics Democrats became a durable force in Washington in the 1970s. They worked through a variety of associations, strategically placed bureaucrats and the federal courts to promote, coordinate, and rationalize their agenda.[42]
- In the late 1950s, the New Right faction began to coalesce within the Republican Party. Over the next twenty-five years it took over the GOP. Despite being the minority party of the era, it became an ideological faction distinct from the older conservatism. It found an electoral base in the suburban South and Southwest, which was the backbone of the putsch that nominated Arizona Senator Barry Goldwater in 1964. After suffering through the Great Society and bridling under the reign of presidents Nixon and Ford, the New Right faction rededicated itself to a longer-term ideological realignment. In the early 1970s, it created a web of think tanks, publications, donors, and organizations in Congress willing to back the cause. These associational efforts paid off handsomely. In 1980, the New Right celebrated the election of one of its own—Ronald Reagan—to the presidency. Over the next decade, Newt Gingrich consolidated the party's transformation in Congress.[43]

Finally, some factions are "mixed cases." Such factions do not fully seek to transform their party but do not believe that the status quo is defensible. Modern Republicans and Half-Breed Republicans fall into this category. Both operated mostly in presidential politics. Both believed that the party status quo was not intellectually justifiable or electorally viable. But neither sought to fully takeover the Republican Party. Therefore, they sought the paradoxical combination of electoral success without a party overhaul.

- Modern Republicans emerged from the expansive growth of corporate managerial jobs in the 1940s and 1950s. They retained close ties with the manufacturing and business communities of the industrial cities. Derisively called "organization men" because they were suburban, college-educated, and economically secure, Modern Republicans shared an understanding of what it took to manage vast bureaucracies. Members of this faction brought these skills to Republican presidential nomination contests, which they dominated throughout the 1940s and 1950s. To win the presidency, they were willing to accommodate the New Deal by accepting greater state in- volvement in the economy, the expansion of federal power over the states, and the legitimacy of labor unions. They had only marginal success in the Senate and almost none in the House of Representatives.[44]

- In the faction-ridden Republican Party of the Gilded Age, Half-Breeds picked- and-chose among the existing policy options in an effort to build a party that stood for moderation, pragmatism, and effective government. Like their Stal- wart rivals, they were also machine politicians, largely from the Northeast and West, but they sought to manage differences within the party and orient it toward the future. To do this, they became key players in the presidential nomination contests of 1880, 1884, and 1888. They also provided some of the votes in Congress to maintain the system of patronage and party regularity.[45]

There is not a hard and fast rule on which type of factions will emerge and what strategies they will adopt. Much depends on their social and electoral bases, organizational resources, ideological commitments, and their party's status as majority or minority.

Although judging success is complex, it might be said that four of the seven change factions had a degree of success in transforming their respective party. Populist Democrats, Liberal-Labor Democrats, New Politics Democrats, and New Right Republicans all managed to significantly alter the character of their party, while Liberal/Mugwump Republicans, Progressive Republicans, Mod- ern Republicans, and New Democrats failed to do so. The most successful status quo faction at preserving their party's character was the Old Guard Republicans. Southern Democrats also held sway for over thirty years and pre- vented the emergence of the Democratic Party as a more liberal party. The Stalwarts seem to have been the least successful status quo faction in control- ling the direction and composition of their party's leadership. The success or failure of these factions can be better gauged by looking at their institutional effects over the course of American political development.

What Causes Factions?

There are five overlapping sources of party factions in American politics. One is the strategic electoral incentives created by the two-party system. Separation of powers, federalism, the Electoral College, and first-past-the-post congressional elections help sustain a two-party system, comprised of two large, diffuse, and porous parties. Only a few modern democracies maintain two-party systems and none of them are as large and diverse as the parties in the United States. Hence, there is ample room for factions to grow and maneuver inside such large parties.

The two-party system provides incentives for factional formation in order to drive the parties toward or away from the political center. Factions have relatively precise ideas about what they would like to see government do that are often to the right or left of the average American. Therefore, some factions seek to pull their party away from the center in order to create the political space to enact their preferences. But when parties pull too far to the extremes of the political spectrum, endangering the chances of electoral victory, other factions emerge to induce the party to seek the political center.

The process occurs because in the American two-party system, when one party gains a majority its coalition necessarily expands, bringing in new groups and interests, creating factions to contest what the party stands for. In contrast, even though parties that find themselves in the minority tend to close ranks, select a strident leadership, and squeeze what resources they can out of their base of support, party competition drives them to factionalize. As the party becomes uncompetitive, a faction is likely to appear in order to try and move the party back into the majority. But the ability to find cracks in the other party's coalition necessarily rubs up against the preferences of the core of the party. Those in the party that seek to make it more competitive will thus run into the old guard, which often resists changes that threaten its power. These party reformers will have a powerful incentive to form a faction to advance their goals and provide them mutual protection. The minority party thus becomes a battle between the larger party seeking to retain its position and a reform-oriented faction seeking to change the party and recapture a national majority.

Intraparty politics drives factions to try to take advantage of two other electoral strategies (Table 1.2). One is to capture a "target" constituency. Such constituencies are groups that are politically disengaged, loosely affiliated with the opposition party, or whose political loyalties have yet to be settled. Factions make concerted efforts to appeal to such constituencies and work doggedly to pass policies that adherents believe will resonate with them. Securing the support of such constituencies can also help the party compensate for potential losses among swing voters in the center. The other is to play to the party's base: that set of voters, organized interests, activists, and intellectuals that are deeply attached to a party's core ideas and interests. The strategy that tempts factional tacticians is to play to the base, hoping to turn out more committed voters than their opponents.

Table 1.2 **Factions Strategic Motivations**

Faction	Center	Base	Target Constituency
Liberal Republicans/Mugwumps	XX		XX
Stalwart Republicans		XX	
Half-Breed Republicans	XX		
Old Guard Republicans		XX	
Progressive Republicans			XX
Populist Democrats		XX	
Southern Democrats		XX	
Modern Republicans	XX		
Liberal-Labor Democrats		XX	XX
New Politics Democrats		XX	XX
New Right Republicans		XX	
New Democrats	XX		

Savvy politicians chose to form, or associate themselves, with factions because they are instruments of differentiation among party elites. They provide a number of powerful cues for the politically active and informed. Factional affiliation can help politicians attract media attention, campaign funds, and a cadre of activists. By affiliating themselves with a faction, politicians can also garner a degree of political cover, which can assist them in their eternal quest to claim credit and avoid blame. Factions thus help structure the party's debate over strategy.[46]

The second cause of factions is ideology. It has long been held that America's big-tent parties were more pragmatic than ideological. Yet, it is for this very reason that factions became the carriers of different ideological currents within the parties. Groups of political actors believe that a factional network will help them promote their conception of the public good. Moreover, factions cannot be understood without examination of their members' objectives. Such an examination sheds light on why factions form because it is nearly impossible to separate ideas and interests into observable causes because ideology is constitutive of interest and vice versa. As E.E. Schattschneider once quipped, "It is futile to try to determine whether men are stimulated politically by interests or by ideas, for people have ideas about interests."[47] Therefore, it is nearly impossible to say which has priority on the faction's agenda or causal precedence in its emergence. Yet, ideational purposes clarify important aspects of factional formation and behavior.

The third source of factions is the geography of American economic development. As Richard Bensel has pointed out regarding the Gilded Age Republican Party, "the influence of uneven regional development . . . tended to fragment the national party into competing factions."[48] Different sections of the United States produced different goods and services, which in turn affected the sorts of demands different regions placed on the federal government. The Northeast and Great Lakes regions were the financial and industrial centers of the nation. The South until the mid-twentieth century remained overwhelmingly agricultural. The Middle West and the Rockies produced major agricultural and mining interests. These differences in productive capacity often translated into stark differences in political outlook.

The final cause of factions is major events, such as wars or economic crises. As David Mayhew has shown, foreign wars can reconfigure domestic politics.[49] For instance, the integration of the armed services in the wake of World War II was an important factor in the consolidation of the Southern Democratic faction. New Politics Democrats cut their teeth in opposition to the Vietnam War. On the home front, major economic crises can drive factional formation. The depression of the early 1890s helped elevate William Jennings Bryan as the leader of the budding Populist faction within the Democratic Party. The Great Depression gave birth to a powerful labor movement that formed one of the bases of the Liberal-Labor faction.

Ultimately, the American political system renders its political parties ill equipped to act quickly and decisively, which provides incentives for factional formation, because factions are more agile and adaptable. Politicians can then tie "causal stories" to their particular factional affiliations and use this symbolic capital in future campaigns. Therefore, barring a major regime change, political operators will find reasons to form factions in the future. Because American parties lack strong disciplined organizations, factional networks forged in the breach perform many of the traditional functions associated with parties. American institutions are to factions what air is to fire, an element without which it instantly expires. Factions are thus sown in the nature of our republic.

Conclusion

The American regime, with its peculiar combination of separation of powers and federalism, gives life to factions but also shapes the conditions for their success or failure at achieving their objectives. Factions must either succeed in changing the public debate and winning elections, or they must change governing institutions from within to commandeer their party. A faction's beliefs about the likelihood of success, and its ability to make long-term political investments, shape its decisions. Yet, factions assess their strength in fluid and evolving conditions. As Nelson Polsby has remarked, "factions . . . arise, not out of the natural bedrock of people, but out of their capacity to calculate their advantage over a protracted period, and their ability to see their best interests in the light of the complexity of the political world in which they exist."[50] The party's status as a majority or minority and the governing institutions (if any) it controls affect the faction's strategic decisions. Therefore, the incentives and ideational factors underpinning the strategic and tactical decisions factions make—and the larger party's response—are at the center of my analysis.

Attention to factions revises our understanding of what American political parties are and how they work. American parties are not simply the diffuse, disorganized blobs with little or no relevance that many have suggested. Nor are they disciplined monolithic blocs that consistently take coordinated and rational action to seek out the median voter and set the congressional agenda. Rather, it is factions that often undertake synchronized action to redefine the party, forcing the more dispersed and amorphous elements to respond. These responses can come from the president, shaping his governing tactics, or from other party members in Congress, changing power dynamics in the legislature. Insofar as factions are the units that infuse American parties with energy and purpose, they are closest to Burke's original definition of political parties as "a body of men united, for promoting by their joint endeavors the national interest, upon some particular principal in which they are all agreed."[51] Ultimately, by trying to command the party in which they reside, factions seek the authority to put their stamp on the nation.

CHAPTER 2

Factions and the Study of American Political Parties

To underscore the theoretical and historical contributions of this book, this chapter situates the study of factions in the vast political science literature on political parties in the United States. I make five moves. First, I lay out the principal debates that have animated students of parties for the last century. Second, I contrast my conception of factions with the leading contemporary theoretical statements on American parties by John Aldrich and Marty Cohen, David Karol, Hans Noel, and John Zaller. Third, I argue that the parties, driven by factions within them, are and have been stronger and more vibrant than they are often depicted. Fourth, I sketch how the faction-driven party claim is "tested" against other views of political parties in the chapters that follow. Fifth, I detail how factions contribute to our understanding of "development," as this notion has evolved in the hands of American Political Development scholars. By building on the insights of previous scholarship, this study challenges, sharpens, and refines them at key points.

The Study of American Political Parties

The scholarly study of American political parties began over a century ago. If one were to include the reflections of statesmen and philosophers, the examination of parties could be traced to the middle of the eighteenth century in England. Most of the analyses of eighteenth- and nineteenth-century parties concentrated on the normative question of whether parties were positive forces or necessarily evils. One line of reflection from James Madison and George Washington to Roberto Michels and Moisei Ostrogorski viewed the very existence of parties as a threat to democratic stability.[1] The best one could hope for was that parties could be narrowly circumscribed. Another group of thinkers—including James Bryce, Woodrow Wilson, Maurice Duverger, Samuel Eldersveld, Pendleton

Herring, and Robert Dahl—held that parties were tolerable if not good for de-mocracy.[2] By the early twentieth century a consensus had emerged that what-ever their drawbacks parties were here to stay and were necessary for democratic government.[3] Schattschneider forcefully summarized this view: "Political parties created modern democracy and modern democracy is unthinkable save in terms of political parties."[4]

In the United States, much of the debate over political parties in the twentieth century then turned on the question of what sort of political parties were most desirable in the American context. The study of parties in the first half of the century was conducted with an eye to reforming those already in existence. For some, such as such as Woodrow Wilson and A. Lawrence Lowell, the parties of the late nineteenth and early twentieth century were too decentralized, nonideo-logical, disorganized, and sometimes downright corrupt.[5] Others—such as Henry Jones Ford, E.M. Sait, Arthur Holcombe, Herbert Agar, Edward Banfield, and Frank Sorauf—expressed greater appreciation for the loose, permeable, and conciliatory aspects of America's homegrown parties.[6] In the postwar period, the "responsible party government" school revived the tradition of criticizing the existing parties in favor of more disciplined and centralized ones.[7]

The mid–twentieth-century debate turned on whether American parties were weak where they should be strong and strong where they should be weak. Reformers generally held that the parties should be more programmatic, more disciplined in legislative action, and more organizationally hierarchical. Factions within them should be eliminated. The defenders of American parties, in con-trast, saw vague campaign appeals, policy compromises, factionalism, and local patronage as the best way that parties could adapt to a diverse society and the institutional particularities of American government.

By the late 1960s these debates had largely run their course. Reform in the direction of the Westminster model was not forthcoming, as it required politi-cally unfeasible constitutional changes. The deterioration of urban machines and the introduction of primaries to nominate candidates in the 1970s (first for pres-idential candidates and then for nearly all other offices) deprived the party orga-nizations of one of their central powers. This sparked a new debate about whether the parties were declining. Never as strong in the right places as reformers wanted, it then seemed that the parties were passing into irrelevance with the loss of formal control over nominations, the rise of split ticket voting, and an increase in the number of self-declared independents in the electorate.[8] The authors of *The Changing American Voter* offered a description of the declining party:

> Party organizations have grown weaker; they are less relevant as
> electioneering institutions than they once were, especially on the
> presidential level. Presidential campaign organizations are created

anew each election. They represent the personal entourage of the candidate rather than a continuing partisan institution. . . . The individual candidates are more independent of party; they run on the basis of their own characteristics and programs, not as representatives of continuing party institutions.[9]

Some observers applauded the prospect of a nonpartisan political world. Others lamented it.

Yet just as the debate over the decline-of-the-parties thesis crested, events once again changed the terms of the discussion. For a variety of reasons—scholars have pointed to the rise of single-issue activists, regional party realignments in the South and the Northeast, Hispanic immigration, income inequality, residential mobility, changing religious values, and the end of the Cold War—the parties in Congress began to behave more like the cohesive parties envisaged by the responsible party government school. In addition, computer technology, changes in telecommunications, marketing, and campaign finance made the national party organizations stronger than ever. Ideological appeals became more direct and consistent. Voters who continued to identify with the parties became more militant.[10] While the number of self-identified independents persisted, a large proportion of them began to vote consistently for one party or the other. The Republican Party became more conservative and the Democratic Party more liberal on nearly all policy issues. Divergences between the parties now occur across social, economic, and foreign policy dimensions.[11] In a word, they are polarized.[12] In the first decade of the twenty-first century, the discussion of parties has turned on whether they were too strong to allow the government to function properly.[13]

Factions and Contemporary Party Theories

Reviewing the history of the scholarly debate about parties reveals that the essential character of American parties remains elusive. In part, this is due to the plasticity of American parties. Analysts are always trying to hit a moving target. The parties have taken highly variegated organizational forms, and a very hazy line separates them from interest groups. Scholars end up emphasizing one aspect or another of the parties at a given point, only to see their center of gravity change. And what the analyst posits as the core of the party goes on to determine how the party should be evaluated. Looking at American parties through the lens of factions helps account for internal shifts within the parties. As we shall see, factions often cause (or exploit) changes in a party's center of gravity.

Using V.O. Key's classic tripartite description of parties, we can map the principal thrusts of the political science scholarship. According to Key, parties exist in government, in organization, and in the electorate.[14] One group of analysts stresses the importance of politicians and office seekers (the politician-centered view).[15] Another focuses on the character of the party organization (the organizational view).[16] And the final group concentrates on interest groups, activists, fundraisers, voters, and other actors engaged in electioneering but who fall outside the official party label (the coalition view).[17] The concept of intraparty factions cuts across these divisions in the definition of parties.

Where analysts put the accent in their definition of parties carries a number of implications in its wake. One is where the analyst is encouraged to look for the major sources of change in the political system. Even more important, it determines whether the party is deemed strong or weak. Some of these implications can be sketched as follows:

1. *Assumption*: Politicians and officer seekers are the core of a party.

   Consequence: The party organization will be weak insofar as politicians run their own campaigns, are highly responsive to voter preferences, and make vague ideological appeals.

2. *Assumption:* Party organization is the central element of a party.

   Consequence: Party strength will vary with organizational capacity. If parties lose formal control over patronage and nominations, they will be weakened and disconnected from voters. If they retain these powers they will be strong and well connected. A weak party has little say over candidate appeals; while a strong party hems in candidate rhetoric.

3. *Assumption:* Outside groups are predominant units within American parties.

   Consequence: American parties are stronger than they appear. Politicians are more responsive to activist groups than the mass public.

Each of these theories of parties and their attendant consequences points out something important but their rigidity forces other important elements into the background. Furthermore, these theories of party rest on the assumption that aside from their ideological positions, America's two parties are situated in the same environment, to which they respond in similar ways.[18]

An advantage of viewing parties as driven by factions is that it cuts across exist-ing definitions. Factions are networks that are comprised of officeholders, organizational officers, and outside groups. Thinking about American parties in this way blends the insights of the previous party theorizing and focuses our atten-tion on the location of the party's energy. Rather than continue the endless discus-sion whether American parties are strong or weak, the examination of 140 years of party history shows that it is the persistent pulling and hauling of factions that give American parties their vitality. In addition, attention to factions reveals radical internal differences between the parties over time. Not only have they lacked organizational symmetry, but during certain periods one party is factionalized while the other is homogeneous; one party contains multiple factions, while the other only has one; one faction in one party is very strong, but those in the other party are weak; and so on. While the assumption of party symmetry is useful for modeling political behavior in theory, it obscures the vast party asymmetry in fact.

Today, there are two leading theoretical definitions of American parties in the scholarly literature. The first is by John Aldrich in his now classic book *Why Parties?* Aldrich oscillates between defining the parties as "the creature of the politicians, the ambitious office seeker and officeholder" and as driven by ac-tivists. My aim in developing the concept of factions is to show how the two are woven together into networks. Rather than move back and forth between these two entities, considering them as parts of factions gives us greater ana-lytical leverage. It is not just that parties help politicians achieve their goals but that factions comprised of politicians and activists collectively unite to achieve shared goals, sometimes at the expense of others in the party. In addition, Aldrich defines activists as those who attend party conventions and caucuses. I employ a more expansive and inclusive definition of activists that includes key outside groups and traces their activity. Finally, I treat not only factions pushing for change (what Aldrich emphasizes in his examination in the role of activists) but also those that defend the status quo.

Marty Cohen, David Karol, Hans Noel, and John Zaller (the UCLA School) have advanced an alternative definition.[19] It shares many elements with parties understood as driven by factions. Therefore, the factional perspective should be contrasted with it. The UCLA School argues that parties are made up of groups that form "coalitions," which are "intense policy demanders." In this view, the party coalition is the party. It is driven by intense ideological commitments. The UCLA School thus distinguishes their definition of parties from the more "politician-centered" view attributed to Schumpeter, Downs, Aldrich, and Schlesinger as well as congressional party scholars such as Cox, McCubbins, Rohde, Sinclair, and Jacobson. Broadly speaking, the latter group argues that the core of a party is elected officials and office seekers who seek to please voters and win elections. Ultimately, the difference between the politician-centered and the group-centered definition of a party turns on where scholars think the life of the party is.

Faction, as employed here, sometimes approaches the UCLA School's notion of a party coalition. Like the UCLA School, the study of factions restores the centrality of actors who do not neatly fit into a party's organizational apparatus. Also like the UCLA School, looking at parties through the lens of faction reveals the importance of ideological commitments for party activity.

There are, however, three key differences. First, my definition of a faction cuts through the divide between the politician-centered versus group-centered views of parties. While it is closer to the latter than the former, it provides an important role for politicians, candidates, and organizational officials, and shows how they are linked to auxiliary groups. The dichotomy the UCLA School sets up between politicians and groups is less important than tracing how that relationship evolves in the hurly-burly of actual politics. That is what this book does. Second, while the UCLA School paints the groups that make up a party coalition as constantly shifting, my conception of factions emphasizes the durability of factional alignments over time. Tracing the history of factions allows us to see the groups that comprise them more clearly. A third issue is that the UCLA School goes too far in defining the party coalition as the whole party. This proposition rules out the possibility of there being multiple coalitions or elements of a party that are not part of the dominant coalition. Hence they often recur in an unspecified way to the concept of faction to deal with negotiations within the parties.[20] My analysis reveals that at many historical points there have been competing factions within the same party. Therefore, rather than standing in for the party as a whole, factions can sometimes be responsible for different outcomes in different institutional settings.

The Factional Perspective

Contrary to the view of parties as constantly fluctuating in their strength and durability, this book argues that the presence of factions within American parties makes them stronger and more durable over time than they are often portrayed. The porousness of American parties is, paradoxically, a source of strength rather than a cause of weakness. Since the Civil War four major changes have been singled out and said to have weakened the parties. These are:

1. *Cause:* Civil service reform in the late nineteenth and early twentieth centuries

   Effect: Decline of state party machines

2. *Cause:* Rise of "amateur" activists in the 1950s

   Effect: Decline of urban party machines

3. *Cause:* Growth of the welfare state in the twentieth century

   Effect: Supplanting of parties' social service functions

4. *Cause:* Introduction of primary elections to nominate candidates

   Effect: Rise of candidate-centered campaigns

Surveying these causes, determining whether parties are strong or weak has often turned on the analyst's conception of parties. Given political scientists' predilection for formal institutions, the loss of patronage and control over nominations would seem to have devastated parties. However, if the analyst concentrates on factions as the driving element within a party rather than the character of the party organization or the resources available to office-seekers, it is apparent that the parties remained pretty consistent over time. The notion of party decline is therefore contingent on how the analyst defines political party. For example, if the measure of party strength is organizational prowess, the Democratic Party in the middle of the last century should have been at a low point. Yet it wasn't. Rather, it was under-pinned by two factions (Southerners and a Liberal-Labor alliance) that were largely independent of the formal organization but that enabled it to control American government.

By assessing parties without attending to factions, analysts have overlooked how parties have remained vibrant. Factions' flexibility allows them to quickly capitalize on new resources when older ones dry up. Factions' efforts to move their party to the right or left to enact their policies closer to their preferences leads them to take action in multiple institutional venues. The salutary result is a more vigorous and stronger party.

To make the case that factions often drive parties, the chapters in this book use the historical record to explore whether the actions of parties are better explained by looking at factions or to other theories of parties. While all party theories are trying to explain party behavior, and therefore forecast many of the same things, the analyses offered here show what can be gained by looking at party factions rather than by employing other conceptions of parties. Ultimately, by working through multiple institutional venues to move their party to the left or the right on the political spectrum, factions instigate a series of other important changes.

In Chapter 3, the question is whether ideological change is more traceable to factions or to parties dominated almost exclusively by vote-seeking politicians. If factions drive parties, then ideological changes should be traceable to changes in factions or to the relative power of factions. If, on the other hand, politicians dominate parties, large ideological changes ought to stem from shifting electoral pressures on officeholders.

Chapter 4 examines whether viewing parties as politician-centered, organization-centered, or factionalized parties better explains presidential nominations. If one focuses narrowly on politicians, one finds that parties have little control over nominations and are thus relatively weak. Likewise, if one focuses, on party officials, one finds that parties have little control over candidate-centered nomination contests. In contrast, if one focuses on factional networks that draw in outside groups—including interest groups, activists, fundraisers, and think tanks—then the party can be said to control nominations. The argument of this chapter builds on some of the claims of the UCLA School.

In Chapter 6, the analysis concentrates on whether changes in the distribution of power within Congress are more traceable to individual members of Congress, the party organization, or party factions. If the party as whole determined the distribution of power, power would be centralized in the leadership, and minority party rights would be minimized. If individual members got their way, power would be radically decentralized and minority party rights enhanced. If factions partially determine the distribution of power, then we would expect greater variation in modes of congressional organization, shifting as they would with the relative power of factions.

Chapter 7 examines the extent to which the parties themselves or factions within them are bigger shapers of presidential action. If voters were central to presidents' fortunes, presidential action would be traceable to the demands of the mass public. What presidents do would be determined by how they either respond to public opinion or are able to reshape it. On the other hand, presidential action may derive more from a president's ability to exploit opportunities in a context shaped by factions. Factions are major parts of the political landscape presidents confront. If the party is unified, the president should have to work with it and deal with its leaders. If, however, the party contains factions, their relative strength and character will alter the president's governing strategies.

Finally, Chapter 8 explores whether policy changes culminating in the building of the American state are more closely linked to factions than to parties conceived of in other ways. If election-oriented politicians dominate parties, policy change should be traceable to electoral shifts. If factions with intense ideological commitments exploit the public's ignorance to drive parties, factions should be found at the root of many policy changes.

In sum, the issue is who decides important matters of American party politics. This book argues that it is usually not simply elected officials and office seekers pursuing votes. Nor is it organizational officials ensconced in the party headquarters. Neither is it constantly fluctuating coalitions of interest groups. Rather it is factions, which are more durable and consistent promoters of ideological visions of American public life.

Factions and Development

The broad historical sweep and wide-ranging institutional concerns of this book distinguish it from much contemporary political science. Of course many scholars share an interest in explaining the development of American politics over time. They have debated whether the nation's political experience should be regarded as containing one, two, or many distinct periods.[21] Louis Hartz considers all of the American political experience to be of a piece.[22] It is held together by the nation's commitment to "Lockean liberalism," and all conflict takes place within this horizon. Although this is a powerful view, it has trouble explaining political change.

A second view of the American political experience identifies a basic division occurring in the late nineteenth and early twentieth century. Prior to the Gilded Age politics revolved around a decentralized system of courts and parties. After that period, the central state acquired major administrative and regulatory authority.[23] In this view, modernization of the economy drove demand for a more professionalized and powerful central state.[24] But given the long time frame that is considered in these analyses—from the Civil War to World War I—this division of American political development hardly constitutes a sharp historical break point.

Finally, the realignment genre posits several periods that are framed by major electoral shifts, occurring approximately every thirty years.[25] In the realignment perspective, some elections were "critical," while the vast majority, were not.[26] These realigning elections were said to take place in 1800, 1832, 1860, 1896, 1932, 1964, and 1980. Other scholars, however, have found many reasons to dispute the claim that these elections are fundamental break points in American political history.[27] To those concerns, one can add factions, which rarely got their start with any of these elections and in many cases existed before and after them.

Analyzing factions over time and across institutional venues dispenses with these debates over periodization. Studying factions undermines the case for clear break points in American political development that are theoretically meaningful; whether those break points occur episodically, as in the realignment schema, or at specific moments such as the late nineteenth century or the

New Deal. Rather, this book treats American politics as a continuously dynamic process of organizing and redistributing political power.

The approach of this book follows the path blazed by Stephen Skowronek in his book *The Politics Presidents Make*.[28] It holds that there are two temporalities at work. On the one hand, many of the big institutional factors in the American political system that cause factions of different types to emerge remain roughly constant. On the other, major changes in national government power, in tele- communications, in the economy, in demographics, and in race relations mean that factions are interested in different issues, communicate differently, and have different social bases. In sum, the American regime produces a variety of factions of similar types yet the context in which they operate changes. Both modes of change are dynamic and developmental.

One payoff of this line of reasoning is that it challenges scholars who assume that both parties are structured and operate in basically the same ways, or who believe that the two parties have deeply different "cultures."[29] Factions of different types have not been evenly distributed across the parties and over time. At certain moments, there are more factions in one party than in the other. Sometimes even a single faction can be more consequential in steering one party than a number of factions in the other party. And despite deeply rooted differences between the two parties, factions within them have been major sources of energy and change.

Furthermore, attention to factions challenges the realignment notion that each period is defined by conflict on a single major policy issue, such as eco- nomic policy in the 1930s. Each critical election is then said to foreground new issue conflicts.[30] James L. Sundquist contended that: "conflict displacement... is *the* defining characteristic that identifies realignment."[31] In these studies of partisan change, positioning near the median voter meant that the parties strove to limit party conflict to a single policy dimension and suppress issues that might splinter their electoral coalition. As Schattschneider put it: "the old cleavage must be played down if the new conflict is to be exploited."[32] How- ever, tracing factional activity shows that there is rarely a dominant issue di- mension and that much conflict persists within and between parties on across economic, social, and foreign policy issue dimensions. Indeed, it is factions that endow parties with multiple issue agendas throughout their histories.

While factions rise and fall, one of the advantages of the broad sweep of this study is to show a degree of continuity in American party life that is often obscured by efforts to mark off certain periods, eras, decades, or ages as impor- tant. Rather than focus on such efforts, the argument here is that factions within the two parties—themselves fixtures of the political landscape since the Civil War—emerge only to later pass out of existence. Despite that conti- nuity, the context in which these factions operate as the society and economy change over time.

CHAPTER **3**

The Conveyor Belts of Ideas

FACTIONS AND PARTY IDEOLOGY

New Institutionalist scholars contend that to understand why things happen in politics, we must first understand what political actors want. However, people cannot always get what they want because the historical context supplies particular rules of the political game. Only outcomes that fall within those rules can be realized.[1] The first step in any analysis, then, is to depict what people want to achieve. Only with a firm grasp of factions' ideological commitments can we then look at the institutional context to determine why they did (or did not) realize their aims. Factions offer a long menu of ideological alternatives. But those alternatives are processed by American institutions, creating a disjunction between the range of alternative courses of action and the responsiveness of institutions to those alternatives. Some factions' preferences dovetail with the context in which they operate and are successful, while others are not.

The effort to modify or defend a party's program means that factions must develop a public philosophy of their own.[2] A party's public philosophy is an outlook on public affairs comprised of four different levels of ideas: fundamental principles, such as natural rights or progress; views about the role of government in society, which designate the areas and extent to which government should intervene; "theories of governance" relating to the distribution of power among institutions and levels of government; and particular policy ideas.[3] A faction will espouse a different recipe, challenging the dominant view within the party on one or all of these levels. This chapter details these challenges.

Tracing ideas to factions cuts through a number of debates about the origins, status, and role of ideas within American parties. The first is that party positions are aggregations of voter preferences and thus track shifts in public opinion.[4] Unlike accounts of political parties that find parties to be highly responsive to voters' demands, examination of factions' doctrines shows that they are often the movers and shakers of elite opinion. Secondly, the notion that factions inject ideas into the parties challenges current theories about the provenance of ideas politics. Contrary to the "issue evolution" approach pioneered by Edward Carmines and James Stimson, which claims that party elites adopt positions before voters do, this chapter argues that by looking at the ideas themselves, it is evident that party elites, insofar as they are affiliated with factions, respond to groups within them.[5] The position advanced here is closer to David Karol's coalition management theory.[6]

A third scholarly debate is concerned with the status and meaning of "liberalism." In one view, liberalism broadly construed is the "boundary condition" for political discourse in the United States.[7] Liberalism, so conceived, holds that men are by nature free and equal. Government is premised on and instituted to secure individuals' rights. It tolerates diverse religious convictions and modes of living. It appreciates conflict among many interests to prevent majority tyranny. It limits government by enumerating its powers in a written constitution and by erecting complex institutional arrangements to slow the policymaking-process. So conceived, the liberal tradition creates the universe in which various representatives of the Left and the Right can wage their partisan battles. Louis Hartz articulated this position in *The Liberal Tradition in America*.[8] According to Hartz, there was neither a truly "reactionary tradition" nor a "revolutionary tradition" in America. All political conflict took place inside the liberal galaxy. Other galaxies such as fascism, socialism, and communism remained unexplored. In this sense, there was little ideological change in America. All kinds of political, technological, and cultural change could occur and still leave the country's core ideological commitments intact. The elasticity of Hartz's thesis makes it hard to disprove. Nonetheless, a number of authors have set out to correct, modify, or enrich Hartz's perspective. J. David Greenstone has argued that Hartz did not pay enough attention to the possibilities generated by the conflicts within liberalism.[9] Another school studies "lost alternatives," which seek to show that American political history could have taken other directions and that there were real alternatives beyond the frontiers of the liberal consensus.[10] A third take is Rogers Smith's "multiple traditions thesis," which shines a spotlight on illiberal strains in American thought.[11]

Factions' public philosophies reveal just how broad the ideological spectrum is in American politics. If there is a "liberal consensus" in America, it is a pretty wide one. In fact, some factions adopt ideas about racial, intellectual, or wealth hierarchies that are at odds with liberal premises. In addition, factional ideological contestation reveals tensions, paradoxes, and contradictions at the heart of "liberalism" broadly conceived. These include, among others, situations requiring the use of state power for antistatist ends; reconciling professional administration with popular participation in government; and seeking to combat discrimination and protect a sphere of individual autonomy. The range of ideas adopted by factions indicates that the parties are far from monolithic ideological blocs.

A fourth scholarly debate is whether American parties are ideological at all. Beginning with Tocqueville, it was long held that American parties were not ideological. Rather they occupied themselves with winning office and dolling out patronage. John Gerring has powerfully challenged this received wisdom, arguing that parties are in fact ideological. This chapter takes a cut at this issue from a different angle. It argues that the parties as wholes are rarely ideological in full. Part of the reason analysts have been reluctant to label American parties ideological is because not everyone traveling under the party label ascribes to the same set of views. When factions contest the party's priorities, they spark battles over what the party should stand for.[12] The description of factional programs reveals that nearly as much ideological debate in American politics occurs within the parties as between them.

A final debate is over why party ideologies change over time. In the Marxist view, ideologies are the product of economic changes, which are concocted ex post facto to justify a set of economic relationships and mask the forces of domination and exploitation. In the sociological view, ideologies change slowly over time due to the evolution of society. The issue evolution approach posits that elites adopt new positions on issues, which eventually trickle down to the masses. Finally, crises, such as wars and natural disasters, recalibrate ideological positions. The great weakness of these and other explanations for ideological change, making it such a tortured subject, is that the outcome to be explained is so diffuse and influenced by so many things. It is important to stress that the claim advanced here is not that factions by themselves "cause" ideological change. Rather, they are simply an important source, among others, for shifting the ideological character of the parties. To make above points, I sketch the most important ideas that made Republican and then Democratic factions act with purpose.

Republican Party Factions

LIBERAL REPUBLICANS

The Liberal Republicans of the Gilded Age sought to make the GOP stand for free markets, efficient government, and rule by well-bred Protestants. According to Eric Foner, "Liberal reform was at one and the same time a moral creed, part of an emerging science of society, and the outcry of a middle-class intelligentsia alarmed by class conflict, the ascendancy of machine politicians, and its own exclusion from power."[13] Liberals generally favored laissez-faire social policies, leniency toward the white South, free trade (or at least a lower tariff), hard money, and civil service reform. To support these positions, the Liberal credo seductively combined great confidence in social science expertise with self-righteous Protestant moralism.[14]

Liberals' ideas operated on all four levels of political ideas. At the foundational level was the positivist conviction that laws governing the political, economic, and social fields—like those in the natural world—could be discerned by reason. Like the French social theorist Auguste Comte, Liberals saw the key to progress as lying in "scientific development," to be implemented by enlightened men with the right pedigrees. When linked to the social Darwinism of the English sociologist Herbert Spencer, positivism provided a scientific justification for economic, if not also political, inequality. Indeed, these "scientific" ideas were drawn upon to limit popular sovereignty, especially when it came to the political power of new immigrants from Southern Europe and blacks in the South.

On the role of the state in society, Liberals' adherence to classical liberalism dictated limited government and free markets. In policy terms, they were proponents of free trade and the gold standard. They also sought to restrain the role of the federal government and return power to the states, even if this meant leaving blacks to fend for themselves in the South. Their theory of governance centered on the claim that the parties and the bureaucracy that they helped staff had become overbearing. Rather, governing authority should be restored to upright professionals. Liberals held that party machines made it impossible for the "best men" to be elected to high office. As Henry Adams put it: "We want a national set of young men like ourselves or better, to start new influences not only in politics, but in literature, in law, in society, and throughout the whole social organism of the country—a national school of our own generation."[15]

The great problem at the core of the Liberal vision was its elitist and antidemocratic assumptions. Liberals wanted to release the entrepreneurial individual. But to do so, they needed state power to dismantle the archaic party system. The greatest threat to American freedom was the patronage system. Because state expansion increased patronage jobs, they called for greater efficiency.[16] Therefore, Liberals advocated for the professionalization of the civil service to reduce corruption. In the words of President Rutherford B. Hayes, Liberals' wish was "to have the business of government done on business principles."[17] Therefore, only certain people could be trusted with state authority. Carl Schurz, a German-born senator, summed up the Liberal position: "as the functions of government grow in extent, importance and complexity, the necessity grows of their being administered not only with honesty, but also with trained ability and knowledge."[18] They sought to reduce the tension between releasing market energies and using state power to deal with corruption by placing power in the hands of an elite comprised of scientists, academics, and professionals. Party reforms would recalibrate the balance between institutions of government.

STALWART REPUBLICANS

Stalwarts sought to defend the patronage system that developed during the Civil War and Reconstruction. In this period, the American state grew rapidly, creating new relationships between business and government. To manage them, parties employed thousands of people. Stalwarts were at the heart of the new business-government nexus. The party's new bosses represented business and fed off it. They promoted state-aided economic development, party loyalty, and concerned themselves with the fate of African-Americans in the South.

After Grant's election in 1868, powerful senators secured control of state parties by managing rival economic and ethnic groups. These "machine" politicians transitioned the Republican Party from the ideological politics of the Civil War era to the professional politics of the Gilded Age.[19] "Government is force," Kansas Senator John J. Ingalls told reformers, "[and] politics is a battle for supremacy. Parties are the armies. The Decalogue and the golden rule have no place in the political campaign. The object is success."[20] Stalwarts' organizational power rested on the control of federal patronage, which oiled political machines and state parties comprised of newspaper editors, postmasters, and revenue collectors. Reared on intrigue rather than ideas, Stalwarts made the party organization the object of loyalty.[21]

To control federal appointments in their states—the "spoils system"— powerful senators created a national network to protect their prerogatives.[22] They defended the system of patronage and "rotation in office" as highly democratic. Senator Joseph E. Brown expressed this view: "This is a republican government; it is democratic in form, and you will have to change the nature of the Government and change human nature also before you will be able to adopt in practice here any utopian theories about civil service."[23] Roscoe Conkling put it in more colorful language, "parties are not built up by deportment, or by ladies' magazines or gush."[24]

Stalwarts resisted the end of Reconstruction.[25] On the one hand, they recognized that the party's heritage as antislavery, pro-Union, and pro–economic enterprise was valuable and that to give up on the South would weaken their position. On the other, Stalwarts did not want to appear obsessed with the South or the fate of blacks. They believed such associations had doomed the Radical Republicans in 1868. Yet, when the Stalwarts supplanted the Radicals, it was the Stalwarts who became the carriers of the doctrine of equal rights. Defeated on the battlefield of intraparty politics, Radicals managed to impose their views upon their conquerors—albeit in a greatly diminished and moderated form. In the hands of the Stalwarts, Radical thought did not have the same life and color. But its themes could be drawn upon either cynically for the sake of winning elections or out of genuine conviction. While Stalwarts were more concerned with the treatment of the freedmen than others within the party, they still sought to make economic and party development the centerpieces of their program. The freedmen's call for equality, social justice, and civil rights took a back seat to the operations of the party machines.

HALF-BREED REPUBLICANS

In the 1880s, Half-Breeds picked-and-chose among existing Republicans proposals in hopes of building a party that stood for moderation, pragmatism, and effective government. Largely from the Northeast and West, they also tended to be machine politicians. However, they sought to manage differences within the party and orient it toward the future by navigating a course between Liberals and Stalwarts. Between 1870 and 1880, especially during the Hayes administration, the battle lines crystallized.[26] Of the three major Republican factions of the period, they were the least cohesive. The Half-Breeds were led, or at least symbolized, by James G. Blaine of Maine.

Historians have described the Half-Breeds as more hesitant supporters of Reconstruction and more restrained in their pursuit of patronage than the Stalwarts. Mark Hirsch characterized Half-Breeds as advocating some reforms but opposing tough Reconstruction.[27] In general, Half-Breeds' differences on policy questions with the other party factions were of degree rather than principle. While usually closer to the Stalwarts ideologically, they were more inclined to make rhetorical gestures in the direction of positions favored by Liberal reformers. Richard Welch has described the public philosophy of the Half-Breed faction as seeking to promote: "economic growth and social harmony . . . expansion of foreign markets, the protection of industry, an improved standard of living for the American workingman, and a national currency system suitable for the needs and safety of American business."[28] Such a set of views, depending on points of emphasis, had broad support among affiliates of every faction in the GOP.

Half-Breeds could occupy the center of the party because many other party members shared these views. They pursued a cooperative strategy, navigating between and playing off the other factions.[29] Less aggressive in their tactics than the Stalwarts, they took the edge off Liberal rhetoric and occasionally pursued similar measures with a more deft political touch. In their clashes with other factions, tone and personal style often differentiated Half-Breeds from Stalwarts and Liberals.

OLD GUARD REPUBLICANS

Informed by social Darwinism, Old Guard Republicans articulated an individualistic philosophy, closely tied to *laissez-faire* economics, which was skeptical of mass democracy and emphasized incremental change and continuity.[30] As Andrew Carnegie famously argued in *The Gospel of Wealth*, while the law of competition "may be sometimes hard for the individual, it is best for the race because it insures the survival of the fittest in every department." He went on to say that: "We accept and welcome . . . great inequality of environment, the concentration of business, industrial and commercial, in the hands of the few . . . as being not only beneficial but essential for the future progress of the race."[31] This was an evolutionary view based on competition among individuals. Modern liberty meant that individuals were free to test their abilities rather than be assigned to a class position. As Carnegie put it: "Freed here from the pressure of feudal institutions no longer fitted to their present development, and freed also from the dominion of the upper classes, which have kept the people at home from effective management of affairs and sacrificed the nation's interest for their own, as is the nature of classes, these [American] masses. . . . called upon to found a new state, have proved themselves possessors of a positive genius for political administration."[32]

Many Old Guard affiliates, including President Taft, studied law at Harvard University with the leading proponent of social Darwinism, William Graham Sumner. In 1883, Sumner asked: "What do the social classes owe each other?" His succinct answer was: "Nothing." Therefore, constraining liberty to promote equality—the position of progressive reformers—would only retard social evolution. Darwinism's tough materialism chimed with industrialization, when large indifferent forces appeared to control man's fate.

For democracy to function properly, a natural aristocracy had to emerge through the struggle to rule the nation. As Taft put it, the "operation of natural laws" would provide some men "the virtues of providence, of industry, and of honesty, and . . . all the other traits and virtues we admire."[33] According to Nicholas Murray Butler, an aristocracy not bound by birth, rank, or wealth should be the true leaders of the nation. Having risen to the top of the heap, only such men were fit to lead society because they understood that moral considerations outweighed the blind struggle; only they would be guided by high morality and civic duty.[34] Despite their amoral premises, conservatives held that moral rectitude determined the socially and economically successful individual. While this individual could come from any social class, people were not equally endowed with the capacity for this sort of behavior.

Other Old Guard affiliates grounded their realism in a Protestant understanding of man's sinful nature. They believed that man's selfishness was a fixture of the natural order. Therefore, conservatives concerned themselves with perfecting an elite to tame popular passions.[35] On such grounds the Old Guard opposed the direct democracy measures championed by Progressives as a recipe for undermining constitutional restrictions on majority rule. As Taft said at a Republican Club banquet in New York in 1912:

> With the effort to make the selection of candidates, the enactment of legislation, and the decision of the courts depend on the momentary passions of the people necessarily indifferently informed as to the issues presented . . . such extremists would hurry us into a condition which would find no parallel except in the French revolution, or in that bubbling anarchy that once characterized the South American Republics. Such extremists are not progressives—they are political emotionalists or neurotics—who have lost that sense of proportion . . . and that clear perception of the necessity for checks upon hasty popular action.[36]

This faction saw itself as the defender of constitutional restraint and the checks and balances that flowed from a realistic assessment of human nature, which, they held, had not progressed. Therefore, conservatives defended the parties, the courts, and the two-term presidential tradition as essential fortifications against overly popular rule. Government could take action to address industrial conditions but it could do so only within constitutional limits.[37]

A corollary of conservatives' foundational views was that government needed a strong hand to guide, domesticate, and direct human energies. The role of the state in the economy should therefore be a prominent one, despite the rhetorical homage paid to individualism and *laissez-faire*. The state could help channel the anarchistic impulses of man by collaborating with business. It should not intervene in the economy to redistribute wealth, but to aid, encourage, and guide the entrepreneur as well as manage the large corporate enterprise. Conservatives were firmly committed to the protective tariff and internal improvements. As historian Lewis Gould has observed, "Protection was more than just an economic policy. In the hands of the Republicans, it also sounded themes of nationalism and patriotic pride."[38] Republicans clung to this position, even when this policy became a potential liability because it favored Northeastern industry, particularly the railroads, at the expense of Southern and Western farmers.[39] In this view, only close ties between business and government could promote sufficient economic development within constitutional strictures.[40]

It is important to stress, however, that conservatives' principles limited what the state could accomplish. Legislation could not change man's sinful nature, and there were clear limits on what the government could regulate. As Taft put it, "There is a line beyond which Government cannot go with any good practical results in seeking to make men and society better."[41] Besides stimulating the economy, the only reason for government intervention was to prevent revolts and anarchy. Because conservatives were seeking to protect the existing order, many of them sought to use the Constitution as a bulwark against threats to social harmony. They wanted to define the Republican Party as the party of law, order, and constitutionalism.[42] Ultimately, conservatives saw and welcomed change more readily in the realm of economics than in the realm of politics.

PROGRESSIVE REPUBLICANS

At the dawn of the twentieth century, Progressives were generally optimistic about the future of man and society. The problem lay not in human nature but in how society shaped and, ultimately, deformed that nature. Peoples' bad habits arose from inequalities created by big business and the "trusts." William James gave expression to this fear of "bigness" in a letter to a friend: "The bigger the unit you deal with, the hollower [sic], the more brutal, the more mendacious is the life displayed."[43] They held that society was in motion for the better and simply needed the aid of wise public policies. Their new foundational principle of "progress" inspired confidence that man could shape society to achieve more equitable outcomes. Progressives believed that change was almost always synonymous with improvement. Progressivism's faith in the future derived from a judgment that the new industrial order was threatening American democracy but that technocratic administration could address the threat. The turn of the century thus marked a moment when large-scale changes would be required to sustain democracy. Government would need greater authority and discretion to improve social life.

The contours of these views first emerged outside the political realm. Few working politicians were directly familiar with the new philosophic arguments being made on behalf of the idea of progress. Most politicians adopted them second- or thirdhand from a distinguished group of intellectuals, which included Lester Ward, John Dewey, Charles Beard, Walter Weyl, Herbert Croly, Richard Ely, and Walter Lippmann. These thinkers boldly sought to supplant the Founders' idea of natural rights with the idea of progress as the basis of the American regime.[44]

According to these writers, who drew from European thinkers such as Hegel, Darwin, and Comte, the idea of progress was taken to be not merely a fanciful hope but an objective fact. They claimed that social scientists could discover the "laws" of history, determine appropriate measures that would speed the developmental process, and help translate them into public policy. This faith in progress inspired confidence in expert guidance. According to Lester Frank Ward, "[S]ociology has ... not only discovered the laws of society; it has discovered the principles according to which social operations take place. ... Sociology has not only established the law of social evolution, but it has found the principle underlying and explaining that law."[45] As Herbert Croly put it, a "better future would derive from the beneficent activities of expert social engineers who would bring to the service of social ideals all the technical resources which research could discover and ingenuity could devise."[46] These experts would supposedly be beyond partisanship, as they would be adapting society to the objective development of history. Ward claimed that social science could produce the right kind of "social control." Rather than the partisan rancor and bureaucratic incompetence produced by the spoils system, in many areas politics could be replaced by "neutral" administration.

Faith in progress inspired hope that the realm of politics could be reduced and that of technocratic management enlarged. The reformer, Walter Lippmann argued in *A Preface to Politics*, had to substitute "attractive virtues for attractive vices. ... Instead of trying to crush badness, we must turn the power behind it to account. The assumption is that every lust is capable of some civilized expression."[47] Therefore, Progressives believed that the state could and should intervene actively in the economy to promote opportunity, equity, and fairness as well as economic growth. As Croly put it in *The Promise of American Life*: "Democracy must stand or fall on a platform of possible human perfectibility. If human nature cannot be improved by institutions, democracy is at best a more than usually safe form of political organization."[48]

Progressives' public philosophy reflected the tension between their faith in the capacity of the people to govern themselves and the need for policy scientists to handle an expanding range of issues.[49] On one hand, they tried to empower the people through a host of direct democracy measures.[50] In their view, there was no longer a need to be skeptical of the people, or to set up a host of checks on their direct rule, as the Constitution did, because the people had matured and industrial conditions demanded a more active government. During the 1912 campaign, Theodore Roosevelt voiced Progressives' desire to return power to the people:

> Are the American people fit to govern themselves, to rule themselves, to control themselves? I believe they are. My opponents do not. I believe in the right of the people to rule. I believe the majority of the plain people of the United States will, day in and day out, make fewer mistakes in governing themselves than any smaller class or body of men, no matter what their training, will make in trying to govern them.[51]

In his campaign for the Republican nomination and then the presidency as the head of the Progressive Party, Roosevelt championed measures of popular rule including the initiative, referendum, recall, direct primary, and quicker constitutional amendment procedures. Progressives hoped that "pure democracy" would generate a national community that could supersede constitutional democracy.[52]

In contrast to their ideals of popular rule, Progressives sought to transfer more decisions to administrative agencies. Progressives sought to bring more policy areas, especially the regulation of the economy, under bureaucratic control. Again, Roosevelt gave expression to this strain of Progressive thought: "we must have government supervision of the capitalization, not only of public-service corporations, including, particularly, railways, but of all corporations doing an interstate business."[53] Only a vanguard class of administrators could address the inequities of large-scale capitalism. "This New Nationalism," Roosevelt said, "regards the executive power as the steward of the public welfare."[54] Progressives aimed to weaken state parties and the corrupt legislatures they dominated by circumventing them with referenda and initiatives. As mediating institutions, the political parties stood directly in the path of the people's direct exercise of power and an efficiently run national community. They needed to be virtually eliminated.

Expert administrators could circumscribe the number of items that required partisan politicians' attention. Croly argued that "Progressive democracy demands . . . an increase in administrative authority and efficiency."[55] As Roosevelt concluded, "The prime problem of our nation is to get the right type of good citizenship, and, to get it, we must have progress, and our public men must be genuinely progressive."[56] The ideal of progressive democracy, Sidney Milkis has written, "would put the American people directly in touch with the councils of power . . . and require administrative agencies to play their proper role in the realization of progressive social welfare policy."[57]

The Progressives' faith in progress, experts, and the people led them to challenge the value of the Constitution. They saw the Constitution's diffusion of power and encouragement of localism and individualism as impediments to an appropriate response to industrial conditions and the realization of a better form of democracy. The Declaration of Independence had established negative freedom, but Progressives believed more was possible. Therefore, Croly called on the American people to adopt a "New Declaration of Independence," that would "affirm the American people's right to organize their political, economic, and social life in the service of a comprehensive, a lofty, and a far reaching democratic purpose."[58] Such a new declaration would overcome the checks and balances that the Founders had put in place to check majorities, making possible positive freedom through majority rule in a new national community.

The Progressive, Albert Beveridge said, "believes that the constitution is a living thing, growing with the people's growth . . . permitting the people to meet all their needs as conditions change."[59]

Ultimately, the aim of Progressives was to centralize national government authority. As they put it in the Progressive Party Platform of 1912, "we advocate bringing under effective national jurisdiction those problems which have expanded beyond reach of the individual States." Not only did they seek to weaken the political parties but also the powers and jurisdiction of the state governments. Such moves, they held, were essential to ensuring democratic self-government in an age of industrialization.

MODERN LIBERAL REPUBLICANS

Liberal Republicans were primarily a pragmatic and strategic faction that did not seek to fully revamp the party intellectually, but rather only to smooth its rough edges. Liberal Republicans were not short on policy ideas but they were without an overarching ideology. According to David Reinhard, "Modern Republicanism amounted to little more than a *smorgasbord* of liberal and conservative offerings. It lacked philosophical backbone."[60] Distinguishing themselves from regular Republicans on the right and Democrats on the left, Liberal Republicans often defined themselves negatively. While they often mused about the need for a comprehensive public philosophy, they never developed one.

Liberals Republicans did not introduce a new foundational principle into intraparty debate. As one journalist remarked about Thomas Dewey's campaign speeches, they showed "no sign of an underlying philosophy." Others held that Dewey showed "no apparent interest in general ideas."[61] Drawn from the managerial class they were neither defenders of tradition nor orthodox in economics. Not surprisingly, they believed in procedure, organization, and practicality—which did not add up to a principled understanding of politics and governance. They sought, instead, to promote an image of confident, cosmopolitan, and forward-looking management savvy. Such an image would help distinguish them from their rivals, which journalist Samuel Lubell called "the coalition of disillusionment."[62]

Liberal Republicans, often out of a sense of *noblesse oblige*, believed that the state should play a strong role in the economy. Hailing from the centers of corporate power, they believed that wise administration could direct a modern economy. (Indeed, it would be strange to discover that business managers did not believe in management). Therefore, Liberal Republicans countenanced the New Deal proposition that modern capitalism required state intervention to protect citizens and tame the ravages of the market.

State supervision of the economy gave the Liberals another *raison d'être*. Who better to manage the economy than those with specialized training and experience running large-scale organizations? Liberals' efficiency, honesty, and integrity, they claimed, best prepared them to manage the modern state. Moreover, for a time, history seemed to prove them right, or so they thought. Increased state involvement in the economy in the 1950s and 1960s coincided with a massive expansion of the economy, which appeared to belie Republican economic orthodoxy.

The biggest issue dividing the Liberals from their intraparty rivals was the role of the United States in the world. The majority of the party favored different strains of "isolationism," while the Liberal Republican faction championed "internationalism," and America's global responsibilities.

NEW RIGHT REPUBLICANS

The New Right began in the 1950s as a small group of intellectuals and reformers in the Northeast.[63] New Right activists, intellectuals, and donors deemed it imperative to directly confront the ideals of progressivism-liberalism. Only through such confrontation could conservatives establish a credible alternative governing philosophy. Different currents within the New Right combined to push the GOP to adopt a vigorous promotion of American interests in foreign affairs, cultural traditionalism at home, and low tax and deregulation in the economic sphere.

The New Right's central thrust was antistatism. As President Ronald Reagan put it: "[The Founding Fathers] knew well that if too much power and authority were invested in the central government . . . not only would liberty be threatened but it just wouldn't work . . . I think during the last decade and before, we've gotten a taste of just what [they were] warning us about. So much power had centralized in Washington that frustration and stagnation ruled the day."[64] To make this case, it drew on four distinct foundational principles: traditionalism, libertarianism, natural right, and biblical faith.[65] Traditionalists held that government planning disturbed a fragile culture; libertarians insisted that it introduced gross economic inefficiencies; neoconservatives deconstructed the policy failures of the Great Society; and religious believers held that the state promoted secularism. These intellectual positions are so distinct that it is a wonder that the New Right was able to cohere. At least in public, however, common opposition to liberalism forced differences in principle into the background and brought shared positions to the forefront.

Traditionalists, sometimes called "paleo-conservatives," took their bearings from a philosophy of history. Unlike the Progressives, however, they looked to the past rather than to the future for inspiration. The central idea was an association of the old with the right. Cultural practices that had worked in the past should be preserved. The burden of proof for any change was on those advocating the change not on those defending the status quo. Thinkers, such as Russell Kirk (who drew extensively on Edmund Burke), made the standard of right the historical tradition of Anglo-American Protestantism. Tradition in this sense was a set of shared cultural practices that had not developed according to a rational plan but rather emerged organically. The traditionalist view was refined, developed, and popularized by writers such as William F. Buckley and George Will.

The second school is libertarianism, which represented a revival of classical economic liberalism. Drawing inspiration from the so-called Austrian School, led by Ludwig von Mises and Friedrich Hayek, the core claim of libertarianism is "spontaneous order." In this view, human affairs naturally work out for the best through the cooperation induced by markets, as long as government does not intervene. As President Ronald Reagan put it: "Did we forget that the function of government is not to confer happiness on us, but just to get out of the way and give us the opportunity to work out happiness for ourselves?"[66] The "invisible hand" works such that by pursuing their own interests, individuals, associations, and firms are led to benefit the collectivity. This position provided a rational critique—rather than an appeal to cultural folkways—of progressive-liberal efforts to plan outcomes in many areas of the economy and society. At the practical level, libertarians also offered technical analyses of the inefficiencies and ineffectiveness of many government programs. Furthermore, the concept of spontaneous order has been applied by libertarians to all social, political, and economic realms, and even inscribed into a philosophy of history. Progress is the working out of spontaneous order in time. Hayek argued that over time the best human practices are selected and those that do not work are discarded. History is thus an evolutionary process.

The third New Right school of thought is neoconservatism. The foundational idea advanced by neoconservatives is natural right. As a political standard, neoconservatives claim they are returning to the ideas of the Founding Fathers and Abraham Lincoln. They also drew inspiration from the German-Jewish émigré philosopher Leo Strauss. Strauss argued that progressivism and traditionalism both sought to anchor the notion of political right in history. The supposed opposition between these two positions, though important, was secondary; the more fundamental choice was between history and nature. Strauss reopened the question, which most thinkers had regarded as definitively settled (in the negative), of whether a standard of right deriving from nature could be known by human reason and would be universally valid rather than culturally circumscribed, however much circumstances might limit its implementation or adoption.[67] Some of Strauss's followers proceeded to defend the doctrine of natural rights not as mere myth or empty metaphysics, but as a plausible account of nature.

Natural right was reintroduced into political debate in the 1970s in reaction to legacies of the Great Society, especially against quota policies, contract set-asides for minority-owned firms, and educational programs centered on multiculturalism. In this spirit, neoconservative thinkers also engaged in an extensive critique of the power of social science to direct society. The critique of the Great Society centered on the idea that government programs based on social science research often led to "unintended consequences" that hurt those they aimed to help. Neoconservatives called for a greater skepticism about the power of government to engineer society according to an *a priori* plan. In the 1970s and 1980s, neoconservatives also began to defend the full panoply of traditional bourgeois virtues against what they saw as misguided tolerance. Modern Liberalism, Irving Kristol claimed, created an "adversary culture" and led to "moral anarchy."[68]

The final school that informed the New Right was religious faith. It was mobilized by a number of fundamentalist Christian sects concerned with restoring moral order. Outraged by Democrats' acceptance of divorce, abortion, premarital sex, homosexuality, feminism, and Carter's leadership (whom they had supported in 1976), Evangelical ministers such as Jerry Falwell, Pat Robertson, and Jim Bakker embraced the New Right.[69] Evangelical Christians sought to bring their religious convictions to bear on policy issues of concern to them.

The second register of the New Right's public philosophy was moral traditionalism. Here the central concerns were speaking up for school prayer, and opposing abortion, school busing, affirmative action, and liberal "permissivism." The attack was on the cultural innovations of the 1960s and 1970s. To counter those trends the New Right sought to reintroduce the republican virtues of federalism, law and order, and family values. For instance, Edwin Meese, Reagan's attorney general, argued that: "Today's 'moral education' fails [because] no one is taught to dislike and certainly not to hate anything. If young Americans are shaped, they are unfortunately shaped to be moral neuters."[70] In this view, the New Right faction sought to place moral debate at the center of the public square.

The third prong of the New Right's agenda was national defense. The New Right Republicans argued for a major defense buildup, playing on patriotic nationalism, a revived Cold War posture, and the Carter administration's foreign policy blunders. New Right adherents believed that the United States had become overly timid in the wake of Vietnam. The result was Soviet aggressiveness that had to be thwarted. The national security buildup the faction favored was then hitched to a continual effort to celebrate the national spirit. As President Reagan put it: "How can we not believe in the greatness of America? How can we not do what is right and needed to preserve this last best hope of man on Earth? After all our struggles to restore America, to revive confidence in our country, hope for our future, after all our hard-won victories earned through the patience and courage of every citizen, we cannot, must not, and will not turn back. We will finish our job. How could we do less? We're Americans."[71]

By the time Reagan was elected, the New Right Republican faction had developed an extensive theory of governance. In its view, government had become overly centralized in Washington at the expense of the states. Congress and the federal courts had arrogated too much power to themselves and needed to be reined in. Congress was encroaching on presidential functions, especially in foreign affairs. After a decade spent creating new rights for a host of groups, the courts had overstepped their bounds and usurped legislative functions.[72] Encouraged by New Politics Democrats' legislative innovations, they had taken over new policy domains to the exclusion of other important political actors. For instance, the policies instituted after Vietnam and Watergate had fenced in the president. To reverse these trends, the executive needed to be strengthened and the state governments empowered. The expanded powers of Congress and the federal courts had converted the states into bureaucratic receiverships. The New Right held that the states could provide a government that was closer to the people, more opportunities for civic participation, and trim the size of government in Washington.

Bound up with the principled aspects of the New Right's ideological commitments is a fierce debate among historians, political scientists and journalists over the role of race in the New Right's development. Critics of the New Right have interpreted the conservative policy agenda as an effort, so to speak, to keep affirmative action white. Calls to limit government, they contend, would cut off the resources necessary to assist minorities. Critics also claim that Republican electoral strategy exploited the racism of some America voters. The so-called Southern strategy began in the 1950s when Eisenhower and the Republican National Committee hoped to build a bi-racial party in Dixie. However, the strategy quickly morphed into one that backed some segregationist candidates and won the votes of racist whites.[73] Exploiting racial issues is said to have continued with Goldwater's opposition to the 1964 Civil Rights Act; Nixon's calls for "law and order"; and Reagan and Gingrich's attacks on "welfare queens." In this view, the GOP did not directly appeal to Southern racism but employed "coded" messages. In critics' eyes, race should decisively shape our understanding of modern American conservatism.[74]

Other scholars have argued, however, that the Republicans' "Southern strategy" and the movement of the white southerners into the GOP column was driven by much more than just racial backlash. Therefore, they contend, race should be given less weight in conservatism's development. These scholars point to issues of timing, electoral competition, and economic development in the creation of Southern Republicanism. In terms of timing, the GOP was successful in the "outer" or "rim" South—in states like Virginia, Florida, Tennessee, and Texas—as early as 1952. In terms of electoral competition, the GOP did not need the South to win presidential majorities between 1952 and 1980, and the rise of two-party competition democratized the region. Finally, some scholars point to economic development and class politics as powerful forces in opening up Southern whites to Republican appeals.[75] Finally, it is clear that GOP policy positions are not inherently racist, neither have its campaign appeals been explicitly so. Therefore, the exact weight and role of race in conservatism's ideological development remains to be determined.

Democratic Party Factions

POPULIST DEMOCRATS

To leverage the Democratic Party, Populists adopted a narrative that pitted the humble common folk against social and economic elites. Underpinning the division of America into the "haves" and the "have-nots," Populists introduced a new foundational principle into the Democratic Party: the biblical faith of evangelical Protestantism. "When you hear a good Democratic speech," William Jennings Bryan wrote, "it is so much like a sermon that you can hardly tell the difference."[76] Faith became an explicit and active force inside the party for the first time. Although Bryan's efforts to draw Protestant voters into the Democratic fold largely failed, the notion of faith was still important to the Populist Democratic faction's self-conception and animating spirit.

Many who took their bearings from faith were apolitical or politically engaged only on specific issues, such as prohibition and child labor. In the hands of Populist Democrats, however, faith was transformed from something concerned primarily with man's relation to the transcendent into a message that made political reform an essential part of Christianity. As Michael Kazin puts it, "Bryan burned only to see religion heal the world," and "preached that every true Christian had a duty to transform a nation and world plagued by the arrogance of wealth and the pain of inequality."[77] In his famous "Cross of Gold" speech at the 1896 Democratic National Convention, Bryan linked the crucifixion to his monetary program. One evangelical cleric went so far as to say that: "[Bryan] is undoubtedly the Moses to lead us out of the land of the gold-bugs."[78] In Bryan's religiously inspired view, Christian faith dictated political engagement.

Faith informed Populist Democrats' conception of equality, which underwent a dramatic transformation. Hitherto the Democratic conception of equality had primarily been understood to mean political equality; that is, quality before the law. But Populists increasingly defined it in socioeconomic terms. Championing the "public economy" and social welfare increasingly came to define the Democratic Party. This new definition of equality led Populists to abandon a century of commitment to antistatism.

The result was a reworking of the concept of rights. Rather than rights being the basis of negative liberty, they became the source of government expansion to provide citizens with various goods and services. More than thirty years before Franklin Roosevelt announced the need for an economic bill of rights, Populists had basically shifted the meaning of rights to include economic rights. They based these changes on the notion that only with a modicum of economic security could individuals exercise their political rights.

With Christian faith having reconfigured the meaning of equality and rights, Populists went on to offer a distinct response to industrialization, which filled the Democratic Party's national programmatic void. In so doing, they sought to wrest the party from the hands of Northern hard-money men and Southern states-rights conservatives.[79] Inspired by the republican desire for the rule of law rather than men, many Populists wanted to draft detailed laws rather than grant bureaucrats the discretion to solve problems. In contrast to the Progressive Republicans' confidence in experts, "Their goal was the broad expansion of the *statutory* state."[80] They took the party of Jefferson, centered on suspicion of government, and converted it into a vehicle for legalistic statism. Populists favored a national state where laws not experts would govern because they retained some of the Democratic Party's traditional skepticism about concentrated power. Hostile to social and economic elites, Populists nonetheless sought a substantial enlargement of federal power to check corporate excesses and recalibrate sectional imbalances. By investing their faith in legalism, they could argue for an empowered state not open to corruption by men and their interests.

In Populists' hands, the Democratic Party increasingly backed the redistribution of wealth, government regulation of the marketplace, and loose monetary policies. Often this was an attack on "bigness." As William Jennings Bryan put it in 1899, "The Democratic Party will continue its attack upon monopoly, whether in the standard money trust, the paper money trust, or the industrial trust." Their campaign materials emphasized opposition to monopolies, government action on behalf of farmers, and greater popular control of government. Populists repeatedly forced conservative Democrats to assent to their legalistic solutions in areas such as railroad regulation, banking, and antitrust.

SOUTHERN DEMOCRATS

Southern Democrats were an ideologically ambivalent faction because they were animated by two distinct goals that were often in tension: preserving white supremacy and modernizing their region's economy. Under the leadership of men like Senator James Eastland and Congressman John Rankin of Mississippi, Southern Democrats pushed sectional solidarity and invoked cherished values of federalism, a Constitution of enumerated powers, and the Democratic Party as a white man's party.[81] As "Cotton" Ed Smith of South Carolina put it, "I have one platform on which I shall live and die—my loyalty to the Constitution, my loyalty to states' rights, and my loyalty to white supremacy."[82] Preserving the "Southern way of life" often meant excluding others from the region, while spurring economic growth entailed inviting outsiders in. Therefore, on one side, they reacted strongly against any policy that even remotely threatened racial hierarchies. On the other, they were tempted by egalitarian and populist measures that assisted working whites. Thus they developed a flexible public philosophy in an effort to simultaneously protect the racial caste system and accommodate demands for economic development.

At the level of constitutional doctrine, the views of Congressman Howard W. Smith of Virginia are instructive. Smith served in the House from 1931–1967 and was a leader of the conservative coalition as Chairman of the Rules Committee from 1955 to 1966. His biographer, Bruce J. Dierenfield, claims that in the fifties Smith was widely regarded as the third most powerful figure in Washington, after President Eisenhower and Speaker Rayburn. Trained in strict constitutional construction at the University of Virginia Law School (1901–1903), Smith fought the expansion of the federal government. He believed that Congress unconstitutionally intervened in business activity through a gross distortion of the commerce clause. The result was a congressional abdication of power to the president and federal agencies, whose regulations Smith saw as illegitimate usurpations of the legislative power.[83]

Southern Democrats' objective was to channel welfare state expansion so that it would not threaten regional norms. They subscribed to a racialist ideology that posited the superiority of whites over other "inferior" races, especially blacks. The fierce commitment to segregation was, according to V.O. Key, Jr., central to understanding the faction's ideological proclivities: "in its grand outlines, the politics of the South revolves around the position of the Negro," and that "the whites of the black belt who have the deepest and most immediate concern about the maintenance of white supremacy" are those who "give the South its dominant political tone." Ultimately, Key wrote, "the bedrock of southern unity" was the region's "prevailing attitude toward the Negro."[84]

Mississippi Senator James Eastland went so far as to claim that Southern soldiers returning from World War II: "desire more than anything else to see. . . . white supremacy maintained."[85] When threatened, Southern Democrats were apt to invoke their ideological principles against federal measures. In the 1940s, as the faction was beginning to form, Peterson Bryant Jarman of Alabama decried one such measure as "an attack on our southern way of life and on white supremacy in which we have every reason to take much pride," and "is really an arrow aimed directly at the heart of the South, which has always been, is now, and must ever be, white supremacy."[86] In the debate over the 1957 civil rights bill, Howard Smith declared: "The Southern people have never accepted the colored race as a race of people who had equal intelligence . . . as the white people of the South."[87] This racialist foundation was deeply at odds with the views held by other Democrats.

Southern Democrats also held a quasi-Burkean appreciation of tradition. During debate on an Alaska statehood bill in 1958, Senator Richard Russell of Georgia voiced to this view:

> It does so happen that a slightly higher percentage of Senators from the Southern states are traditional in their political outlook. . . . As a general rule a majority of us do not favor change for the sake of change. . . . In the sense that I am opposed to change for the sake of change . . . I gladly plead guilty to being a conservative.[88]

The traditionalism of the South was given its fullest expression in a 1930 book, *I'll Take My Stand: The South and the Agrarian Tradition.*[89] In this mode of thought, the old ways were strongly correlated with the right ways. The burden of proof for any reform initiative rested with the reformers; the old ways consistently received the benefit of the doubt.

Southern Democrats argued for a narrowly tailored role of the national state in the economy and social affairs. As Russell put the matter: "We [Southern Democrats] are generally opposed to excessive spending of public funds. We try to be very cautious in considering legislation which might lead the country down the road to state socialism."[90] Rather than a comprehensive national welfare state, they called for a limited one predicated on means-tested programs and private charity. A system of federal grants-in-aid to the states— which would handsomely benefit the South because it was the country's poorest region—could then be administered locally in such a way as to respect regional differences. Local control could also ensure that national social policy was subordinate to the dictates of the market and would not interfere with the racial issue. Given the absence of labor unions, businesses would find good investment opportunities in the South.

LIBERAL-LABOR DEMOCRATS

Liberal-Labor affiliated intellectuals were the inheritors of a vaguely articulated confidence in bureaucratic expertise that had emerged during the Progressive Era and been revived and reinforced during the New Deal.[91] Liberal-Laborites advocated an expansive role for the central state to address the nation's economic and social problems. However, thinkers associated with the Liberal-Labor faction tended to push controversies over ideological commitments to the background. In the face of Fascism, Nazism, and Communism, Liberal-Labor affiliates made a strategic retreat from strong claims about progress and faith—especially when these ideas had the effect of casting the American past in a harsh light. Instead, they adopted a pragmatic stance and a more traditionally American idiom relatively unencumbered by high-toned theoretical doctrines. "The recipe for retaining liberty is not doing anything in one fine logical sweep," Arthur M. Schlesinger wrote, "but muddling through."[92]

Moreover, the writers that informed the faction's thinking were generally skeptical of any strong theoretical foundation for political life. Such foundations, they held, were dangerous when introduced into political life, as they could be sources of fanaticism. In light of Stalinism, World War II, and the Cold War, they articulated a disillusioned creed, grounded in a sinful human nature, and praised pragmatism, moderation, and pluralism.[93] Reinhold Niebuhr best expressed the skeptical liberal faith in *The Children of Light and the Children of Darkness*. According to Niebuhr, there were no moral certainties in the political world. Therefore, only democratic pluralism could restrain the contrary temptations of utopianism and cynicism. "Man's capacity for justice makes democracy possible," he wrote, "but man's inclination to injustice make democracy necessary."[94] Arthur Schlesinger, Jr.'s bestseller, *The Vital Center*, gave popular expression to this realist view.[95] Ultimately, only in an open, democratic public square, could different convictions be tested and dangerous ideas tamed.

The emphasis on prudence marked a major shift away from the idealism and moralism of Populist Democratic rhetoric. The Liberal-Labor faction held that the investment of such faith in the common people to "humanize" capitalism was a misguided romantic delusion.[96] John Kenneth Galbraith argued that there was no need to fret over capitalism, since Keynesianism could successfully manage it.[97] In any case, economic deprivation was no longer the principal problem. Major class antagonisms had declined, a proletarian revolution was not in the cards, and conflict at the picket line was declining. According to University of Berkeley educator Clark Kerr, "The battles (in the new knowledge society) will be in the corridors instead of the streets, and memos will flow instead of blood."[98] Prudent management, not moral indignation, was the order of the day.

Yet, this did not temper liberals' ambition for state action to solve problems. In an age of increasing prosperity, liberalism's agenda expanded well beyond that of the 1930s. Arthur Schlesinger argued that the New Deal welfare state combined with Keynesian economic management spelled the completion of "quantitative liberalism." The new task for liberals was to usher in "qualitative liberalism," which would "oppose the drift into the homogenized society." It would also "fight spiritual unemployment as [quantitative liberalism] once fought economic employment. It must also concern itself with the quality of popular culture and the character of lives to be lived in our abundant society."[99] Such aspirations for government action became the basis for Lyndon Johnson's Great Society. According to Johnson, the Great Society would "build a richer life of mind and spirit," a society not "condemned to a soulless wealth."[100] Furthermore, the realization of Johnson's program would mean "nobody in this country is poor," and that the aged would enjoy lives with "meaning, purpose, and pleasure."[101]

The great tension at the heart of the Liberal-Labor faction's vision—one confronted by Mugwumps and Progressive Republicans before them—was between the desire for individual flourishing and the felt need for statist management to create the conditions for that flourishing. Wilson Wyatt, the first national chairman of the Americans for Democratic Action, expressed the demands for a larger state role in underpinning human development:

> [We reject] the view that government's only responsibility is to prevent people from starving or freezing to death. We believe it is the job of government to function to lift the level of human existence. It is the job of government to widen the chance for development of individual personalities. It is not enough for society to guarantee physical survival of its inhabitants; it must also nourish the dignity of an individual human being.[102]

Therefore, along with a respect for the individual, especially the creative individual, liberals also tended to embrace economic planning. They sought to reduce the tension between these two aspirations by proposing to place power in the hands of scientists, academics, artists, and professionals that could govern in a way that was good for both leaders and the led.

Underpinning the faction's agenda was a broader set of convictions. On the role of government in society, Liberal-Laborites advocated an expansive role for the central state in solving the nation's economic and social problems.[103] They were confident that technocratic management could manage an industrial economy. This was evident in the Democratic Party's platform positions on economic issues between 1952 and 1964.[104] Yet, the Liberal-Labor faction gave the economic interventionist position new content and meaning. They sought to broaden the party's agenda to include a host of social groups and political issues that did not fit into the populist socioeconomic categories of the opulent rich versus working stiffs. It wasn't the middle classes that needed attention but the desperately poor. No longer was poverty seen as the result of economic causes but rather as a social pathology that could be addressed by an array of subtle policies.

Liberal-Labor advanced a theory of governance that called for greater control of the federal government over the states; more national, internally coherent, and ideological political parties; and, at least under Eisenhower, a stronger policy-making role for Congress vis-à-vis the president. Only a centralized, truly national state could manage a modern economy, enlist the states as administrative units, and equitably distribute goods and services. In 1947, Arthur Schlesinger, Jr., voiced the political strategy of building an expansive welfare state brick by brick: "There seems no inherent obstacle to the gradual advance of socialism in the United States through a series of New Deals."[105] Only such a state could, in President Johnson's words, achieve "not just equality as a right and a theory but equality as a fact and a result."[106] Liberal-Labor rejected the Southern Democrats' vision of a welfare state that relied on means-tested programs run by the states, private charity, and stop-gap federal programs.

To achieve Liberal-Labor's aims, Congress required reform. Liberal-Labor believed congressional reform was a means to correct what they deemed the endemic weaknesses of Congress—its incapacity to act quickly, its inability to plan, and its propensity to delegate power to the executive.[107] The primary obstacle was the decentralized committee system, dominated by conservative Southern Democrats.[108] Not surprisingly, the faction found the idea of British-style parliamentary parties congenial.[109] Disciplined parties would speed lawmaking, enhance Congress's ability to plan, and give the legislature more power when dealing with the president.

Liberal-Laborites also sought to bring a host of new policy ideas onto the public agenda. They adopted a broad set of policy priorities that stretched far beyond the self-interest of unions. Internationally, they adopted a strong anticommunist position and favored a firm response the Soviet Union in the Cold War. Domestically, Liberal-Laborites sought to "complete" the New Deal, pressing for greater rights for African-Americans and unions, national health care, urban renewal, and macroeconomic intervention. By the 1960 election, the Liberal-Labor faction had established the legislative program of the national Democratic Party. As James L. Sundquist put it: "the Democratic program that was presented to the country in 1960 was truly a *party* program . . . the substance of the program had been written with unusual precision and clarity during the [previous] eight years—eight years that at the time seemed endlessly frustrating but that were, in retrospect, extraordinarily fruitful."[110] By laying the intellectual and rhetorical foundations, the faction's networking and lobbying operation had remade the Democrats' policy platform. The shift in priorities and its meaning for the party's public image was not lost on Liberal-Labor's rivals, the Southern Democrats, who protested loudly and repeatedly about the direction of the party.

NEW POLITICS DEMOCRATS

Although the New Politics faction was inspired by high-minded ideals—such as social justice, compassion, diversity, and individual autonomy—it did not seek to link these values to a strong theoretical foundation. To the extent that they were interested in foundational principles, the "spirit" of the views espoused by the New Left informed New Politics Democrats. It also gave their mode of expression a certain tone and style at odds with the older Liberal-Labor faction. New Left thinkers advanced a view of historical development that held that the country was declining and headed toward a nightmarish technological society that would produce an alienated citizenry. America's moral decline could only be reversed by a cultural and political revolution. According to the New Left, America's large state bureaucracies and corporate enterprises destroyed authentic personal relations and had to be overthrown in favor of "participatory democracy."[111] "The goal of man and society," the Port Huron Statement proclaimed, "should be human independence: a concern . . . with finding a meaning in life that is personally authentic." To achieve their aims the New Left grounded their views on a conception of historical development that combined visionary optimism with deep pessimism about the present.

New Politics Democrats did not go to the New Left's extremes of either pessimism or optimism. Nevertheless, the ideas of the New Politics were, as Richard Harris and Sidney Milkis argue, directly "traceable to New Left critiques of the American political economy."[112] The "ideological bridge" between the two was constructed out of materials from the environmental and consumer movements. Each movement linked the New Politics to the more assertive New Left foundational position. Moreover, the frenzied political atmosphere of the 1960s socialized many New Politics types in ways that made such causes ready-made vehicles for their suspicion of capitalism.

In the 1970s, New Politics Democrats also introduced another foundational notion: identity politics, or multiculturalism. Under this banner, political action should take its bearings from the essences of oppressed groups. This view divided the social and political world between the sexist, racist, and imperialist mainstream culture dominated by white males and a soon to be liberated plurality of oppressed groups. Because women and people of different races, ethnicities, and sexual preferences were said to have different ideas and values, each group required their own political representation as well as social and intellectual space apart from the dominant ethos to flourish. After affirming their authenticity, these groups would revive a moribund American society. The new liberalism held that a cadre of enlightened lawyers, program administrators, and others in the "caring professions" was needed to protect victimized groups from a supposedly virulent majority.

Rather than completely reject American society, militate for revolution, or form a counterculture within it, New Politics Democrats sought to use the state—retooled for greater popular participation—to intervene extensively in the economy and society. Despite being deeply suspicious of the establishment in government and business, New Politics Democrats sought to penetrate these arenas and transform them. They wanted to make the state more professional and responsive, especially to certain victimized constituencies, and simultaneously enhance public participation in government decision making. Their vision was of a powerful administrative state run by experts that was also highly democratic and open to citizen input. To Environmentalists, consumers, the poor, minorities, gays and lesbians, women, and the disabled all required state attention—but could also be counted upon to participate in the policy formulation of that attention.

NEW DEMOCRATS

Just when they no longer had to contend with the Southern faction bent on preserving "states' rights" and segregation, the Democrats Party found itself in the curious position of being more united but low on intellectual fuel. New Politics Democrats had given the party a certain image with their defenses of affirmative action; "the right to be different"; the right to clean air, water, and welfare; and stress upon large social and economic forces as the "root causes" of crime, racism, and poverty. New Politics had become expert at satisfying various constituencies but inept at promoting an overall notion of the public interest. As one party leader put it, "The problem is the public's perception of the Democrats. The problem is that we are the party that can't say no, that caters to special interests and that does not have the interests of the middle class at heart."[113] One of the founders of the Democratic Leadership Council, the New Democrats' clearing house, Senator Lawton Chiles (D-FL) recalled that: "When some of us began talking about the future course of our party, the one thing that troubled us was that our party had become the party of caucuses. A caucus for every group but Middle America."[114] In response, New Democrats sought to use new ideas as a source of political change.

Will Marshall of the Progressive Policy Institute laid down the gauntlet to the Democratic Party: "The party's old faith, New Deal progressivism, has run its course. . . . This has left Democrats without a clear governing philosophy that can infuse the party with an impelling sense of common purpose. . . . What is needed today is a new overarching creed."[115] A new creed is what New Democrats have purported to offer.

The public philosophy developed by New Democrats was ultimately more strategic than philosophic. New Democratic thinkers did not devote a great deal of time and energy to establishing the theoretical foundations for their beliefs. For the most part, they sought to tap into the old faith in historical progress that had provided an anchor for the party under Woodrow Wilson. Indeed, deciding to name their think tank the "Progressive Policy Institute" indicated that the appeal to progress was designed, at least in part, to counter the dour notion of historical decline associated with the Left since the 1960s. New Democrats wanted to be seen as optimistic and forward-looking without expending too much effort explaining why they were. It is fair to say that New Democrats were deeply committed to a version of liberal democracy without being too concerned with the philosophic foundations of their version.

New Democrats laid out distinct positions that departed from the party mainstream. Regarding the role of government in society, they sought to shift the party position toward less state involvement and greater friendliness to market-based policy solutions. A large redistributive welfare state should not, in their view, be the party's primary objective. Rather, New Democrats called for using market mechanisms in certain areas, such as health care and environmental regulation, and increasing bureaucratic efficiency. According to New Democrats, there was a new breed of government administrators, armed with a new set of managerial techniques, and they could be trusted to serve the public interest.[116]

Breaking with organized labor, they promoted free trade and deficit reduction as the best ways to spur economic growth. New Democrats macroeconomic prescriptions began with fiscal discipline. They emphasized entrepreneurship and innovation spurred by job training and educational opportunity. These recommendations were anathema to Liberals who believed that economic growth could be produced by increasing public investment, using state power to foster a climate for private-sector job creation, and protecting existing jobs from overseas competition. New Democrats were at their best when it came to advocating technocratic solutions to policy problems. They championed a host of new policies, including welfare reform, deficit financing, volunteerism, and crime reduction.

On cultural values and foreign policy, however, New Democrats were slow to develop coherent, broadly agreed upon positions. They did not feel particularly threatened by the counterculture because they believed that it had been converted into consumerism. Yet, New Democrats re-evaluated that position in 1990s when it became obvious that cultural issues would remain salient. They then began to argue that the party needed to downplay hot-button issues and take a more moderate line when moral and cultural issues were raised. But this was a strategic rather than a principled move. Again, New Democrats approach to issues such as gay rights, abortion, affirmative action, and stem cell research was tactical rather than philosophic.

In foreign affairs, they criticized the larger party for supporting pacifist isolationism, but these themes were largely rhetorical devices and were not objects of intense scrutiny by New Democratic thinkers. The neglect of international affairs was understandable; aside from a few flashpoints, foreign policy was not a major agenda item in the 1990s. Moreover, although New Democrats were concerned about the Carter Administration's legacy in foreign affairs, they cared more about domestic policy. One of the factors leading to the factions demise in the early twenty-first century was the inability of its members to develop a common approach to the new threat of Islamic terrorism and instability in the Middle East.

Conclusion

Looking at the parties through the prism of factions' ideological commitments challenges a number of perspectives on party ideology. Some analysts have held that social class drives party ideology, pitting the common folk against cultural and economic elites. Another school claims that ethnoreligious conflict underpins party alignments. Finally, realignment theory posited that critical elections reconfigured the parties' ideological positions.

The study of factions suggests that none of these perspectives provides a coherent synthesis of American party ideologies. A few factions, such as the Populist and Liberal-Labor Democrats did make class-based appeals but such ideas are not at the heart of the other ten factions' ideologies treated here. Similarly, ethnic, racialist, and religious convictions have been present for the Southern Democrats, Populist Democrats, Progressive Republicans, and the New Right but they have not dominated these factions' ideological discourse. Finally, factions' ideological positions and their stability over long periods of time fail to coincide with the timing of critical elections posited by the realignment school.

The above survey of factions' doctrines shows that rather than being constrained by a binary choice between two monolithic parties, the American system contains within it a highly variegated plurality of ideologies carried along by factions operating beneath the party labels. Factions are agents that provide strategic movement in the political realm, responding with greater agility and subtlety than the parties taken straight. Factional networks are vehicles for taking up ideas, which often developed outside the government institutions, and bringing them into the public sphere. Considering factions as ideological networks helps us see the interaction and connections between the political tasks of mobilization and organization.

For some factions ideas are a primary motivation, making it difficult to adapt or abandon them; others treat ideas as means to certain ends, such as recasting their party's reputation and winning elections. The different way factions conceive of and treat ideas can have important effects on their strategies and tactics. Furthermore, factions' ideological agendas are important party resources. They provide ideas and narratives that party members can draw upon. Ideas that redefine the public debate on an issue can play a significant role in political change. Therefore, factions can change the balance of power within a party and its ability to compete with the other party. Ultimately, a faction's character has consequences for the political system as a whole.

CHAPTER 4

Selecting a Party Leader

FACTIONS AND PRESIDENTIAL NOMINATIONS

In countries with runoff presidential election systems, such as France or Brazil, factions form their own parties, which can negotiate deals between the first and second rounds. The United States, however, only has two parties. These parties are forged on the anvil of factional competition over presidential nominations. Factions often influence whom the parties designate as their standard-bearer. Their motive to secure the nomination for one of their own is obvious: It is a fulcrum with which factions can leverage their party and move it along the Left-Right political spectrum. The selection of a particular candidate is central to prioritizing certain policy initiatives and thereby shaping the "brand" of the party to which they belong.

Factions want a candidate with views close to, if not identical with, their own. The party as a whole needs a candidate who can win the general election. It is the competing values of orthodoxy and victory that induce tension between factions and the party during the nomination process. To outmuscle their rivals within the party, factions employ a wide variety of tactics, such as media campaigns, grassroots mobilization, delegate credentials challenges, and patronage promises. Each faction's goal is to secure enough support from the rest of the party to win the nomination. After that point, however, greater support dilutes the benefits of a candidate's factional alignment. Sometimes the fights between factions lead the party to choose a compromise candidate. Such choices, of course, still reflect the influence of factions on determining the nominee.

This chapter makes three claims and pursues them though the historical record. One is that factional conflict at the nomination stage is—appearances to the contrary—a sign of party strength rather than weakness. Contrary to Austin Ranney, factional competition prior to selecting a nominee evinces party vitality.[1] The Democratic Party of 1948 was riveted by Southern and Liberal-Labor factions, but Harry Truman still managed to win the general election. The Republican Party of 1912 was split by factions but quickly recovered. The strength of a party with factions can be seen in the fact that most of the time factions support the nominee, even if he is not their first choice. General elections show that factionalized parties are still capable of waging (and even winning) a campaign. Factional conflict does not cause the party to end in ashes.[2] The analysis here comports in large measure with the UCLA School's characterization of the nomination process as reflecting "weak structures, strong parties."[3]

Another point is that factions have endowed the presidential selection process with much more continuity than most analysts have found.[4] Despite major changes in the mode of presidential nominations over the last one hundred and forty years, factions have consistently been important pieces in the presidential nomination puzzle. They have been particularly important actors in an institutional arena where the rules of the game have never been stable. Nearly every cycle brings into play changes in those rules. Since the 1870s, factions have regularly schemed to change party rules and state laws to improve their prospects. Factions are a source of continuity in the midst of so much institutional change. The fact that there is no clear location of authority to determine the rules of the presidential selection process has allowed factions to exploit the consequent uncertainty. Even though new institutional arrangements are supposed to provide new structures and redistribute power to new locations, the finding of this chapter is that factions are consistent players in the process.

Political scientists have engaged in extensive debate about how, when, and why parties' nomination structures have changed. In the traditional view, there have been three modes of presidential nomination since 1832. The first was the convention model (1832–1912). In it, powerful state party leaders controlled the selection of delegates and dominated the "smoke-filled rooms" around the convention site. Decision-making power was said to be in their hands. Aspirants to the White House did not campaign openly for the nomination. Instead, they pursued an "inside" strategy, which entailed persuading party leaders that they could win. In 1912, the convention model underwent a slight modification, as some states introduced primary elections or otherwise reformed their method of selecting convention delegates in ways that made the process more transparent. These reforms allowed candidates to pursue an "outside" strategy, which entailed demonstrating their popular support by winning primary elections. But even within this so-called mixed system (1912–1968) state party leaders still had the final say at the convention. In 1972, however, control of the nomination by party leaders was brought to an abrupt end within the Democratic Party. Reforms led many states to adopt primary elections, which handed the power to pick the nominee to primary voters. These changes dramatically weakened the power of state party leaders, as candidates created their own ad hoc organizations and campaigned openly for the nomination. The Republican Party soon mimicked the Democrats, ushering in the "candidate–centered" system (1972–present).

For scholars who adopt an organizational definition of a party, only the arrangements from 1832 to 1968 can produce a strong party. It was during this period that the organization controlled the selection of nominees and was underpinned by powerful party organizations and leaders in the various states. For those who adopt the politician-centered definition of parties, the post-1972 candidate-centered system shows that parties are the creatures of office seekers and are responsive to voters, and that party strength declined with the end of the leader-dominated party convention. Furthermore, according to the office-seeker definition of parties, popular leaders should be able to dominate the candidate-centered system. The factional perspective claims that these organizational changes are less important than is often assumed. Because factions are active in the nomination debate prior to the convention in both the convention and candidate-centered systems, the specific rules of the system do not strengthen or weaken the party. The contest among factions also means that powerful candidates are unable to force themselves on the party.

Finally, the historical account presented here suggests that the decline-of-parties thesis—as seen through the lens of presidential nominations—is wedded to a questionable historical periodization. Howard Reiter has pointed out that most nominees between 1928 and 1968 were chosen on the first ballot, which suggests that the nominee was chosen prior to the convention.[5] Aaron Wildavsky, James Q. Wilson, and Everett Carll Ladd, Jr., have shown that activists had become much more important elements of convention politics by the 1960s.[6] Even at their peak in the late nineteenth and early twentieth centuries, powerful patronage parties existed in only a few states and cities, which meant that party leaders at the convention probably exercised less control, and that amateur activists were more important, than is often assumed.[7] Finally, presidential aspirants had begun to form entities resembling their own campaign organizations prior to the convention as far back as William Jennings Bryan in 1896. Therefore, what scholars often take to be new elements—uncontested conventions, the rise of ideological activists, and the creation of candidates' own ad hoc organizations—predate the reforms of the 1970s. If the party was never as strong during the convention period, it is not nearly as weak in the candidate-centered system. Conversely, if candidates and activists were stronger well before the 1970s, the changes inaugurated in that decade were less dramatic. Attention to factions underscores these continuities.

From the end of the Civil War to the present, factions have engaged in similar activities, assisting candidates in important tasks, such as securing funds, campaign staff, and high-profile endorsements. They provide candidates with ideas and endow them with at least the appearance, if not always the reality, of momentum. By channeling various elements and energies within the parties, factions help shape their destiny.

Examining presidential nominations over the 132-year period from 1872 to 2004 (33 nominations for each party), slightly less than one-quarter of the nominees (16 of the 66) could be considered the heads of factions at the time they were placed at the top the ticket. This comports with the findings of other political scientists that if one faction dominates nominations over the strong objections of another, it is unlikely to enjoy great success.[8] Nine men captured these sixteen nominations (Greeley, Bryan, Willkie, Dewey, Goldwater, Humphrey, McGovern, Reagan, and Clinton). These factional champions have a poor track record when it comes to winning the White House. Only two, Reagan and Clinton, made it to the Oval Office. This record of factional activity suggests that few champions of factions win the nomination, and even fewer win the presidency. Seven nominees were affiliated with a faction when they were nominated and seventeen unaffiliated. Thus one-third (23 of 66) of the nominations were either the champions of factions or seen as being closely affiliated with a faction. In nearly two-thirds of the cases, factions were a consideration. Only twenty-eight of the nominations occurred when there were no factions in the party.

The third claim of this chapter is that factions perform three important roles in the presidential selection process. One is as gatekeepers, where their aim is to block candidates affiliated with their rivals. The goal is to raise the political costs for their opponents in hopes of nominating one of their own or finding a compromise choice that owes the faction something. A second role is to enable their champion or an affiliated candidate to win the nomination. To secure the nomination for their champion, factions use tactics of elite bargaining, grassroots mobilization, and media campaigning. Sometimes, they even go so far as to attempt to change the rules of the nominating process itself. The third role is as dissidents, where factions defect from their party and become the source of splinter parties (treated in the next chapter). Since the turn of the last century, third parties have often been the result of a faction that develops within a party only to emerge during an election cycle under their own name. Most twentieth-century third parties were short-lived and focused almost exclusively on the presidency, in contrast to antebellum third parties, which indicates something of their factional origins.

As the cases discussed below demonstrate, a faction's tactics often depend on its size, position, and ideological commitments. Larger, better-established, and more pragmatic factions tend to adopt blocking strategies. Smaller, newer, more ideological factions tend to be enablers, who try to take over the party by nominating their candidate, or if frustrated to defect into splinter parties.

Table 4.1 **Relation of Presidential Nominees to Factions**

Year	Nominee	Nonfactionlized Party	Head of Faction	Affiliated	Nonaffiliated
1872	Grant (R)			XX	
1872	Greely (LR/D)		XX		
1876	Hayes (R)			XX	
1876	Tilden (D)	XX			
1880	Garfield (R)			XX	
1880	Scott (D)	XX			
1884	Blaine (R)			XX	
1884	Cleveland (D)	XX			
1888	Harrison (R)	XX			
1888	Cleveland (D)				XX
1892	Harrison (R)	XX			
1892	Cleveland (D)				XX
1896	McKinley (R)	XX			
1896	Bryan (D)		XX		
1900	McKinley (R)				XX
1900	Bryan (D)		XX		
1904	Roosevelt (R)				XX
1904	Parker (D)				XX
1908	Taft (R)			XX	
1908	Bryan (D)		XX		
1912	Taft (R)			XX	
1912	Wilson (D)				XX
1916	Hughes (R)	XX			
1916	Wilson (D)				XX
1920	Harding (R)	XX			
1920	Cox (D)	XX			
1924	Coolidge (R)	XX			
1924	Davis (D)	XX			
1928	Hoover (R)	XX			

Table 4.1 (continued)

Year	Nominee	Nonfactionlized Party	Head of Faction	Affiliated	Nonaffiliated
1928	Smith (D)	XX			
1932	Hoover (R)	XX			
1932	Roosevelt (D)	XX			
1936	Landon (R)	XX			
1936	Roosevelt (D)	XX			
1940	Willkie (R)		XX		
1940	Roosevelt (D)				XX
1944	Dewey (R)		XX		
1944	Roosevelt (D)	XX			
1948	Dewey (R)		XX		
1948	Truman (D)				XX
1952	Eisenhower (R)		XX		
1952	Stevenson (D)				XX
1956	Eisenhower (R)		XX		
1956	Stevenson (D)				XX
1960	Nixon (R)				XX
1960	Kennedy (D)	XX		XX	
1964	Goldwater (R)		XX		
1964	Johnson (D)				XX
1968	Nixon (R)				XX
1968	Humphrey (D)		XX		
1972	Nixon (R)				XX
1972	McGovern (D)		XX		
1976	Ford (R)				XX
1976	Carter (D)				XX
1980	Reagan (R)		XX		
1980	Carter (D)				XX
1984	Reagan (R)	XX			
1984	Mondale (D)	XX			
1988	Bush I (R)	XX			

(continued)

Table 4.1 (continued)

Year	Nominee	Nonfactionlized Party	Head of Faction	Affiliated	Nonaffiliated
1988	Dukakis (D)	XX			
1992	Bush I (R)	XX			
1992	Clinton (D)		XX		
1996	Dole (R)	XX			
1996	Clinton (D)		XX		
2000	Bush II (R)	XX			
2000	Gore (D)			XX	
2004	Bush II (R)	XX			
2004	Kerry (D)				XX

* This list only includes the nominations of the two major parties. I exclude factional candidates that launched third-party campaigns, such as Roosevelt in 1912, Thurmond in 1948, and Wallace in 1968.

Gilded Age Factions

From the end of the Civil War to the election of 1888, the Republican Party was rent by factionalism. The contest among three factions—the Liberals (Mugwumps), Stalwarts, and Half-Breeds—had a powerful effect on the nominating politics of the period. The clash of factions led to the victories of dark-horse candidates Rutherford B. Hayes in 1876 and James Garfield in 1880. The hotly contested nomination of James G. Blaine in 1884 weakened him in the general election against Democrat Grover Cleveland. These nominations occurred in a period of close party competition for the White House. Hayes lost the popular vote to Samuel Tilden in 1876, Garfield eked out a victory in 1880, and Blaine lost narrowly to Cleveland in 1884.

After the Civil War, the largest and most powerful of the GOP's factions, the Stalwarts, drove the Liberal faction from the Republican fold in 1872. In addition to dominating states with a large number of Electoral College votes, such as New York, Pennsylvania, and Illinois, Stalwarts could also rely on the support of the South because they subsidized the Southern Republican Party with federal patronage. In 1876, however, the Stalwarts entered the presidential selection process in a weakened position. The Grant administration's scandals had tainted them. In addition, they were divided over favorite senators Roscoe Conkling (New York) and Oliver P. Morton (Indiana). Because Stalwarts lacked someone who could pose as a "reformer," they were forced to cooperate with Liberals to block the selection of their nemesis, James G. Blaine. Blaine's moderate policies and captivating personality earned him broad support. Yet, questions about his health and concerns about his involvement with several railroad companies weakened his candidacy. Lacking strong support in any quarter, Conkling and a group of reformers were able to block his candidacy.

The blocking activity of rival factions allowed a relatively obscure governor to emerge as the party's presidential nominee. With the leading candidates of the three major factions (George Edmunds, Conkling, and Blaine) deemed unsuitable, the GOP was forced to look elsewhere for a nominee. Hayes emerged victorious because he was acceptable to all party factions. For Stalwarts, he had remained loyal to Grant in 1872 and had been endorsed by the Grand Army of the Republic. For machine politicians hungry to retain control of federal patronage, Hayes's proven ability to win elections made him satisfactory.[9] Liberals founds his positions favoring civil service reform, hard money, and leniency toward the South congenial. Had they known that Hayes had written the following in his diary in 1875, they would have cheered: "I do not sympathize with a large share of the party leaders. I hate the corruptionists . . . I doubt the ultra measures relating to the South, and I am opposed to the course of Gen. Grant on the 3*d* term, the Civil Service, and the appointment of unfit men on partisan or personal grounds."[10] In a come-from-behind victory over a number of convention ballots, Hayes defeated Edmunds, Blaine, Conkling, Morton, and Benjamin Bristow (another Liberal favorite).[11]

Four years later, in 1880, Hayes had withdrawn from the race citing his own beliefs about terms of presidential service (but it is also unlikely he would have been renominated, given strong Stalwart and Half-Breed opposition). Factional gate-keeping facilitated the emergence of another relatively unknown politician, James Garfield, as the GOP standard-bearer. As early as the summer of 1878, Stalwart newspapers began calling for Grant to run again. When he returned from a world tour in the fall of 1879, he was arguably the most popular political figure in the country. Conkling, John Logan of Illinois, and Simon Cameron of Pennsylvania, known as the "Triumvirate" or "Great Syndicate," organized his renomination effort well in advance of the convention. Their efforts approximated the personal organizations candidates would develop in the twentieth century.

To secure convention delegates, the Stalwart strategy was to secure the South, win the West, and control New York, whose convention votes were a major step toward securing the nomination. To win over reluctant delegates, Conkling promised posts in a future Grant administration. At the convention, the Triumvirate sought to impose the unit rule (according to which a majority of a state's delegates could force the entire delegation to cast its votes for one candidate). If the rule had held, Grant probably would have won. But there was enough time before the convention for opposition to mobilize.[12]

Liberals stridently opposed another Grant term. They favored Treasury Secretary John Sherman or Vermont Senator George Edmunds. Yet, the real opposition to a third term for Grant came from the Half-Breeds. The Half-Breed faction solidified in the run-up to the 1880 Republican convention, and Blaine threw his hat in the ring. Having already been passed over for the nomination in 1876, Blaine was a formidable candidate. Half-Breeds organized a National Blaine Club; and small Blaine Clubs appeared throughout the country. These efforts support the notion that amateur activists were engaged in the nomination process well before the 1960s. When the June convention arrived, Blaine already controlled almost half the committed delegates.

As the GOP headed into the 1880 convention, one historian has estimated that through their factional networks Conkling and Blaine controlled about 85 percent of the convention votes.[13] This level of preconvention organizing suggests that candidates developed something close to personal campaign operations to enlist support. Consequently, the Republican Convention in Chicago was one of the most savage displays of intraparty strife in American history. For thirty-four ballots, Grant's and Blaine's support remained nearly identical. Grant's support was based on the Stalwart strongholds of the South, New York, and Pennsylvania. Blaine's support, as in 1876, was spread across the nation. Sherman and Edmunds, the Liberal candidates, found their backing in the Northeast.

Stalwarts and Half-Breeds fought over credentials, voting rules, and organization. When Stalwarts tried again to pass a unit rule for delegate voting, Garfield, the chairman of the Rules Committee, who was affiliated with the Half-Breeds, championed a rule allowing each delegate to vote individually. This hurt Grant's chances because it released anti-Grant voters in Illinois, New York, and Pennsylvania. For thirty-three ballots the candidates deadlocked. On the thirty-fourth and thirty-fifth ballots, a massive shift in favor of Garfield occurred. On the 36th ballot, he received a majority of 399 votes to 306 for Grant, and 42 for Blaine.

Garfield's victory was the result of factional conflict. Before the convention, he hadn't even been dignified with dark horse status. Esteemed within the party, he was virtually unknown to the general public. Because Garfield had secured the nomination with a combination of Liberal Republican and Half-Breed support, he recognized his debt to the latter by making Blaine his most trusted campaign advisor and later Secretary of State. To compensate the Stalwarts and heal party divisions, Garfield offered a New York Stalwart the vice-presidency, tendering the nomination first to Levi Morton, who, on Conkling's orders, turned down the position. Garfield then approached Chester A.

Arthur, who accepted over Conkling's objections. President Hayes rejoiced at Garfield's selection:

> There is much personal gratification in it. The defeat of those who have been bitter against me. The success of one who has been uniformly friendly. The endorsement of me and my Administration. The endorsement of civil service reform. The sop thrown to Conkling in the nomination of Arthur, only serves to emphasis the completeness of his defeat.[14]

In 1884, the Stalwarts again found themselves in a difficult position. After Garfield's assassination by a deranged job seeker, Arthur had become president. He disappointed Stalwarts by signing the Pendleton Civil Service Act. In addition, Conkling had died, which weakened the New York organization. Consequently, "Black Jack" John Logan was the only Stalwart candidate in the field. But other Stalwart's such as Thomas Platt and Grant did not strongly support him. Therefore, the Stalwart-Liberal combination was unable to stop Blaine's nomination as they had in the two previous contests. Demonstrating that factional conflict does not permanently fracture parties, the Stalwarts fell in line behind the man from Maine, who nominated Logan as his vice-presidential candidate. Unable to block a "machine ticket" in the convention hall, however, Liberals—then called Mugwumps—determined to stop it at the voting booth by shifting their support in key swing states, such as New York, to Democrat Grover Cleveland. The *New York Times* called Blaine an "utter scoundrel" and predicted that he would lose New York where Liberals were such a strong force.[15] A young Theodore Roosevelt reacted harshly to Mugwump action in the 1884 election, saying, "The Goo-Goo and Mugwump idiots are quite as potent forces for evil as the most corrupt politicians."[16]

From 1872 to 1884, factionalism was the determining element of presidential nominating politics in the Republican Party. With three factions vying for supremacy within the party, the result was extremely close general elections, as Liberals bolted the party in 1872 and 1884. But this did not greatly damage the party's long-term prospects, as it won the presidency in 1888 and again in 1896, 1900, 1904, and 1908. Factional conflict sustained a vital and vibrant party, rather than serving to enfeeble and emasculate it. Factions' gate keeping also facilitated the emergence of compromise candidates in circumstances that were as President Hayes described them, "in no respect extraordinary save in the closeness and consequent uncertainty of the result[s]."[17] Finally, the activity of the GOP factions in these nomination contests slowly served to erode the antebellum tradition of the leader-dominated convention and encourage a more candidate-centered politics.

Old Guard and Progressive Republicans

The 1912 presidential election was one of the most spectacular in American history. The battle for the Republican presidential nomination began in the congressional elections two years earlier. The Old Guard faction, which had dominated the party since the 1896 elections, was intent on retaining control. In January 1910, the Republican Congressional Campaign Committee, headed by Old Guard congressman William B. McKinley (R-IL), announced that it would officially oppose Progressives in the summer primary elections and only endorse "straight" or "loyal" Republicans. President William Howard Taft joined the conservatives in a "well planned and generously financed campaign to root insurgency out of the party by defeating progressive representatives for renomination in primaries in the Middle West."[18] Taft agreed to Nelson Aldrich's proposal to establish a fund to elect "orthodox Republicans," and personally called a meeting in Iowa to strategize. The administration and the Old Guard carried out similar operations in Kansas, Nebraska, Washington, Wisconsin, and California. In each state networks of "Taft Republican Clubs" were formed to support "regular" Republicans against Progressives in the primaries. This anti-Progressive effort employed federal patronage and sent "standpat" orators to the region. Intraparty bitterness was so great that some of the Republican state conventions ended in raucous brawls. Again, these efforts indicate the activist engagement and extensive ad hoc organizational activity long in advance of the convention.

However, the election results of 1910 made grim reading for Old Guard Republicans. The Old Guard's effort to purge the party of insurgents backfired badly. In primary battles between Progressive and Old Guard Republicans, conservative candidates lost almost every contest. Some Progressives interpreted the results to mean that their attempt to take over the Republican Party was succeeding.[19]

After the disastrous 1910 elections, the Old Guard took other steps to head off the Progressive insurgency. Former President Theodore Roosevelt had been the wild card in American politics since his return from Africa in the summer of 1910. President Taft sought the former president's endorsement, but Roosevelt refused to commit to his renomination. Instead he began gearing up to challenge Taft, either by supporting the Progressives' titular leader Wisconsin Senator Robert La Follette, or by trying to claim that mantle for himself. Taft responded decisively to the threat by organizing state conventions before the Progressive forces had a chance to mobilize and quickly captured Southern Republican convention delegates. At these conventions Taft's lieutenants made lavish patronage promises to beleaguered Southern Republicans. Although Taft was likely to lose in the general election if renominated, he doggedly pursued the prize.[20] Taft's organizational maneuvers were those of a presidential aspirant in the candidate-centered system. As Sidney Milkis has pointed out, Taft was the first sitting president to actively campaign to be renominated. Taft himself said: "I feel humiliated that I, as President of the United States, am the first one that has had to depart from the tradition that keeps the President at home during political controversy."[21]

Once Roosevelt supplanted LaFollete as the titular leader of the Progressive faction, he tried to capitalize on his continental reputation. The new device of primaries to select convention delegates, adopted in fifteen states by 1912, allowed Roosevelt to display his popularity among voters. He sought to make the direct primary a national issue and win enough popular support (and delegates) such that a critical mass of Republican regulars would switch from Taft to him at the convention. But even after creating an extensive personal organization and winning these primaries, the Rough Rider was well short of the number of delegates needed for the nomination. Of the 1,078 total delegates, only 360 were chosen by direct primaries, the rest were selected through traditional state conventions and caucuses, which heavily favored Taft. Nonetheless, Roosevelt waged an innovative campaign that enlisted a variety of outside groups—especially reformers in the Social Gospel movement—in its support.[22]

Despite Roosevelt's popularity and primary victories, the best that his lieutenants could do was challenge the Southern delegates' legitimacy at the convention. Even with Roosevelt breaking tradition to appear at the convention in person, these credentials challenges failed. After the Taft forces selected New York Senator Elihu Root chairman of the convention, virtually all the disputed delegates were decided in favor of Taft.[23] An embittered La Follette also refused to release the thirty-nine delegates pledged to him, which might have elected Wisconsin Governor Francis E. McGovern chairman of the convention and opened the possibility of resolving delegate disputes in Roosevelt's favor, thus eliminating the last possibility of a Progressive *coup* at the convention.

Ultimately, Taft controlled a bitter Chicago convention and secured the nomination. A course of events foreseeable eighteen months before the election—a party split and Democrat Woodrow Wilson's victory—soon came to pass. But the decline of the convention itself as the locus of decision making, which had been driven by the Republican factionalism of the late nineteenth century, was completed by the factional campaigns of 1912. While the final decision was made at the convention, the Old Guard and Progressive factions of the party ushered in the first truly candidate-centered nomination campaign in American history.

Populist Democrats

The Populist faction profoundly influenced the Democratic Party's presidential nominating politics of the Progressive Era.[24] Populists took their case into presidential politics, nominating William Jennings Bryan in 1896, 1900, and 1908. Bryan has the dubious distinction of being the only candidate to be nominated three times by a major party and to lose in the general election all three times. Yet, Populists discovered that securing the presidential nomination for a champion of a faction led to a quick and dramatic change in party platforms and campaign rhetoric.[25] To secure the nomination in 1912, Woodrow Wilson adopted a new progressive outlook and established strategic links with Populist Democrats.[26] The Populist faction was instrumental to the nominations of both Bryan and Wilson.

Economic depression and defeat in the 1894 midterm elections provided the opportunity for an emergent faction to take over the Democratic Party's presidential apparatus. Dissatisfaction with Grover Cleveland's administration gave Bryan and the Populists a chance to win the nomination. With their eyes fixed on 1896, the reformers' principle objective was to secure the presidential nomination of one of their own. To secure delegates and pressure state party leaders, Populists who supported free silver created new associations, such as the American Bimetallic League, the National Bimetallic Union, and the National Democratic Bimetallic Committee. Among the leaders of this movement were Senators James Jones of Arkansas, David Turpie of Indiana, and Isham Harris of Tennessee.[27] In the fall, they met in Washington to lay their plans for the campaign, forming a national committee to recruit and organize free silver Democrats for the purposes of taking over the party organization. In addition, Populist Democrats saturated the country with articles, pamphlets, essays, and books to advance their agenda.

Despite this budding organizational infrastructure, Bryan worked alone. Indeed, his efforts resembled the creation of an individual campaign apparatus seen in the post-1972 period. "While the Democratic National Bimetallic Committee shouldered the burden of reorganizing the party internally," Stanley L. Jones has written, "Bryan individually took on the larger task of rallying the great multitude of free silver voters, who were not traditionally Democrats, into a silver Democratic party."[28] Bryan's speeches in Congress and throughout the nation made him a powerful national voice for reform. He made a special effort to network with the recently elected Populist Party legislators in Congress and gained control of the Democratic and Populist parties in his home state.[29] In 1895, Bryan toured the South and West promoting free silver and establishing a personal following within the Democratic Party. From his home in Nebraska, Bryan sent fellow Democrats and Populists articles and copies of his speeches. He also exhorted them to take up the cause of silver and broader reform.[30]

Bryan's aim was to take over the Democratic National Convention. He tirelessly pushed two goals to make his nomination possible: first, that silver delegates comprise a majority of the convention, and second, that they be uncommitted to any candidate. Beginning with Bryan's "Cross of Gold" speech, which distinguished him as presidential timber and inspired the writing of a radically new party platform, Populist Democrats took over the Democratic National Convention in three of the next four cycles.[31] Bryan was, however, soundly defeated in the general election by Republican William McKinley. In the "battle of the standards," McKinley received 7.1 million votes to 6.5 million for Bryan. McKinley won 23 states for 271 electoral votes; Bryan took 22 states and 176 electoral votes.

In 1900, Bryan's nomination was a foregone conclusion.[32] However, another defeat in November returned him to the speaking circuit. To keep the Populist message alive in those lean years, Bryan founded a magazine, *The Commoner*. The organizational efforts of his brother and the magazine helped maintain the faction's network. In 1904, the Democratic Party nominated New York Judge Alton B. Parker as its presidential standard bearer to satisfy conservatives from New York and Southern Bourbons alienated by the party's economic radicalism and two consecutive defeats. Populists only had a list of second-stringers as potential nominees—including Senators Francis M. Cockrell and William Stone of Missouri, Mayor James H. Head of Memphis, and Judge Walter Clark of North Carolina. The Eastern press dubbed them, "Bryan's Little Unknowns from Nowhere."[33] None of these candidates were able to make headway against Parker at the convention.

Immediately after Parker's defeat, Bryan and Populist Democrats began planning for 1908. By nomination time, according to Lewis L. Gould, "Bryan had achieved ascendancy among Democrats that approached possession of a personal machine within the party."[34] Bryan's titular leadership rested on his magazine, which sold 140,000 copies a week, and a massive mailing list of like-minded voters. Although the resources the faction commanded for popular mobilization and intraparty bargaining were sufficient to win the nomination, Taft beat the Commoner in the general election worse than McKinley had.[35]

In 1912, it was the power of Bryan's titular leadership, his de facto control of the party's nomination, and a desire to tap into his following, that transformed Woodrow Wilson, previously a Cleveland Gold Democrat, into a progressive presidential candidate. Bryan's dramatic interventions at the Democratic National Convention in Baltimore led the delegates to include many progressive measures on the platform on which Wilson would run. John M. Cooper concludes that, "Wilson inherited from William Jennings Bryan a reformist Democratic Party, which he refined and solidified as a coalition of less advantaged groups seeking to advance their interests through the welfare state."[36] Without being a product of the reform forces in the party, Wilson chose to affiliate himself with them. A year before the convention, Wilson had said that "No Democrat [could] win whom Mr. Bryan does not approve."[37]

In the battle for the nomination Wilson was surprised when the Populist-affiliated Speaker of the House, Champ Clark, decisively defeated him in primaries in Illinois, Massachusetts, and California. Wilson also found his Southern support shaky as Tom Watson of Georgia and J.K. Vardaman of Mississippi supported Alabama Representative Oscar Underwood. Therefore, as Cooper puts it, "Wilson had no choice but to play the reformist, antimachine, anticorporation cards."[38] But Bryan was cool on Clark, who had allied himself with more conservative Democrats such as Judge Parker. With Bryan's support at a boisterous national convention, Wilson scored a major come-from-behind victory. It took forty-six ballots. Yet, such intraparty conflict did not fundamentally weaken the party. After Wilson's election Bryan said: "Mr. Wilson is the best modern example of Saul of Tarsus. . . . He has been soundly converted."[39]

From 1896 to 1912, Bryan and the Populist faction used insider bargaining and media campaigns to control delegates to the Democratic national conventions. Indeed, it was the combination of Bryan's factional support and his communication skills that overawed his rivals. And this was before the rise of modern telecommunications, which are said to have abetted the candidate-centered character of modern nomination politics. Although Populists operated within the convention system, with the limited exception of 1912, they combined mass mobilization of later presidential nominations campaigns with the more traditional insider bargaining techniques.

Modern Liberal Republicans

Between 1940 and 1956 "modern" or Liberal Republicans dominated the GOP's presidential selection process. The public's general support of the New Deal welfare state gave Liberal Republican candidates an entrée.[40] While their regular Republican colleagues opposed Franklin Roosevelt and all his works, the Liberal Republicans' task was to move the party toward the political center. The nominations of Wendell Willkie (1940), Thomas Dewey (1944 and 1948), and Dwight Eisenhower (1952 and 1956) were meant to give the party centrist appeal. These factional candidates were accepted but not embraced by the rest of the party because they held out the possibility of winning the White House and making inroads into Democratic areas. The

GOP's minority status enhanced the Liberal faction's position in the party's presidential wing.

Coming into the conventions of the period, Liberals could count on solid support in the Northeast, which totaled roughly a third of the convention vote, and states in the Midwest and West with progressive traditions. To defeat their rivals, Liberal Republicans either blocked Southern delegations through credentials challenges or co-opted them with patronage promises. Willkie and Dewey pioneered this preconvention approach to winning a delegate majority. Again, in 1952, by replacing Senator Taft's southern delegates with Eisenhower supporters after credentials challenges, the General captured the nomination by a narrow margin. Liberal Republicans' strategy was thus to lock up key regions prior to the convention and force the battle to hinge on the South—the region most likely to abandon party orthodoxy in favor of a winner. This required the faction to mobilize new activists. In the months prior to the convention, the Willkie campaign held public rallies and organized local Willkie-for-President Clubs. Indeed, Howard Reiter takes the Willkie campaign to be the harbinger of the candidate-centered system.[41] William G. Carleton argues that: "The nomination of Willkie defied all of the old rules."[42]

The 1940 Republican presidential selection process was an opportunity for Liberal Republicans to divide and conquer. The contest came down to a struggle between Willkie (who had been a Democrat until 1938) and the GOP regulars' Robert Taft (Ohio). Willkie relied on the support of clubs organized by partisan amateurs, publishers, financiers, and media magnates.[43] Willkie's support from Wall Street was crucial. Its law firms and investment banks lobbied Republicans across the country to support him at the convention. But Taft retained the allegiance of many elected officials, especially fellow congressmen. Despite Taft's support in the Midwest and the South, Willkie forged a winning coalition of the Atlantic seaboard and the Pacific Coast. By winning the party's nomination, Willkie attracted a new generation of urban, middle-class liberal activists to the Republican Party.

After Franklin Roosevelt defeated Wilkie in 1940, the task of consolidating Liberal Republicanism fell to Dewey, who became governor of New York in 1942. Dewey appealed to that slice of the American professional class that supported internationalism abroad and limited social reform at home but disliked the Democratic Party because of its racist southern faction or its alliance with labor unions.[44] Dewey's organization exercised predominant influence at Republican nominating conventions throughout the 1940s, and his home state of New York became the most fertile soil for Liberal Republicanism. It produced such lights as Senator Jacob Javits, New York City Mayor Fiorello La Guardia, and Governor Nelson Rockefeller. As a source of campaign funds and media power, as well as its position in the Electoral College, New York was essential to Republican strategists in presidential elections.

Liberal Republicans were able to prevail at national conventions between1940 and 1956 because of their solid support in the Northeast. To this sum they added the progressive strongholds of Michigan, Minnesota, Oregon, and California. They won these delegations because they often controlled the governorships of these states and the Republican Governors' Association. In 1952, there were thirty-two Republican governors, a majority of whom could be considered Liberal Republicans.

In 1952, for the fourth straight time, the Republicans selected the most electable candidate rather than the one who reflected the party mainstream. That year, Dewey convened a meeting of twenty-five Republican governors to line up support for Eisenhower. While Liberal Republicans celebrated the victory of an affiliate who owed them a good deal, their control of the Republican Party began to crumble. Eisenhower's triumph over Taft concealed the faction's weakness inside the party. For many Republicans, Eisenhower became an apologist for FDR and a target of Barry Goldwater and his followers in the late 1950s. The General simply wasn't an authentic or "real" Republican.

In 1960, Vice President Richard Nixon followed the Liberal Republican script for securing the presidential nomination. Yet, Nixon realized that the elements Liberals had relied upon were weakening. Therefore, during Eisenhower's second term he solidified his relationships with party leaders across the country. Nixon made a point of courting conservatives by campaigning and raising money for them. These activities and Nixon's relatively conservative reputation necessitated a meeting with the leading Liberal Republican, Governor Nelson Rockefeller of New York. Nixon flew to New York and met with Rockefeller. They produced a compromise statement on disputed policy issues. Conservative Republicans were furious at what appeared to be another bow to Liberal Republicanism. Arizona Senator Barry Goldwater called Nixon's compromise the "Munich" of the GOP. Although there was little that could stop Nixon from winning the nomination, the episode embittered many on the Right. After Nixon's nomination in 1960, no other candidate with Liberal Republican connections would ever again be nominated for president.

The Liberal faction's organizational efforts displayed many features of later periods of presidential nominating politics. The campaigns were centered on candidates who were often more personally popular than was their party. Outside groups, such as corporate lawyers, editors, and middle management provided important resources not linked to the official party. Each campaign drew in new activists. In sum, while Liberal Republicans still needed to work at the conventions of the period to secure victory, the desire of the party to win the presidency overrode concerns about ideological orthodoxy.

New Right Republicans

The 1964 Republican nomination demonstrates that activists aligned with factions could potentially play a major role in the nomination process well in advance of the formal change to the candidate-centered system, which, for the GOP, did not fully occur until the late 1970s. A faction could thus determine a great deal well before any primaries or the convention itself. After a divisive nomination process and crushing defeat in the general election in 1964, the party recovered to win three of the next four presidential elections.

In the 1960s, the New Right faction staunchly opposed Liberal Republican candidates such as Pennsylvania Governor William Scranton and Nelson Rockefeller. In the fall of 1961, a group of New Right activists met at a Chicago motel to plot a takeover of the GOP's presidential nominating system. Led by F. Clinton White, a savvy tactician and strategist, the New Right engineered Arizona Senator Barry Goldwater's nomination for president by the Republican Party in 1964. Their strategy was to gain control of the party by securing a delegate base that combined the Midwest, the Southwest, and the North. White coordinated a handful of obscure rank-and-file organization men, tapping contacts from his service as chairman of the Young Republicans. The group announced the Draft Goldwater movement in April 1963. The initial strategy was simple but effective. First they encouraged the candidacies of numerous favorite sons to deny Rockefeller delegates. Then they saturated the press and the Republican Party with messages that Goldwater could win. Consequently, no other candidate was able to secure a majority of delegates before the convention.

One condition that helped the New Right stymie their rivals was that for the first time in thirty years there was not a popular Liberal Republican in the race. Rockefeller lacked appeal to GOP primary voters. Henry Cabot Lodge refused to enter the fight. And William Scranton did not throw his hat into the ring until it was too late. The widespread view that President Lyndon Johnson was invincible also helped Goldwater. Ultimately, many New Right Republicans were so intensely committed to the defeat of a moderate candidate to compensate for years of frustration in presidential politics that other considerations were overridden.

By the summer of 1964, after a few primary battles, the delegates headed to the convention with Goldwater as the clear favorite. To secure delegates, the Goldwater movement took over precinct meetings, county and state committee meetings, and state party conventions. Their aim was to select conservative delegates ahead of time who would vote for Goldwater at the convention. Working within a system of indirect local elections favored White's strategy, since the most conservative activists participated at the precinct level. Despite a concerted effort by Scranton to "Stop Goldwater," which induced many Republican politicians to refuse to appear with him on the stump, Goldwater secured enough delegates to ensure his nomination.[45]

After Johnson's crushing defeat of Goldwater in 1964, however, none of the New Right's victories in the 1966 election were enough to empower the faction in the GOP's presidential politics of 1968. For many activists, California Governor Ronald Reagan still lacked sufficient experience to command the entire party. The faction simply lacked candidates to compete. Although the New Right was not thrilled by a Nixon candidacy in 1968, it took steps to block Rockefeller.

The Watergate scandal elevated House Minority Leader Gerald Ford to the White House. Yet, Ford's appointment policies deeply alienated the New Right. Affiliates were particularly incensed by his selection of Rockefeller to be vice president. In addition, the appointment of other Liberal Republicans, such as Scranton to his advisory staff and Charles Goodell to head a program for amnesty for Vietnam draft resisters, offended the New Right. Ford's policy choices, such as support for the Equal Rights Amendment, increased budget deficits, and his refusal to meet with Alexandr Solzhenitsyn were cause for more outcries. Consequently, as William C. Berman argues, "By the time Ford made plans to run for the GOP nomination in 1976, he had to confront . . . a massive bloc of discontented voters inside and outside of his own party, who were looking for a white knight to lead their charge against an allegedly bankrupt Republican presidency."[46] The president had failed to quell a factional revolt within his party.

In the 1976 Republican nomination contest, Reagan led the New Right forces into battle against President Ford. Reagan was still remembered for what was known among his supporters as "the speech" at the 1964 Republican National Convention, where he told the country: "the issue of this election [is] whether we believe in self-government or whether we abandon the American revolution and confess that little intellectual elite in a far distant capital can plan our lives for us better than we can plan them ourselves."[47] In 1976, Reagan secured the backing of New Right politicians such as Idaho Senator James McClure, South Carolina Senator Jesse Helms, Illinois Congressman Phillip Crane, and governors James Edwards of South Carolina and Meldrim Thomson of New Hampshire. He was also endorsed by most of the activist base as well as the faction's intellectuals and their periodicals. The Reagan campaign's strategy was to win a few early primaries to establish himself as a serious contender. But Ford foiled this plan by narrowly beating him in New Hampshire and then handily in Florida. Analysts speculated that Reagan's conservative economic positions, especially his discussion of social security's problems, damaged his campaign. In addition, Reagan's early selection of Pennsylvania Senator Richard Schweiker to be his running mate—a Liberal Republican—offended conservative supporters of Reagan's candidacy. Ford went on to win other important primaries and secure the nomination in a close vote at the convention (Ford 1,187 to Reagan 1,070). Ford's loss to Carter, however, set the stage for a New Right candidacy in 1980, as the 1976 campaign allowed Reagan to win wider name recognition, build organizational ties, and develop a longer contributor list. As Paul Laxalt, a Nevada Senator and the chairman of Reagan's campaign, put it: "though we lost we really won."[48]

By 1979, the New Right was poised to once again nominate a presidential candidate of their own. In March of that year, Laxalt helped form the Reagan for President Committee. A dozen senators and congressmen and over 350 prominent Republicans joined him. Reagan also commanded the fundraising power of many PACs established in the 1970s. After George H.W. Bush upset Reagan in the Iowa Caucuses, Reagan found his stride, defeating Bush in a number of states until he finally withdrew from the race. To assuage moderates in the party, and soften his image as the champion of a faction, Reagan later selected his rival as the vice-presidential candidate. Reagan thus left the Republican National Convention with a party unified behind him. In November, Reagan carried 44 states and won 489 electoral votes. The head of a faction had been elected president.[49]

The 1988 GOP primary contest featured one early surprise but resulted in the predictable outcome. Vice President George H.W. Bush was the heir apparent to Reagan, but his moderate image and policy positions did not inspire the New Right. Some conservatives from the Reagan administration leaked to the press that if Bush stumbled in the primaries, they would support try to recruit Laxalt to run for president.[50] Indeed, all Bush's challengers—Kansas Senator and Majority Leader Bob Dole, New York Congressman Jack Kemp, televangelist Pat Robertson, and Pat Buchanan—attacked him from the right. Bush's worst fears appeared to be coming true after he came in third in the Iowa Caucuses behind Dole and Robertson. It was only thanks to a win in New Hampshire that Bush was able to stave off the implosion of his campaign. Bush also invested heavily in the Southern states to erect a "firewall" after New Hampshire. The victory in the Granite State and significant campaign activity in the South were enough to force his poorly funded rivals out of the race. Ultimately, the New Right had to settle for Bush. The nominee then tried to shore up his support with conservatives by inviting Buchanan to speak at the Republican National Convention, who delivered his now famous "culture war" speech.

Because the New Right was successful at mobilizing activists, exploiting modern campaign techniques, and securing the nomination for one its own both before and after the transition to the candidate-centered system, it makes the strongest case for the continuity factions provide in the presidential selection process.

Liberal-Labor Democrats

The Liberal-Labor faction was the only centralizing mechanism in the Democratic Party's presidential campaigns. Organized labor distributed money, leaflets, telephone banks, and provided polling services, campaign researchers, seasoned strategists, and canvassers.[51] Its' electoral efforts included voter registration drives and get-out-the-vote campaigns. The Committee on Political Education (COPE) pulled so many voters into the Democratic Party that "labor functioned [in the 1950s and1960s] as the most important nation-wide electoral organization for the Democratic Party."[52] In some areas of the country, according to Byron Shafer, labor entirely displaced the organizational apparatus of the Democratic Party.[53] Labor's efforts on behalf of state and local officials made it a formidable power in the delegate selection process for the Democratic National Convention.

The AFL-CIO leadership often attended and was usually in close contact with strategically placed operatives at the Democratic conventions from 1956 to 1972. Indeed, AFL-CIO President George Meany believed he had a de facto veto over the Democratic Party's presidential and vice-presidential nominees.[54] At a minimum, the party professionals (until 1972) were conscious of the need to select a candidate approved by the AFL-CIO.

In the "mixed system" of presidential selection that prevailed from 1912 until 1972, state party leaders chose the majority of delegates to the national convention, while a minority was chosen in primary elections. This system of elite bargaining enhanced labor's power, since labor organizations were very powerful within many state parties. According to Taylor Dark, organized labor became the Democratic Party's central powerbroker.[55] David McDonald of United Steelworkers described his activity at the 1960 Democratic National Convention in Los Angeles, as follows:

> I chivvied and bullied and pleaded and traded and threatened and maneuvered on the convention floor to get [Kennedy] votes ... I delivered the hundred Steelworkers votes, prodded the Pennsylvania delegation (headed by a Catholic who thought a Catholic couldn't win) into voting as a bloc for Kennedy, and perhaps convinced a scattering of other from the depths of my own conviction.[56]

The 1960 and 1968 presidential nominations were the great tests of the faction's influence. (The 1964 Democratic convention was fittingly called "a dreary wasteland of Lyndon-knows-best.") The 1960 campaign was the most active labor had ever been in presidential nomination politics, which was also the first truly competitive contest since 1952.[57] Despite initially favoring Senator Hubert Humphrey (D-MN), union leaders soon decided to throw their weight behind John F. Kennedy. Meany, Reuther, and other labor leaders took up Kennedy's cause behind the scenes. They assisted him in several primaries and in rounding up support within state delegations. Labor's activity was instrumental in defeating the Southern congressional leadership's opposition to Kennedy.[58] The faction was able to block the challenges of candidates favored by their Southern competitors. Throughout the preconvention campaign, ADA liberals, who wrote articles in influential magazines in support of Kennedy, assisted labor.[59] The faction's flexibility made it an ideal vehicle in the "mixed system" of presidential selection.

After Johnson withdrew from the 1968 presidential nomination race, labor quickly switched to their longtime ally Humphrey. At the 1968 Democratic Convention in Chicago, amidst protest over the Vietnam War, the AFL-CIO played its powerbroker role to the hilt: Party contacts were tapped to yoke together a delegate majority for Humphrey. As David Broder observed: "never before has the national labor federation become so openly involved at so early a stage in the fight for the Democratic presidential nomination."[60] The AFL-CIO could claim to influence a third of the delegates, given the power of state and local office holders who were indebted to labor for campaign support. Spread among many delegations, labor delegates provided intelligence to COPE director Al Barkan, who promoted Humphrey's candidacy. Despite strong opposition from the emerging New Politics faction that supported Eugene McCarthy, labor pulled off a coup for Humphrey.[61]

The Liberal-Labor faction viewed Humphrey's nomination as a great victory. But to others in the party, labor's actions seemed like a raw power play. Labor's refusal to endorse McCarthy "deeply alienated other factions within the Democratic Party, including the newly insurgent [New Politics] forces of youths, minorities, women, and the opponents of the Vietnam War."[62] The emotions unleashed would come back to haunt unions, as they provided the fuel for a new faction that would ultimately undermine labor's special role in Democratic presidential politics. As Barkan put it, "The biggest reason for staying out of the primaries is that you're forced to pick and choose among your many friends."[63] Moreover, candidates could cut labor leaders out of the bargain and appeal directly to rank-and-file members in primary campaigns.

This problem became evident almost immediately. Labor's nonendorse-ment of George McGovern in 1972 arose from what J. David Greenstone described as labor's "cultural ideology . . . differences on foreign policy, and such cultural issues as permissiveness, the work ethic, and social and sexual deviance."[64] But, as one operative said, it also stemmed from the fact that "the one thing the AFL-CIO can't forgive McGovern for is the one thing he can't do anything about: if he's nominated he won't owe labor anything."[65] The rise of a new faction meant that labor's position in the presidential selection process had been undermined.

The decline and fall of the Liberal-Labor faction in the 1970s changed the role of organized labor in presidential nominating politics. The labor move-ment was also changing, as it came to be dominated by public employee unions, who were more white collar, racially diverse, and closer to gender parity. Consequently, labor's values also began to shift in the direction of a new liberalism and away from more traditional material concerns. Nonethe-less, the party remained viable. Carter won the presidency just four years after McGovern's defeat.

New Politics Democrats

New Politics Democrats interpreted the 1968 presidential election process to mean that Democrats must move to the left to galvanize new voters. Strategic divisions provided New Politics reformers a window of opportunity to orga-nize and advance their agenda. They sought to shift the party to the left by al-tering the Democratic Party's presidential selection procedures. In 1972, the insurgent faction helped engineer the nomination of Senator George McGov-ern, possibly the most left-wing candidate in the party's history. McGovern's victory in the nomination contest marked a high point for the New Politics liberalism.[66]

The New Politics Democrats blocked their rivals using newly minted proce-dural rules that instituted primary elections as the way candidates secured del-egates at the convention. Between 1968 and 1972, New Politics Democrats spearheaded massive changes in the party's organizational operation. They hoped that the rules changes they instituted would effectively block more con-servative Democrats in the future, opening the way for their type of candidate. The effect of these changes was to allow New Politics supporters of McGov-ern—who had served on the committee that designed the changes and best understood them—to block challengers within the party.

Therefore, it was a faction that effectively decided the 1972 nomination contest by working well in advance of the official process (the primaries or the convention) to change the party rules in ways that favored candidates aligned with it. This factional technique would have been familiar to factions of previous eras, who worked assiduously before the process began to manipulate state party rules to ensure the right slate of delegates. Therefore, even in the first truly candidate-centered presidential selection contest, it was in good measure a faction that set the table for McGovern's victory. The affiliated activists did the rest during the primaries.

Maine Senator and 1968 vice-presidential nominee Edmund Muskie was the party establishment's candidate. Washington Senator Henry "Scoop" Jackson represented the party's center-right. Hubert Humphrey also joined the fray late and became McGovern's chief obstacle to winning the nomination. Yet none of these candidates could defeat McGovern. In nearly every state, he was able to mobilize more white-collar activist support. Only Alabama Governor George Wallace was able to generate much grassroots enthusiasm. But his campaign was abruptly finished when an assassin's bullet paralyzed him. Strong showings in Wisconsin, Florida, Massachusetts, Pennsylvania, and Ohio put McGovern in a commanding position. In each state, McGovern was able to expand his base to include key groups coveted by Muskie, Wallace, or both. Bruce Miroff argues that McGovern's organizational savvy and his supporters' enthusiasm explain his success.[67] The final test between McGovern and Humphrey came in California. After a hard-fought contest, McGovern emerged victorious, which ensured his nomination at the convention. Four short months after this triumphant moment, Nixon crushed McGovern in the general election.

Yet, New Politics Democrats' hope was largely realized four years later, in 1976, when the party nominated Georgia Governor Jimmy Carter and the American people elected him president. Although New Politics types were initially skeptical of Carter, he did not disappoint them. In 1976, the McGovern-Fraser reforms began to take full effect, as over thirty states held primaries compared to just twenty-one in 1972. The Democrats' presidential selection process of 1976 hewed most closely to the ideal of the candidate-centered system. In this respect, while the New Politics faction slowly came around to Carter, his personal campaign operation was the driving force to a greater extent than the other cases examined here.

Using the new primary system, and greatly assisted by the Watergate scandal, Carter defeated George Wallace in North Carolina, Scoop Jackson in Pennsylvania, and Morris Udall in Wisconsin. Despite the late entry into the contest of Idaho Senator Frank Church and California Governor Jerry Brown, Carter was able to secure enough delegates to win the nomination. In the short term, at least, the system put in place by New Politics Democrats achieved their desired results by blocking the conservative or establishment candidates

(Wallace, Jackson, and Udall). Of course, Carter was greatly assisted in securing New Politics support by the fact that Massachusetts Senator Edward
Kennedy had decided not to enter the race.

Carter capitalized on being a political outsider unfamiliar with Washington and rode a wave a cynicism about politics that swept the country in
the 1970s. Carter's penchant for moral leadership appealed to New Politics
sensibilities. Unwilling to take a firm stand on many issues during the nomination contest, Carter stressed values in his primary campaign. He argued
that American government needed a strong dose of integrity, honesty, and
compassion. These themes resonated with New Politics Democrats' conception of political leadership.[68] Nonetheless, Carter's campaign for the
nomination remained slightly isolated from the New Politics faction, which
to the extent it was active on his behalf, worked at the grassroots to round
up primary voters. In this regard, 1976 most closely approximated the
decline-of-parties thesis, where a candidate ran and won without the support of the party organization, the establishment in Washington, or a party
faction.

New Democrats

If imitation is the sincerest form of flattery, New Democrats paid the New
Politics Democrats high tribute. New Democrats sought to change the party's
presidential nomination process to defeat their opposition, just as New Politics
Democrats had done in 1969–1972. They believed the nomination system
favored liberal activists and placed the eventual nominate too far to the left to
be able to credibly move to the center for the general election. In anticipation
of the 1988 presidential election, the overhead agency for New Democrats, the
Democratic Leadership Council (DLC), helped engineer "Super Tuesday"
(March 8, 1988), when Democrats in twenty, mostly Southern, states held primary elections on the same day. New Democrats resorted to a technique
familiar to convention-era factions: manipulate the rules to gain advantage.
These efforts were undertaken well in advance of the formal nomination
process and were meant to take the emphasis off the candidates' personal organizations. The DLC's hope was that more conservative Southern voters would
dilute the influence of Iowa and New Hampshire, forcing candidates to the
center of the political spectrum. It hoped this would boost the fortunes of the
New Democrats' preferred candidate, Tennessee Senator Al Gore.

This strategy failed because it increased the visibility of Jesse Jackson, the
faction's chief rival.[69] Super Tuesday demonstrated that New Democrats
could not secure the nomination for one of their own simply by changing the

nomination rules. While Gore won four states on Super Tuesday, Jesse Jackson won five, and the eventual nominee, Massachusetts Governor Michael Dukakis, came away with Florida and Texas. While a large number of the elected officials associated with the DLC were from the South, it was clear that a political strategy that depended on primary voters in the region could not be the pivot to leverage the party. Democratic primary voters, even in the South, were more liberal than New Democrats anticipated. After the 1988 nomination and convention, the National Democratic Party seemed to have made the DLC irrelevant. However, after Dukakis' defeat in the general election, New Democrats could legitimately contend that they were more necessary than ever.

After a failed effort to tinker with nomination rules, the DLC sought new ways to field a presidential candidate to run on its program. DLC Director Al From recruited Arkansas Governor Bill Clinton to become the organization's president in 1990 and created the Progressive Policy Institute. From boldly told Clinton in Arkansas: "If you take the DLC Chairmanship, we will give you a national platform, and I think you will be president of the United States."[70] Two years later, Clinton ran for president as a "New Democrat." He skillfully used the organization's resources and contacts to launch his bid for the Democratic nomination. The DLC apparatus was especially important for a largely unknown governor of a small state. Clinton was an ideal New Democratic candidate, insofar as he had a wonkish grasp of policy detail and the ability to cogently express it to average voters.[71]

Events favored Clinton. In the primaries, he had the good fortune of facing largely second-tier competition. Most of the heavyweight contenders—such as Al Gore, Mario Cuomo, and Richard Gephardt—dropped out in the face President George H.W. Bush's 90 percent approval ratings in the wake of the American victory in the Persian Gulf War. With Paul Tsongas running to his right and Jerry Brown to his left, Clinton positioned himself in the center.[72] Prior to the nomination contests in Iowa and New Hampshire, the *Washington Post* gave him frontrunner status. Despite nagging questions about his marital infidelities and personal history, Clinton was hard to characterize as a sixties leftist because his message was that of a moderate DLC member from a conservative southern state.[73] The *San Francisco Chronicle* claimed that Clinton's winning the nomination represented "a historic and dramatic shift for the party."[74] In the general election campaign, he followed DLC prescriptions, even selecting follow DLCer and moderate Tennessee Senator Al Gore as his running mate. He tamped down social issues and played up the fact that if Americans "worked hard and played by the rules" they would get ahead in life. In his "New Covenant" convention speech, Clinton declared: "We offer opportunity. . . . We demand responsibility."[75]

Even in the candidate-centered system, Clinton relied extensively on a factional network, first, to launch his campaign, and second, to provide him with policy ideas and rhetorical tropes. Therefore, rather than exclusively rely on his own organization, Clinton used the DLC to raise funds in Washington and connect him to activists in the states. This resembled some of the organizational operations that predated the candidate-centered system.

Conclusion

Contrary to the view that changes in modes of presidential selection have dramatically altered the character of the parties, this chapter has shown that factions have operated in similar ways across time, creating greater continuity in how these contests work than a focus on the "rules of the game" would lead one to believe. Attention to factions also challenges the view that parties have declined since the changes enacted in the nominating process in the 1970s. Finally, by looking across such a broad historical sweep, it becomes evident that parties are not weakened by factional conflict in the nomination process. They can be deeply divided and riddled with conflict and still succeed in the general election.

Insofar as presidential selection is largely determined by elites, factions can play an outsized role. Surveys of party activists have revealed that they tend to be closely attuned to slight variations in candidates' positioning and ideological appeals. Factions help activists within a party sort out their preferences and then provide resources for their favorites.

An historical perspective on the role of factions in presidential nominating politics enriches the discussion of how each of the different nominating systems has functioned and how changes to it might (or might not) lead to different outcomes. If factions have played a role regardless of the system and insider elite candidates have dominated the field, we might speculate that changing the current rules, whatever other positive benefits that might have, will not stop factionalized elites for trying and probably getting their way in the new system. The reality is that factions within America's two big-tent parties have been significant sources of continuity. And they have helped make the parties stronger, not weaker, by vigorously contesting party nominations for president.

CHAPTER 5

Breaking Up the Party

FACTIONS AND SPLINTER PARTIES

If factions are unable to secure the nomination for one of their own, negotiate a compromise candidate, or block an unsatisfactory nominee, they have only one remaining option: exit. On such occasions a few factions have formed splinter parties. As James Q. Wilson and John DiIulio put it, "factional parties are created by a split in a major party, usually over the identity and philosophy of major party's presidential candidate."[1] Such separations are often dramatic divorces—even if the parties eventually get back together. Long ago, V.O. Key detailed the circumstances in which splinter parties created by factions could have their greatest impact. According to Key:

> [American political history offers] striking illustration[s] of the strategic position that may be won by minor parties and of their potential influence on the programs of the major parties. . . . Not every minor party can club a major party into acceptance of its policies. To do so the third-party must have its strength concentrated in close states, and the nationwide contest as a whole must be regarded by party leaders as close. Otherwise, the splinter group carries no threat to the fortunes of the either major party candidate.[2]

The conditions for factional parties exercising power as described by Key applied in five cases: 1872, 1884, 1912, 1948, and 1968. In 1872, Liberal Republicans bolted the GOP to nominate *New York Tribune* editor Horace Greeley. In 1884, when they were called Mugwumps, Liberals supported Democrat Grover Cleveland, rather than Republican James G. Blaine. In 1912, insurgents bolted the GOP to nominate Theodore Roosevelt on a Progressive Party ticket. When segregation came under direct threat, some Southern Democrats launched quixotic splinter parties in 1948 (Strom Thurmond's Dixiecrats) and 1968 (George Wallace's American Independent Party). In

87

each case, factions found the system of presidential selection stacked against them. In some instances their effect was magnified by the alignment of forces in the presidential election.

Creating a splinter party for an election cycle or two is a risky move that factions occasionally make in hopes of changing their party's preferences and shifting its reputation to the left or the right. This chapter discusses factions that believed that by creating their own party they could refight the battle they lost at the nomination stage. Looking at the cases treated here, splinter parties are rarely able to affect the left-right shift of their party of origin that they seek. Liberal Republicans efforts in 1872 brought few changes to the Republican Party's policy choices or public image over the next four years. After the Bull Moose campaign of 1912, the GOP remained a solidly conservative party. And the Dixiecrat and Independent Party campaigns of 1948 and 1968 did little to force the Southern Democrats agenda onto the larger Democratic Party. Despite their limited impact on their original party, these factional parties have provided dramatic spectacles in American politics.

Factional parties' limited influence on their party of origin results, most obviously, from the fact that they must oppose their own party during the campaign. In order to re-enter their former party in the wake of defeat, the bolters must do so on its terms. Furthermore, even if a splinter party candidate demonstrates the popularity of some of the faction's policy preferences, the larger party has ample time to co-opt and digest them before the next presidential election cycle. The two conditions for splinter party influence, according to Key, are the strength of such parties in swing states and a nationally close election. Even with these conditions met in the cases analyzed here, these splinter parties have been unable to influence the programs of the parties that gave birth to them. Let us examine each case in turn.

Liberal Republicans

In 1871, it was clear that Ulysses S. Grant would be renominated and that Liberals lacked the resources to take over the convention. Liberals estimated that their position within the party system increased the chances that they could achieve their goals by splitting the party. Therefore, they tried to make the necessity of a new party apparent to the nation, and sought, throughout the 1871–1872 congressional session, to expose the scandals of the Grant administration.[3] Liberal Senators met frequently with activists outside of Congress. Missouri Senator Carl Schurz became the most zealous and effective promoter of a splinter party strategy.[4] He organized associations and clubs throughout the North and South to bring together the "best men" from both parties.[5]

The Democratic Party's attitude was important to Liberal strategists. In fact, they hoped to commandeer a weak and disorganized party because a new party would only be viable with Democratic support. Liberal tacticians recognized that the discredited and marginalized status of the Democratic Party offered a unique situation. Schurz negotiated in secret with the Chairman of the National Democratic Party August Belmont in an effort to fuse the two parties behind the Liberal ticket. Other Liberals went further. In Ohio, New Hampshire, and Connecticut, they tried to dissolve the Democratic state parties and rebuild them as Liberal entities. When Democratic leaders assessed the situation, they saw the choice as between a possible victory with the Liberals or certain defeat. Therefore, delegates at the Democratic National Convention endorsed the Liberal platform and presidential nominee.[6]

To the astonishment of many, the Liberal Convention in Cincinnati nominated Horace Greeley. The editor of *The Nation*, E.L. Godkin, described Greeley as "a conceited, ignorant, half-cracked, obstinate old creature" and held that his election would be "a national calamity of the first magnitude ... the triumph of quackery, charlantry, and recklessness."[7] His nomination exposed the Liberals chief problem: the lack of a credible national standard-bearer. Liberals suffered acutely from a malady that has plagued nearly all splinter parties in American politics: the dearth of quality candidates. There were a large number of candidates competing for the nomination, but they all had significant liabilities. Greeley had a history of erratic judgment and was not a serious promoter of the Liberal ideology. To Liberal intellectuals, the convention had nominated an eccentric who opposed free trade and hard money, was uninterested in civil service reform, and had supported bizarre causes such as vegetarianism. Schurz believed his nomination deprived the Liberal movement of "its higher moral character" and asked him to withdraw.[8] Greeley's journalistic career was also a political liability. All of the different, and at times conflicting, positions he had taken were in print, making him easy to attack. Republicans easily pilloried his shifting positions during the Civil War and Reconstruction.[9] The nomination decision doomed both the Liberals' effort to become a viable third party as well as their prospects for taking over the Democratic Party. The election results were decisive: Grant crushed Greeley in the fall.

A dozen years later, Liberals, then called Mugwumps, again played the role of defectors. A leading Mugwump periodical wrote:

While the issues upon which Republican and Democratic parties have been long arrayed against each other have in great part ceased to be prominent, it must not be forgotten that a new generation of voters, which has grown to manhood since the war, will appear at the polls this year. Their votes will be very effective in determining the results, but they will not be affected by the consideration which hold old Republicans and Democrats to their party allegiance. These new voters regard chiefly principles and persons.[10]

With near parity in party strength in 1884, the Mugwumps sought to play each party off the other for maximum benefit. Their strategy was to leverage the Republican Party by threatening to bolt it, while keeping open the possibility, should they shift to the Democrats, of cashing in on electoral debts. In the run-up to the GOP convention, Mugwumps began to organize politically in the swing states. The aim of these organizational efforts was to "establish such communication between Republicans throughout the country, and especially in the doubtful states." This would allow them to "lay before the Convention, with authority, representation of Republican sentiment fitted to prevent unwise nominations, or should such be made, to impose the responsibility for defeat on such candidates on those who nominate them." Mugwumps urged the party to "take every proper measure to promote the nomination of a Republican candidate who is a satisfactory exponent of the progressive spirit of the party, and who would command the hearty support of independent voters."[11]

The Blaine-Logan "machine ticket" that emerged from the Republican National Convention in 1884 horrified Mugwumps, who bolted the party to join the Democrats. In their eyes, Grover Cleveland stood for civil service reform and honest government. Because the election would be determined by small fluctuations in key swing states, the Mugwumps' decision to split the party took on great significance. Due to its importance in the Electoral College, New York became a major battleground, where Mugwumps fought regular Republicans. To win the presidency that year required a minimum of 201 Electoral College votes. Democrats could count on roughly 150 votes and Republicans on 180 votes in their core states. Securing victory therefore required winning some combination of four swing states (New York, Indiana, New Jersey, and Connecticut). After a bitter campaign, and a few tactical errors in New York by the Blaine campaign—in particular the famous Delmonico's dinner and the Blaine's refusal to distance himself from the "Rum, Romanism, and Rebellion" alliteration—Cleveland emerged victorious. Because Cleveland won New York by only 1,143 votes, Mugwumps claimed that their defection had moved New York into the Cleveland column.[12] Out of the 1,670,175 votes cast in the Empire State Cleveland's margin of victory represented 0.1 percent of the popular vote.

Progressive Republicans

From 1884 to 1912, factions were largely inoperative in Republican presidential nomination contests. The selections of McKinley (1896 and 1900), Roosevelt (1904), and Taft (1908) were largely foregone conclusions. In 1912, however, Taft was considered the head of the Old Guard faction, and Roosevelt was widely viewed as a champion of Republican Progressivism.[13] Taft's victory over Roosevelt for the GOP nomination caused a defection of Progressives into a third party, which ensured Woodrow Wilson's victory in the general election. The former New Jersey Governor captured 435 Electoral College votes and 42 percent of the popular vote. At the head of the Progressive Party ticket, Roosevelt came in second, winning 27 percent of the popular vote. Taft came in third. While factional conflict within the Republican Party in the first two decades of the twentieth century had a major impact on only one presidential contest, that impact was profound. It did not, however, leave a lasting mark on Republican policy positions or the party's reputation.[14]

Events portending a party split followed fast on the heels of the 1910 elections. In the immediate aftermath of the elections, forty-seven Progressive Republican members of Congress declared themselves unbound by the positions of the Republican Conference and thirteen Senators demanded recognition as a separate unit of the Republican Party entitled to their fair share of committee assignments.[15] In December 1910, La Follette and others formed the National Progressive Republican League (NPRL), indicating their intention to wrest the nomination from Taft. By the spring of 1911, the still decidedly Western character of the NPRL revealed one of its weaknesses.[16] The League was largely unsuccessful recruiting more than a handful of Eastern progressives. Many members quickly realized that bringing Roosevelt onboard could alleviate this problem and give the faction a national character. Yet, Roosevelt held his cards close to the vest throughout the summer of 1911, conferring with advisors at his home in Oyster Bay and writing a few articles in the *Outlook*.

During a speaking tour in the late summer, Roosevelt proposed ideas—such as increased government regulation of corporations, restriction on child labor, workmen's compensation, as well as income and inheritance taxes—the sum total of which came to be known as the "New Nationalism." While Roosevelt tempered his rhetoric in the East, conservatives reacted with outrage and progressives with delight. In December 1911, Roosevelt privately allowed friends to create a campaign organization for the Republican presidential nomination. After La Follette gave a poor speech in February of 1912 and Roosevelt stated publicly that he would seek the nomination, many of La Follette's supporters' switched allegiances. This finished La Follette's bid for the nomination; the embittered senator then accused Roosevelt of dividing the progressive faction.

As recounted in the last chapter, Roosevelt first tried to lead the progressive forces to victory within the Republican Party. The new device of primaries to elect convention delegates allowed Roosevelt to tap into his popularity with the public. In the "mixed" system of presidential selection, Roosevelt pursued an "outsider" strategy.[17] He sought to win enough popular support so that some Republican regulars would switch from Taft to him. Yet when it became clear that Taft would win the nomination, many Roosevelt delegates left the convention hall and met at a nearby hotel. Hiram Johnson, the California progressive, declared that the Progressive Party would be formed forthwith. Roosevelt later announced that he would lead the new party. However, the new party faced all of the traditional biases of the American political system against third parties, making its campaign a difficult one. As the prospects for a Progressive Party victory dimmed with Wilson's nomination by the Democrats, many Republicans—even the eight governors who had written Roosevelt encouraging him to seek the Republican nomination—remained in the Republican fold. Indeed, most incumbent Republican politicians who had supported Roosevelt up to the convention did not follow him into the Progressive Party. This freed the Progressive Party, and Roosevelt himself, to become more radical during the campaign.

The national campaign that ensued was in many respects anticlimactic after the dramatic battles within the GOP. Despite Progressives' optimism after the election of 1910, their bid to take over the GOP failed. The splinter party assured the election of Woodrow Wilson and aided the Democrats in securing majorities in both houses of Congress. The constraints of the two-party system meant that once they lost the bid for the Republican nomination, the costs of forming a splinter party dictated that only the most die-hard Progressives would bolt the party. Those who remained in the Republican Party were weakened and forced to cooperate with the existing party structure. Those who left the party had either to find a new home or accept the party's conditions for re-entry. To a substantial extent, Roosevelt's defeat in the election of 1912 spelled the end of progressivism as a political and ideological movement inside the Republican Party. Furthermore, Wilson co-opted some of the Progressive Party's platform and was supported by some Republican progressives until World War I. By 1916, the Progressive Party had largely disintegrated. Some supporters returned to the Republican fold, others backed Wilson. One of Roosevelt's advisors recollected:

> For all its legal status, the Progressive party cannot really be said to
> have been a political party at all. Rather, it was a faction, a split-off frag-
> ment of its mother star, the Republican party, which like a meteor
> flamed momentarily across the sky, only to fall and cool on the earth of

solid fact.... The lesson taught by the Progressive incident seems to be a familiar one: that a party cannot be founded without a definite cause, or solely on the personality of an individual. To survive the hardships of the initial years, a new party must be a party of ideas, not of man.[18]

While Sidney Milkis has made a strong case that the Progressive Party was indeed a party of ideas, the party still found it difficult to get out from under the towering shadow of Roosevelt. Ultimately, the biggest impact of the Progressive Party was not on the Republican Party from which it emerged but on the Democratic Party under Woodrow Wilson, who adopted and implemented a healthy portion of its program.

Southern Democrats

Prior to 1936, Southern Democrats were, in a sense, the Democratic Party. The two-thirds rule, requiring a super majority to select the party's presidential nominee ensured that the South could always veto candidates it did not like. As one Southern governor explained, "We have always felt that since we never have a candidate from the South, we should at least have the right to veto a fellow whom we do not like."[19] However, this bargain came to an end in 1936 when FDR arranged for the party to abolish the two-thirds rule. Henceforth, Southern weaknesses in presidential politics, Northern disregard for Southern preferences, and a desire for recognition of those preferences sparked two independent Southern presidential campaigns. Strom Thurmond led the first in 1948 and George Wallace the second in 1968. These men and their supporters were among those in the South most resistant to change and unsatisfied with pragmatic attempts to hold the line against measures emanating from other factions within the Democratic Party. Dramatic action, they held, was called for to stop their party's transformation. Based on this belief, governors from the South, leading small bands of followers, formed new parties as the vehicles for their presidential ambitions. Both Thurmond and Wallace hoped that by contributing to the defeat of the Democratic nominee they could earn respect and force the national party to pay closer attention to Southern demands in the future.

In principle, these were objectives that could be broadly endorsed by many Southern Democrats, even if they could not, for practical reasons, publicly support these candidacies. Most Southern Democrats were unwilling to follow Thurmond or Wallace out of the Democratic Party. The short-term advantages of connections with a presidential administration outweighed long-term threats to the racial status quo. Support for the national Democratic ticket also meant economic programs that served Southern interests. If they joined a splinter party, Southern congressmen and senators would jeopardize their seniority privileges and committee appointments. Thurmond and Wallace both played on racist ideology but victory was too unlikely for other Southern Democrats to make long-term investments of political capital.[20]

Thurmond was enlisted as the "Dixiecrat" candidate at an ad hoc convention in Alabama held a week after a number of Southern delegations stormed out of the Democratic National Convention during a speech by Hubert Humphrey in which he called for an end to segregation and support for black civil rights. Thurmond's campaign was a vigorous protest against the national establishment and the increasing attacks by that establishment on racial segregation in the South. During the campaign, the Dixiecrat said, "There's not enough troops in the Army to force the Southern people to break down segregation and admit the Negro race into our theaters, into our swimming pools, into our homes, and into our churches."[21] Thurmond won four Deep South states, 39 Electoral College votes, and more than one million votes (2.4 percent of the popular vote). However, in the states Thurmond won he was not listed on the ballot as the States' Rights Party candidate but as the Democratic Party candidate.

George Wallace, on the other hand, began his attempts to win the presidency as a factional candidate seeking the Democratic Party's nomination. He entered and won a number of primaries in 1964. Only when it became evident that he would never win the nomination did he decide, in 1968, to run on the American Independent Party ticket. Wallace won five Southern States and 10 million popular votes but not enough to alter the outcome of the election. Four years later, he returned to the Democratic fold and sought again to win the Democratic nomination until he was crippled by an assassin's bullet. He made his final bid for the Democratic nomination in 1976, coming in third behind Georgia Governor Jimmy Carter and California Governor Jerry Brown. Both the Thurmond and Wallace campaigns were expressions of a Southern insurgency against the Northern establishment.[22]

Neither Thurmond's nor Wallace's independent presidential campaigns achieved their stated objective of throwing the election to the House in order to secure concessions from the Democratic Party. Nor were they able to change the ideological trajectory from their party of origin.

Conclusion

None of the factions-cum-splinter parties were able to win the White House. Few won many Electoral College votes. None was able to force an Electoral College "tie" and throw the election to the House of Representatives. With the possible exception of George Wallace in 1968, none of the factional presidential candidates were able to mobilize large voting blocks that they could use as leverage within their party. Consequently, none of these campaigns had a lasting impact on their original party's reputation or left-right positioning.

For the most part, factional candidates in presidential elections have been quixotic affairs. As third-party candidacies, they are different from those third parties that emerge from a grassroots movement (e.g., the People's Party) or parties created by single individuals (e.g., Ross Perot's Reform Party). In fact, factional splinter parties appear to have less effect on the two major parties than most of the third parties in the other two categories. Nonetheless, factional splinter parties have often been opportunities for insurgent factions to blow off steam and express their frustration with the party establishment.

CHAPTER 6

Power Distributors

PARTY FACTIONS IN CONGRESS

Ever since the American Political Science Association's 1950 report on political parties, political scientists have been investigating whether parties are the agents that direct America's Congress.[1] Some have found that American parties are powerful actors, comparable in strength to parties under the so-called Westminster model. Others hold that congressional parties exercise little or no influence on legislators' decisions—that it is not the party but the individual member who is the central actor in congressional politics. Yet, factions do exist between the "responsible" party and the lone legislator. This chapter argues that factions often tie together a number of members of Congress—forming a cohort that is smaller than the party as a whole—and attempt to redistribute power within in the legislature. The analysis concentrates on why factions adopt particular strategies and their consequent implications for the allocation of power and resources in Congress. Shifting power in Congress is a means for factions to reposition their party on the Left-Right political spectrum and realize their policy preferences.

American parties rarely act like Roman phalanxes. Nor are they simply aggregations of individuals. This essay will look beyond the debate over whether parties matter—they do in some ways—and instead study their internal character.[2] In doing so, it is constructive to move beyond functionalist approaches, which hold that parties are products of their environment, responsive to exogenous changes in the political economy.[3] These approaches have too often treated parties as reflections rather than agents of change, thereby overlooking different patterns of change within each party.[4]

Instead, a systematic treatment of what occurs *within* America's congressional parties puts certain properties in sharper relief. Because our parties are neither as strong as some suggest nor as weak as others hold, factions are often important actors within them. "More commonly," Charles O. Jones has observed, "we have had factionalism with organizations of convenience (called political parties) designed to promote factional interests."[5] These factions are usually informally organized through networks that link members of Congress to party activists, interest groups, and intellectuals in efforts to control the policy-making process. Factions have also created new organizations, such as the Democratic Study Group or the Conservative Opportunity Society, to gain power and shape members' policy preferences. To further advance their goals, factions shift the distribution of power in Congress—even sometimes going so far as to change the institution's rules. Yet, their strategies to achieve their objectives vary. Sometimes factions centralize power; in other instances they decentralize it. Most often they pursue these strategies informally under the existing procedural rules. Occasionally, however, factions resort to formal procedural changes to enhance their position and defeat their rivals. Either way, factions are key players in determining the power of the party caucus, the leadership, committees, subcommittees, and outside groups in the legislative process. In this way, factions help determine what measures make it onto the agenda and whether they are voted up or down.

Factions have been intimately involved in the creation and destruction of congressional "regimes"—the different modes of distributing power in Congress. These regimes usually find their fullest expression in the House, with the Senate adopting more limited versions. Scholars have identified five forms of congressional organization in the twentieth century. The first was the strong Speaker system or "Czar rule" in the House (1890–1911), which began under Speaker Thomas Reed (R-ME) and fully flowered under Old Guard leader Joseph G. Cannon (R-IL). The next was "party government" (1912–1914)—the reign of the majority party caucus—instituted by Populist Democrats and President Woodrow Wilson. Then came the "era of the barons" (1915–1975)—decentralized rule by powerful committee chairman—imposed and directed by Southern Democrats. The fourth mode emerged in the late 1970s when New Politics Democrats' reforms resulted in "subcommittee" government. And finally, a return to the strong Speaker emerged in the 1980s and was consolidated by Newt Gingrich (R-GA) and the New Right Republicans after 1994. In what follows it will be shown that the efforts of factions at institutional innovation have had major consequences for the policy-making process.[6]

The friction generated by factions has consequences for congressional party competition. Factions' activity moves their party along the Left-Right political spectrum, which in turn shapes the opportunities, incentives, and constraints of the other party. Congressional party factions either push the parties closer together (by moving to the center) or pull them apart (by moving to the extremes). The power of congressional parties cannot be gauged solely by looking at competition between the two parties; one must also account for what happens within them.

Finally, the study of congressional parties since the Civil War reveals a decline in factionalism in both parties at the dawn of the twenty-first century. The age of polarization has ushered in a new era of party government, where the parties are increasingly united and opposed. Both parties have become more ideologically homogeneous, and there no longer exist elements in either party that overlap the political center. The party leadership has also gained new formal and informal powers to control the rank and file. Therefore, even though New Democrats (or Blue Dogs) claim that centrism is their goal, their voting records show that they are more liberal than almost all Republicans. In sum, polarization is bad news for factions.

The Argument

This chapter seeks to address the following questions: Why do some factions seek to decentralize power? Why do others seek to centralize it? Why do they sometimes try to formally change the institutions rules to achieve power redistribution and other times proceed informally, using existing rules? There are, in effect, four strategic options that a faction can pursue: formal centralization, formal decentralization, informal centralization, and informal decentralization. Tracing the process by which factions chose to place themselves in one of these categories (or not) provides a much richer picture of factions than the common perception that factions only serve to weaken parties.

Each outcome is conceived here as the result of the interaction of a faction's goals with the situation in which the faction finds itself. Put differently, which strategy a faction adopts depends on the particular combination of "micro" (individual) and "macro" (contextual) variables that comprise each case. At the micro level, a mixture of electoral, policy, and power-base considerations drive faction members. Members of Congress belong to a faction because they believe that their adherence helps them achieve certain goals. Factions thus become vehicles for members to pursue their own electoral interests by shifting the party's ideological positioning and image to the right or to the left. The coordination functions factions perform can also help members realize what they deem "good" public policy. And finally, factional affiliation can help members secure key power bases—such as subcommittee chairmanships—that will enhance their power over politics and policy.

At the macro level, three factors impact factions' strategic choices: (1) whether the faction is in the majority or the minority party; (2) the faction's size; and (3) its organizational capacity (or the strength of its network). Depending on the context, one or more of these variables can play an important role in factions' strategic choices about how to redistribute power in Congress.

These contextual variables are causal mechanisms—the processes or pathways through which factions' goals must pass and which determine their strategy.[7] The explanation of the interface of factions' goals with contextual factors is at the heart of the analysis.

Given the number of cases, it would be foolish to offer a model that would "predict" which strategies factions choose. This is because to an important degree factions' strategic choices are bound by events and contingency. A more sensible approach is to produce descriptive inferences about how factions have adopted their strategies for redistributing power. Such a method yields a device for providing order among the vast detail of the historical record. By treating groupings not always hitherto treated as factions under that label, a synthetic arrangement of the agents clamoring to redistribute power in Congress over the course of a century and a half emerges.

Factions and the Distribution of Power in Congress

The best way to understand these factions is to study their activity in Congress over the course of the twentieth century. To maximize their influence, factions develop new organizations and communications networks that forge ties among members as well as link them to outside groups. By designing, honing, and refining measures, they try to shape the congressional agenda and the policy-making process to enhance their power. Factions seek to secure policy outcomes in line with their preferences, in order to defeat their adversaries, and better fit themselves to wear the banner of "reformer." But to do these things the rules of legislative game must operate in their favor.

What is ultimately at stake is the locus of power within the institution of Congress.[8] Factions seek to shift the distribution of power within each chamber and the institution as a whole. Factions sometimes do this informally, using existing procedures. At other times, however, they initiate changes in procedural rules to privilege their position. The distribution of power in Congress changes when power is centralized or decentralized. Therefore, depending on the situation, factions work to centralize authority in a few hands or disperse it among a larger number. There are two ways to centralize authority in Congress. One is by giving more power to the leadership; the other is by giving more power to the party caucuses. To disperse authority, power must be invested in the committees (or subcommittees) and the leadership and party caucuses weakened. A redistribution of power can be accomplished informally, as factions position themselves on the political landscape to take advantage of the existing rules of the Congress. The Old Guard Republicans and Southern Democrats adopted this strategy; the former to

Table 6.1 **Faction Strategic Choices**

Formal Centralization	Formal Decentralization
Liberal-Labor Democrats	Progressive Republicans
New Right Republicans	
Informal Centralization	Informal Decentralization
Old Guard Republicans	Southern Democrats
No Clear Choice	Mixed Cases
Liberal Republicans	Populist Democrats
New Democrats	New Politics Democrats

centralize power, the latter to decentralize it. On the other hand, mobilizing a coalition to formally change Congress's procedural rules can change the balance of power. Progressive Republicans, Liberal-Labor Democrats, New Politics Democrats, and New Right Republicans took this route.

The result of this analysis is a typology of factions and strategies (Table 6.1). Three factions sought to centralize power: The Old Guard Republicans did so informally, while the Liberal-Labor Democrats and New Right Republicans did so formally. Three factions tried to decentralize it: the Progressive Republicans formally, Stalwart Republicans and Southern Democrats informally. The Populist Democrats and the New Politics Democrats are mixed cases since they alternated between decentralization and centralization as well as formality and informality. Finally, the Gilded Age Liberal and Half-Breed Republicans, and the Modern Republicans and New Democrats have been frustrated in their efforts to adopt a strategy to redistribute power in Congress.

INFORMAL CENTRALIZATION

The Republican Old Guard dominated Congress in the first decade of the twentieth century. As a majority faction in the majority party, they pursued the electoral goals of keeping the party to the right and preventing a Progressive takeover, the policy goal of fending off business regulation, and the power-base goal of controlling the congressional leadership positions and key committee chairmanships. The faction managed this feat by using existing chamber rules to informally centralize power in both the House and the Senate. In the House, the Old Guard took charge under Speaker "Uncle" Joe Cannon (1903–1911). Cannon exploited to their full extent the rules passed by his predecessor Thomas Reed.[9] He and his allies controlled the Rules Committee and the appointment of members to chair and sit on other committees. Therefore, Cannon not only controlled the flow of legislation but other legislators' careers.

Like his Old Guard colleagues, Cannon had little patience for reformers of almost any stripe.[10]

A distinctive aspect of the Old Guard faction was its ability to centralize authority in the notoriously individualistic Senate. The "Senate Four"—Nelson Aldrich (R-RI), William Allison (R-IA), Orville Platt (R-CT), and John Spooner (R-WI)—organized and directed the chamber. Their control rested on four things: sheer leadership skill, domination of the committee assignment process, command of the powerful Rules and Finance committees, and direction of major sources of campaign cash from Wall Street. Aldrich was "a genius in the art of legislative bargaining, a master of senatorial organization, the head of a clique that determined legislative programs and organized committees, his position was commanding beyond that of almost any senator in generations."[11] He became the "unofficial leader of the Republican Party" and Allison became the central figure in the party apparatus in the Senate, becoming the chairman of the GOP Conference and the Steering Committee. Aldrich and his associates secured seats on the most important committees and controlled the committee appointments of other senators. As Progressive Republican Albert Beveridge (R-IN) observed, "These men and their disciples rule the Senate through the packing of important committees with their creatures."[12] The impact of the Senate Four's control over national policy was an increase in party discipline. The centralization of Senate leadership under the "Allison and Aldrich faction" was effected almost completely informally.[13]

A minority faction in the minority party, the Populist Democrats played along with Progressive Republicans and contributed to a modest formal decentralization of the House. When, after the elections of 1912, they became the majority faction in the majority party, they sought to informally centralize power in both houses of Congress. Prior to 1912, their aim was to move the Democratic Party to the left and bolster its reform credentials to increase their electoral position. The aim was to make the party synonymous with reform. Yet, after 1912, Populist reformers sought to advance their policy program, which required them to recentralize power in Congress. This was not simply the Populist Democrats behaving as the majority party (although that is certainly part of the explanation) but rather as a faction with particular ideas about political parties, responsible government, and collective action.

The Populist Democrats of the Progressive Era first opposed and then embraced centralization. When they were in the minority, they collaborated with Progressive Republicans to formally decentralize power by defeating Speaker Cannon. They believed that the speaker was using the Rules Committee to enforce party discipline and exclude the minority party from shaping legislation. In their 1908 platform, Democrats criticized "Cannonism," which had become associated with machine politics backed by business interests affiliated with the GOP. Attacking the speaker offered Democrats a chance to capitalize on these symbols and cast themselves as reformers. Ultimately, Populist Democrats provided the votes to overthrow Speaker Cannon and change the rules of the House of Representatives.

The defeat of Cannon had a profound effect on the operations of the House during Wilson's first term. Indeed, it inaugurated what many scholars of Congress have seen as a short-lived but distinctive congressional regime of party government. The power wrested from the speaker had to be located somewhere; so when Democrats became the majority party, that somewhere became the party caucus. Prior to the move against Speaker Cannon, Democrats had adopted a set of internal party rules that allowed a two-thirds majority to bind all members of the caucus. Therefore, the caucus could not only set party policy but also enforce it. After Wilson's election, Oscar W. Underwood (D-AL) made the caucus the instrument of the president's attempt at parliamentary governance.[14] According to Randall Ripley, "Underwood thoroughly agreed with [President] Wilson in believing in a unified party working together to pass a definite program. For him, a binding caucus was the natural way to govern a legislative party. This device allows debate within the party but also allowed the party to present a completely united front to the opposition party."[15]

Party government worked as follows. During the 62nd to 63rd Congresses, Democrats met in caucus to settle their positions on policy, which members were then bound to support on the floor. Measures were considered first by Democratic members of the relevant committees (excluding Republicans), presented to the entire caucus for a vote, and only then revealed to the full House membership and the appropriate committees, essentially for ratification. Less formally, the Senate adopted the same procedure under the leadership of John W. Kern (D-IN).[16] The House and Senate Democratic caucuses, not the floors of the two chambers, became the place where legislation was debated. Much of Wilson's program, the New Freedom, was passed this way. Yet, after two years of caucus-government, many complained that the new technique was more authoritarian than Cannonism. Innovative as it was, government by party caucus did not endure past 1916. The central point remains that by transforming their party, a minority faction helped engineer a significant shift in the distribution of power within the Congress and its principal means of operation.

FORMAL CENTRALIZATION

In the 1950s and 1960s, Liberal-Labor Democrats tried to formally change congressional rules to centralize power.[17] As a minority faction in the majority party, they pursued the electoral goal of moving the party to the left to capture supposedly unmobilized liberal voters. They also sought to enact a specific policy program to "complete" the New Deal and provide civil rights to African-Americans. In addition, they sought to make the party caucus and congressional leadership posts new power bases from which they could command their Southern Democratic adversaries. They deemed congressional reform necessary because the fragmented and decentralized committee system slowed legislation and empowered conservative Southerners. Influenced by the idea of "responsible party government" advanced by some academics, they sought to strengthen the congressional party caucus. A majoritarian party organization would come at the expense of Southern committee chairs and rural legislators. Liberal-Laborites anticipated that centralization of the party caucus would increase the likelihood of passing their preferred policies.

Michael Foley argues that although Senate Liberals were largely ineffective at changing the chamber's rules, they managed to transform the folkways of the institution.[18] This was in large measure due to the shift of power away from Southern conservatives and toward Northern Liberals, especially after the 1958 elections. In the House, the faction pursued its goals by creating one of the most powerful informal groups in congressional history: the Democratic Study Group (DSG).[19] In particular, the DSG focused its efforts on weakening the power of the Rules Committee, which by the late 1950s had become an arm of the conservative coalition of Southern Democrats and rural Republicans. The DSG took a two-pronged approach. One tactic was to push for changes in the Democratic Party Caucus's procedures, which in turn might mean changes in the House's overall rules. The other was to take their case public. The faction's strategy was to put media pressure on reluctant Democrats and gain attention inside and outside the Beltway. Liberal-Labor's overall goal was to defeat their Southern Democratic rivals.[20]

The biggest thorns in the side of Liberal-Labor were Chairman "Judge" Howard Smith (D-VA) and his House Rules Committee, which controlled the floor agenda, established the amount of time spent on each piece of legislation, and determined what rules would be used in considering a bill.[21] The committee consisted of twelve members, at least half of which (all four Republicans and two Democrats) were conservative coalition affiliates. Appointed to the committee in 1933, Smith became chairman in 1954 when Democrats recaptured control of the House. Along with Edward Cox (D-GA) and William Colmer (D-MS), Smith became an informal leader of Southern conservatives. He pushed his powers over legislation to the hilt. In the late 1950s, he denied hearings on about twenty bills in each term. On legislation he opposed, Smith would often simply retire to his Virginia farm—where his family had lived since before the Civil War—and refuse to schedule a hearing. For instance, in 1959, he used this tactic to cause a year's delay in the consideration of a civil rights measure. Smith's position handed Southern Democrats an effective veto over legislation they opposed. To force legislation out of the Rules Committee, Liberal-Labor was forced go to extraordinary lengths.[22]

After John F. Kennedy's election, the DSG set its sights on reforming the Rules Committee. They launched a massive publicity campaign to shine a spotlight on the power of conservative Southern committee chairs. Liberal-Labor placed a host of reform options on the table. President Kennedy and Speaker Sam Rayburn signed onto increasing the number of members on the committee. Expansion would weaken the power of Chairman Smith, who had said that he aimed to block parts of President Kennedy's New Frontier. The resolution to enlarge the Rules Committee (H. Res. 127) was reported by the Rules Committee by a vote of 6 to 2 on January 14, 1961, with only committee Democrats in attendance. Chairman Smith and Colmer cast the dissenting votes. Following an hour of debate on the resolution on January 31, which included impassioned pleas from Speaker Rayburn and Chairman Smith on opposing sides, the House voted 217 to 212 to enlarge the Rules Committee from 12 to 15 members. Two years later, the House voted again to expand the committee. This mild reform smoothed presidential-congressional relations with a Democrat in the White House and prepared the ground for the passage of the Kennedy-Johnson domestic program. Nonetheless, the Liberal-Labor faction's goals for weakening the Southern committee chairs power remained largely unrealized. It would not be until the mid-1970s that Southern Democrats would finally be defeated.[23]

Beginning as a minority faction in the minority party, New Right Republicans used formal and informal means to centralize authority in the House. The New Right set out to shift the GOP to the right in order to elect more members dedicated to their policy agenda of small government, decentralization, and traditional values. This electoral goal was linked to New Right conservatives talk about "revolution" in the 1980s under Newt Gingrich's direction because a formal redistribution of power would enhance their reputations as reformers. Such a revolution would entail taking over their party and filling power bases, such as key committees, with the faithful. Therefore, they were not content, like moderate Republicans, to broker deals with Democrats to satisfy their constituents. They opposed a decentralized party apparatus that allowed, even encouraged, such horse-trading. In the early 1980s, Gingrich founded the Conservative Opportunity Society in the House and his own political action committee (GOPAC) to recruit, train, and fund conservative candidates.[24] At the time, Gingrich was seen by many of his colleagues as a peripheral figure. Ten years later he became the House GOP leader. Combined with the members of the Republican Study Committee—a conservative organization modeled on the DSG founded in the 1970s—nearly three-quarters of House

Republicans belonged to a conservative association by 1992. The explanation for this development, according to John Pitney and William Connelly, was that "[t]hrough the elections of the 1980s and early 1990s, the faction that favored Gingrich gained members, while the opposing faction shrank."[25] This was in no small measure due to Gingrich's use of the media—especially C-SPAN—and his own formidable organizational genius.[26]

The electoral goals of the New Right had always been linked to policy goals, which favored centralization. Therefore, the desire for a centralized House came before the stunning GOP victory of 1994. Elected speaker that year, Gingrich restructured the Republican House Conference and consolidated his position within it. A new Steering Committee was created to centralize the party leadership's control over committee chairmanships. Gingrich was then able to secure the votes for his preferred committee chairs without deferring to the seniority rule. In addition, formal House rules were changed to cap a committee chair's tenure at six years. Gingrich and his allies also adjusted committee jurisdictions and abolished three committees that supposedly served Democrats. Their strategy was a direct assault on committee power in the name of promoting the Contract with America.[27] The new Republican majority succeeded in empowering the party leadership and imposing greater centralization within the committees in particular and the House in general.

Once in the majority, the goals of the New Right legislators were to enhance their reputations as reformers and to make the House a more streamlined and effective governing institution. The latter, in particular, would enable to them to quickly pass the conservative agenda that had been prepared over the previous decade. The legislative session of 1995 was consumed with a flurry of activity to place the policies proposed in the Contract on the House agenda, gain them national attention, and then quickly pass them. The leadership imposed strict deadlines for committees to move Contract legislation to the floor to be voted on. The results were striking: in the first three months of 1995, the House passed 124 measures (compared with 53 in 1981) recorded 302 roll call votes (compared to 23 in 1981). The new mode of party government in the House produced a flurry of legislative activity.[28]

INFORMAL DECENTRALIZATION

From 1872 until Roscoe Conkling's retirement in 1884, Stalwart Republicans generally pursued an informal decentralization strategy. As the dominant of three factions in the majority Republican Party, Stalwarts were especially powerful in the Senate. At the time, Senators were elected by state legislators. For many Stalwarts to be chosen senator required controlling their state parties, which were powerful organizations. To direct patronage in their states,

Stalwarts sought to maintain the Senate as something of a federation of state party bosses that, as George Frisbie Hoar (R-MA) remarked in 1877: "each member kept his own orbit and shone in his sphere, within which he tolerated no intrusion from the president or anyone else."[29] The object of decentralization was to give the Senator-Boss control over patronage within his state.

In the late nineteenth century, the Senate had not yet created the posts of majority and minority party leaders. Hence there was no need to struggle over who would occupy them. Moreover, the rough ideological consensus among Republicans meant that centralization was not necessary to line up majorities on important votes. While tensions did exist within the party over agenda priorities, Reconstruction, the tariff, and monetary policy, these debates usually played themselves out in presidential nominations. Therefore, factional leaders staked out decentralized power-bases or fiefdoms over which they could rule. Led by Conkling, the Stalwarts who ruled in the Senate periodically emerged to confront presidents when they disagreed over appointments, patronage, and organizational matters—issues that were not usually subject to roll call votes. During the Hayes and Garfield-Arthur administrations, the Stalwarts thus structured congressional-presidential relations.

As the majority faction in the majority party, Southern Democrats are the only faction that has pursued an informal decentralization strategy. They sought to keep the party to the right of center—where they believed the median voter in America was to be found—and ensure their electoral supremacy regionally. In policy terms, they sought to prevent the growth of a powerful national government that could interfere with the racial status quo. And the conquest of committee chairmanships through seniority provided members with access to a vast number of power bases. The overall advantage of decentralized power in Congress is that it allows a faction more opportunities to play a sort of balance power politics by voting with, or threatening to vote with, the opposition party. As one of the best-organized factions, with subtle but effective internal lines of communication, Southern Democrats skillfully used this technique to leverage their party. Using informal networks, the faction redistributed power within the institution. The way Congress was made to operate might be described, in William White's words: "as the South's unending revenge upon the North for Gettysburg."[30]

Southern Democrats present the unique spectacle of a faction that exploits existing institutional rules to decentralize authority. Thus John Rankin (D-MS) was able to threaten his northern colleagues while opposing an antilynching bill in 1940: "Remember that southern Democrats now have the balance of power in both Houses of Congress. By your conduct you [northern Democrats] may make it impossible for us to support you for important committee assignments, and other positions to which you aspire."[31] They transformed the operation of Congress by commandeering committee chairmanships. Domination of Congress was the Southern Democrats' response to the New Deal shift in power in favor of executive power. They were able to achieve this because Southerners hailed from a one-party region and were usually the longest-serving members on most committees, guaranteeing them control of the most important chairmanships. In the 1930s, they capitalized on the rules that Congress had adopted in the wake of the Republican Czars and the Democrats' experiment in party government, which weakened centralized authority. The fragmentation and decentralization of Congress in the 1940s and 1950s gave Southern conservatives abundant opportunities to block or shape legislation in their favor.[32]

Southern Democrats also established communications networks that familiarized affiliates with parliamentary procedure and the details of many legislative proposals. Older legislators would take on apprentices and mentor younger members from their region. They would often gather to plot legislative strategy over bourbon and water. These informal channels served as "schools" for southern legislators, which transmitted congressional norms and folkways as well as shaped their preferences.[33]

To enhance their position, Southern Democrats—like the other factions such as the Progressive and Modern Republicans—were willing to work across party lines. To an unprecedented extent, Southern Democrats cooperated with conservative Republicans to form the "conservative coalition."[34] An informal formation that skillfully manipulated parliamentary procedure, the coalition empowered Southern Democrats to shape public policy and the development of the American state in profound ways. This bipartisan bloc of conservatives often discussed strategy and lined up votes. It developed informal lines of communication and a handful of recognized leaders. "We did not meet publicly," Howard Smith recalled after his retirement, "The meetings were not formal. Our group met in one building and the conservative Republicans in another. Then Eugene Cox, or Bill Colmer (D-MS) or I would go over and speak with the Republicans. Or the Republican leaders might come see us. It was very informal."[35] The coalition either vetoed liberal initiatives or shaped them to fit its preferences. Southern Democrats thus occupied the pivotal position in a quasi-three party system in Congress. When Southerners and non-Southern Democrats both approved measures they became law; when Southerners dissented, they failed or were rewritten with Republicans.[36]

FORMAL DECENTRALIZATION

As a minority faction in the majority party, Progressive Republicans tried to formally decentralize the House. To enhance the electoral fortunes of likeminded candidates, especially in the West and Midwest, Progressive Republicans sought to move the GOP to the left. In policy terms, they believed that decentralization of power in Congress would give independent and entre-preneurial legislators more room to maneuver and more opportunities to take credit. The control of new power bases, especially in the committees, would give them access to badly needed resources.

Consequently, they spearheaded the insurgency to overthrow Speaker Cannon in 1909–1910. Progressives sought to expand the Rules Committee, remove the speaker from that committee, and take away his control of com-mittee assignments. The speaker had the power to deny recognition on the House Floor, to select the members of the Rules Committee (Cannon was a member of this committee), and to appoint all committee members and chairs. By 1909, the Republican speaker's aggressive centralization of power had worn thin with Progressive Republicans and Populist Democrats.[37] According to David Rohde, "He used his powers ... as a vehicle for rewarding allies and pun-ishing dissidents. Control of the Rules Committee permitted him to determine which bills got to the floor, and his power as presiding officer enabled him gen-erally to dictate their fate once there."[38] Attacking the speaker offered Progres-sives a chance to earn symbolic capital by casting themselves as reformers. Decentralizing power in the House would offer more legislative opportunities for younger Progressive congressmen to advance their goals. According to Eric Schickler, "Subverting Cannon's power as Speaker . . . united members pur-suing a mix of ideological, power base, and ... partisan objectives."[39]

After much maneuvering, Progressives worked with Democrats to finally pass significant changes to the House Rules in 1910. They removed the speaker from the Rules Committee, doubled the size of the committee from five to ten, and stipulated that Rules Committee members be elected by the entire House rather than the majority party caucus. Yet, Cannon could still select other committees' members and chairs, and influence the flow of legislation in the House. Nonetheless, these reforms weakened the power of the speakership and restricted majority party control over legislation.

In the 1970s, New Politics Democrats were a minority faction within the majority party. They opposed the remnants of the committee system and sought to expunge the waning influence of conservative committee chairs. To achieve these aims, they called for decentralizing reforms, enshrined in a "sub-committee bill of rights." These measures showed New Politics Democrats to be more interested in legislative individualism than in party majoritarianism. The consequence of the New Politics reforms was a decentralization of power in the House, as the new powers were given to subcommittee chairmen. The New Politics Democrats nearly achieved the legislators' dream: every member a chair of some committee.

The changes inaugurated by New Politics Democrats came in three stages. First, after the passage of the Legislative Reorganization Act, the Democratic Caucus decided in 1971 that committee chairs could be selected by criteria other than seniority. Although this change had no immediate effect on the power of the sitting committee chairman, it did set an important precedent. The one attempt by New Politics Democrats to unseat a committee chairman in 1971 failed. However, New Politics Democrats were suspicious of any centralization of power, even in the congressional party caucuses. Therefore, their next step was to push for substantial decentralizing measures. In 1973, the caucus adopted a subcommittee bill of rights, which granted subcommittee chairs autonomy from the committee chairs, opening their hearings to the public, and allowing them to hire their own staff. This, in effect, made subcommittees the new locus of legislative power and weakened the centralizing effect empowering the party caucus might have had. Rather than become the tools of the majority in the caucus, committee chairmen were now hemmed in by an array of permanent subcommittees with their own staff, jurisdiction, and other resources. Ultimately, these reforms significantly decentralized power within the House.

Finally, in 1975, the Democratic House Caucus set its sights on reducing the power of the Ways and Means Committee, in particular its power to make committee assignments. Chairman Wilbur Mills's (D-AR) personal problems created an opportunity for change. New Politics Democrats wanted to shift the power to make committee assignments to the Democratic Steering and Policy Committee, which they believed would be more responsive to the caucus. The party accepted this proposal and also enlarged the Ways and Means Committee from 25 to 37 members. The House Democratic Caucus also made other changes. They gave the speaker control over the Rules Committee with the expectation that it would turn Rules into an instrument of the majority party caucus. Finally, the caucus directly challenged individual committee chairmen. In the end, three chairmen lost their positions in a vote of the Democratic Policy and Steering Committee. For many analysts, the centralizing steps taken in 1975 spelled the end of the committee era and the power of Southern Democrats in Congress. For the next decade the House would try to recentralize power as the decentralizing reforms instituted by the New Politics Democrats proved unwieldy.

FOUR FRUSTRATED FACTIONS

Neither the Liberal nor the Half-Breed Republicans of the Gilded Age could mount a serious effort at redistributing power in Congress. The former simply lacked the numbers in the House or the Senate to undertake serious action. In the long term, the latter probably paved the way for the major centralizing reforms that Thomas Reed enacted in 1888 to bring order to the House, but prior to that they were largely ineffective. From 1872 until 1888, power was extremely decentralized—bordering on chaotic—in the House. No one controlled the order or limits of debate; minorities could easily obstruct debate by refusing to answer roll. On the floor when members wanted to listen to a speaker they had to gather closely around him to be able to hear over the din produced by all sorts of other business being conducted. Few proposals were made by the parties, whose caucuses meet sporadically and infrequently.

The Half-Breeds had their institutional home in the House of Representatives. Yet, so complete was Republican domination of the House that Half-Breeds had few incentives to develop more elaborate party mechanisms to control the few dissenters.[40] Instead, they sought to centralize power informally to line up votes on important measures. Their tactics were largely consensual, since they aimed to split the difference between Stalwarts and Liberal Republicans. The rough consensus that prevailed on policy issues between the two largest factions contributed to the institutionalization of parties in Congress in the late 1870s, which provided the grounds for increased party unity on roll call votes in the 1880s and 1890s. Consequently, Half-Breeds halfheartedly pursued centralization due to their position inside a relatively ideologically united Republican party in the House. Cooperation also prevailed in the Senate.[41]

When it comes to redistributing power in Congress, Liberal Republicans of the mid-twentieth century and New Democrats both had difficulty settling on a strategy or set of objectives. As a minority faction in the minority party, Liberal Republicans made some halting steps toward centralization but ultimately preferred to exercise their influence as individuals. In the House, Liberal Republicans made a furtive attempt at creating an organization modeled on the DSG. Faction affiliates in the House formed the Wednesday Group as a forum for discussion and coordination among like-minded members in 1963. Six junior congressmen formally organized the group: Lindsay (NY), Morse (MA), Sibal (CT), Tupper (ME), Ellsworth (KA), and Mathias (MD). The desire to work more effectively with the Kennedy Administration led Liberals to form the new organization. Indeed, it was their cooperation with congressional Democrats, especially on the reform of the Rules Committee in 1961, that drove Liberals to seek new forms of mutual protection. Initially, it seems the new organization was supposed to provide political cover for members that wanted the benefits of cooperating with Democrats.[42]

The Wednesday Group never proved to be an effective vehicle for Liberal Republican aspirations in the House. Its members lacked the numbers and ideological discipline to be power brokers in the Republican Conference.

Unlike the DSG, the Wednesday Group was never able to clearly define its role or provide the kind of information, coordination, and ideological symbolism for its members. It functioned more as a support group than a means for providing services to members in ways that could enhance their power in Congress. The failure of Liberals to sway their party's leadership elections was indicative of their ineffectiveness. In 1964, during a House Republican leadership change, the Liberal candidate for conference chairman and party whip, Peter Freling-huysen (R-NJ), was soundly defeated for both positions by mainstream candidates. After this defeat, Liberals never again challenged the party leadership. Consequently, the Wednesday Group gave up on organizing members to vote as a distinct bloc and sought to provide services to its members.

In the late 1960s and 1970s, the Senate became the last refuge of Liberal Republicans. In 1967, Hess and Broder estimated that Liberals represented, perhaps, fifteen of the thirty-six Republican Senators.[43] In the 1966 and 1968 elections, Liberals gained seats and were able to constitute a solid power base from which to affect policy. Barbara Sinclair found that on a whole range of issues, Liberal Republicans diverged from the rest of Senate Republican Conference.[44] Liberals supported limited economic intervention and the continuation of welfare state programs and were indifferent to the cultural and moral issues that began to appear on the public agenda. Given their suburban constituencies, they helped smooth the passage of environmental and consumer protection legislation. In the individualistic Senate, however, Liberal Republicans were able to work more effectively with moderate Democrats. But they were never able to forge an organizational apparatus, and their influence remained highly personalized.

The New Democrats have been both a minority faction in the majority party (1986–1994) and a minority faction in the minority party (1994–2006). Yet, under neither condition did they determine how they thought power should be exercised. Some favored centralization to limit the power of liberal interest groups; but others worried that since those same interest groups were tied to the majority of the party, centralization would enhance their position. Ultimately, New Democrats did not take significant steps to push for a significant redistribution of power. New Democrats primarily focused their attention on winning the presidency. Although many members of Congress were members of the Democratic Leadership Council (DLC) and personally identified themselves as New Democrats, they did not organize themselves inside the legislature. Unlike labor unions in the 1950s and 1960s or public interest lobbies in the 1970s, the DLC did not provide a reliable coordinating mechanism or whip system to line up votes on important legislation. It had some success shaping members' preferences through policy briefings but this found only limited expression in roll call votes.

The oldest organization of centrist Democrats is the Blue Dog Coalition in the House. While this group is slightly to the right of New Democrats on issues such as gun control, abortion, and immigration, it overlaps substantially with the newly created New Democratic group. Congressmen Cal Dooley (D-CA), Jim Moran (D-VA), and Tim Roemer (D-IN) established an ideological home for New Democrats in the House by forming the New Democrat Coalition in 1997. With only 43 members this group remains a distinct minority within the Democratic Caucus. In the spring of 2000, Senators Evan Bayh (IN), Bob Graham (FL), Mary Landrieu (LA), Joe Lieberman (CT), and Blanche Lincoln (AR) founded the Senate New Democrat Coalition (SNDC) to provide a unified voice for New Democrats in the Senate. Today, the SNDC has approximately 20 members.

Nonetheless, the overriding political condition affecting New Democrats' behavior in Congress is polarization, which increases the incentives to toe the party line. Over the past half-century, a *Congressional Quarterly* analysis of roll call votes demonstrates, Democrats in the House were never more unified than in 2005.[45] And only in 1999 and 2001 were Senate Democrats more united than in 2005. Overall, party-unity scores show that Congress is becoming more divided by party on more issues more often, turning compromise into a dirty word. In sum, current institutional and partisan conditions are hostile to factions. Congressional Democrats have powerful incentives to vote together and to discipline any breaks in the ranks. Again, as the minority party for most of the first ten years of the new century, the Congress has proven a hostile environment for faction politics.

To succeed in redistributing power, a faction's party must gain a majority in at least one chamber of Congress. Factions fail because they are not in the majority (Liberal Republicans), because they remain too small a minority within their own party (New Democrats), or because they are unable to work across party lines on a consistent basis as a means of leveraging their respective parties. Success at changing the balance of power can result in significant legislation that favors the faction's conception of the party and helps to move its image along the Left-Right political spectrum. Failure, of course, produces neither of these outcomes.

Conclusion

Contrary to the common view of factions as negative and destabilizing forces, American party factions have been sources of health that invigorate the political system. Some factions contribute to the centralization of power in Congress by trying to homogenize the preferences of party members. If the conditional party government model is correct, factional activity helps explain how the condition of homogeneous preferences is often achieved. For instance, this is evident in the decade-long takeover operation of the New Right Republicans in the 1980s and early 1990s. Other factions try to decentralize power to create the space for heterogeneous preferences and policy entrepreneurship, or to act as veto players. Theses ends were evident in the activity of the Progressive Republicans, New Politics Democrats, and Southern Democrats. Moreover, rather than fragmentation and disintegration, the internecine battles between factions pushing in opposite directions has probably been a source of stability within the American Congress.

The structure of the Congress gives rise to factions. The power of individual legislators, the institution's constitutional mandate to set its own rules, and the need for coordinating mechanisms provide members of Congress incentives to form party factions to achieve their goals. Unlike members of many parliaments, American congressman exercise real power as individuals—even the lowliest House freshman has more freedom of action than a backbench MP. On the other hand, parties organize both the House and Senate. Procedural mechanisms determined by the majority party, especially in the House, make parties powerful governing instruments. The oscillation between individual and minority rights, on the one hand, and party power and majority prerogative, on the other, provide the space for the emergence of factions. Factional activity in congressional politics shows that a faction's beliefs about the likelihood of success shape its decisions. Yet, factions make assessments of their prospects in constantly changing circumstances. As the above cases suggest, the party's status as a majority or minority and the chamber in which it is embedded affect a faction's strategic decisions.

Attention to factions contributes to our understanding of how American congressional parties work. Parties are not simply useful labels without impact on legislative outcomes as some have suggested. Nor are they disciplined British-style blocs that undertake coordinated action to set (or oppose) the congressional agenda. Rather, it is factions that often take synchronized action, transforming the internal character of the party and forcing others party members to respond. The responses of other members of Congress can change the institution's power dynamics. Insofar as factions are the units that infuse American parties with energy and purpose, they try to command the legislative branch in order to put their stamp on the nation.

CHAPTER 7

Shaping the Situation

FACTIONS AND PRESIDENTIAL GOVERNANCE

Few American presidents have viewed their office as a ceremonial post. Rather, they have sought to win accolades by constructing a legacy worthy of historical memory. Because presidents are ambitious men, there is a powerful temptation to pin the causes of presidential success or failure on individual traits of particular presidents.[1] Yet factions, as key parts of the political landscape, can both facilitate and frustrate presidential ambitions. A president's debts to, association with, or distance from a faction within his own party can shape his choices. This is especially the case when a faction is a major force in the nomination process, in the halls of Congress, or both. In many instances, presidential governance is a game of give and take with factions, as they present presidents with governing opportunities and constrains. A president's relation to factions within his party thus shapes his policy priorities, strategies, and governing tactics.

While the issue of how factions structure the political context of presidential governance has received scant attention, the president's ability to influence policy making has been the subject of much scholarly investigation. Four aspects of the president's policy influence have received extensive treatment. First, scholars have scrutinized the president's legal powers—such as the veto and executive order.[2] A second line of inquiry treats the differences in the president's ability to influence foreign and domestic policy. The most frequent conclusion being that the president has a greater likelihood of getting his way beyond the water's edge.[3] Third, scholars have examined whether and how the president uses his political party to mobilize support.[4] Finally, scholars have explored how the president's connection to the mass public and his ability to deal with members of Congress affect policy making.[5]

The last group can be subdivided into those who examine presidents' "insider" strategies of bargaining with elites, and those who "go public," employing electronic communications to appeal directly to the people.[6] Scholars disagree whether the president can shape policy through rhetorical appeals to the citizenry. Some are optimistic about his ability to do so.[7] Others are less sanguine. They hold that public appeals rarely work because they "fall on deaf ears," as George C. Edwards put it.[8] Jeffrey Tulis and Joseph Bessette contend that even when the public hears such appeals *and* causes members of Congress to respond, the result is undesirable because policy makers then pay heed to the ill-informed mass public.[9] Yet, Brandice Canes-Wrone has argued that presidents' engagement with the public does move policy in the direction of public opinion and that that movement does not lead to bad public policy.[10]

Rather than continue this debate over the rhetorical presidency, this chapter returns to the insider or institutional approach. It shifts the focus from the personal characteristics of the president and his abilities to an analysis of the president's relationship to political elites.[11] While presidents may or may not be responsive to the mass public, and may or may not be able to move it in the direction of their preferences, they are often preoccupied with factions in Washington.[12] I argue that factions are major factors in presidential decision making. Presidents often secure change by exploiting opportunities in a context shaped by factions. Rather than rhetorical prowess in guiding public opinion, successful presidents recognize and take advantage of circumstances as they find them. Whatever a president's political skills or personal goals, he must take stock of his situation, weigh the costs of possible courses of action, and make decisions in light of that situation. Much of presidents' work is therefore on coalition building to win the support of a few actors to advance their initiatives.[13] This means working directly with Congress. As Lyndon Johnson once put it: "There is only one way for a President to deal with Congress, and that is continuously, incessantly, and without interruption."[14] Or as Richard Neustadt has argued, "The President and Congress are at once so independent and so intertwined that neither can be said to govern save as both do."[15]

Yet, only some presidents are saddled with the responsibility of dealing with one or more factions within their party. Others are blessed by not having to confront a factionalized party (Table 7.1). Since 1868, fifteen of the twenty-six presidents have found themselves in a factional situation, while only eleven presidents have escaped that circumstance. This is significant insofar as presidents are often judged by how well, or how poorly, they handle factions.

Factions can help presidents formulate policies, inspire public opinion, mobilize supportive outside groups, and spearhead legislation in Congress. Some of the clearest examples of this include Populist Democrats, Liberal-Labor Democrats, New Right Republicans, and New Democrats. In contrast, factions can stymie presidential initiatives by galvanizing opposition, using parliamentary procedure, and otherwise raising the political costs of action. The most notable cases of this are the Liberal Republicans and Stalwarts of the

Table 7.1 **Presidential Situations vis-à-vis Factions**

President	Factionalized Party	Nonfactionalized Party
1. Grant	XX	
2. Hayes	XX	
3. Garfield	XX	
4. Arthur	XX	
5. Cleveland		XX
6. Harrison		XX
7. Cleveland	XX	
8. McKinley		XX
9. Roosevelt	XX	
10. Taft	XX	
11. Wilson		XX
12. Harding		XX
13. Coolidge		XX
14. Hoover		XX
15. Roosevelt	XX	
16. Truman	XX	
17. Eisenhower	XX	
18. Kennedy	XX	
19. Johnson	XX	
20. Nixon	XX	
21. Ford	XX	
22. Carter		XX
23. Reagan		XX
24. Bush		XX
25. Clinton	XX	
26. Bush II		XX

*In the cases of Wilson, Carter, and Reagan, a faction had largely taken over the party when they took office, so I coded them as not confronting a factional situation.

Gilded Age, Old Guard and Progressive Republicans of the early twentieth century, and Southern Democrats in the 1940s and 1950s.

The extent to which a president is forced to reckon with a faction in his own party depends on three conditions. One is the faction's strength in Congress.

Another is the extent to which the president's nomination and campaign were linked to a faction. The last is whether there is more than one faction within the party. Based on these conditions, there are four basic strategies the president can adopt. Presidents who govern in periods of factionalism must choose between acting as a faction's champion, appeasing a faction, playing the role of referee between competing factions, or assertively opposing a faction.

For instance, in situations where a faction is a powerful force in nominating contests, strong in Congress, and there are other factions present, a president can choose between championing one faction or playing referee. For instance, Rutherford B. Hayes chose to oppose the Stalwarts by siding with the Liberal Republicans, while James Garfield and Chester Arthur acted as arbiters among the Gilded Age GOP factions. In contrast, if the faction is strong in the nominating process but weak in Congress and no other factions are present, the champion of a faction will try to compensate the faction with appointments and other under-the-radar maneuvers. Ronald Reagan and Bill Clinton both arrived in the White House in such a context. Hence they sought to play the role of referee, arbitrating between the faction and the larger party. Presidents risk, in this situation, indictment by allied factions for not being "true" to their factional commitments. Hence the New Right saw conspiracies that kept "Reagan from being Reagan" and New Democrats held that Clinton had "sold out" to the liberals in his party.[16]

This mode of categorizing the situations in which presidents find themselves and the governing strategies they adopt in light of them differs from the leading approaches to the subject. Stephen Skowronek and Charles O. Jones have both developed categories to capture the president's situation that hinged largely on the incoming president's relation to his predecessor.[17] The accent here is on the factional character of the political landscape. The analytical scheme offered here is not meant to supersede prior accounts but rather to add theoretical richness. This chapter traces the history of presidential-faction interaction through these conceptual lenses.

Presidents and the GOP Gilded Age Factions

In the twenty years after the Civil War, the executive branch was the weakest in the national government. The idea of legislative supremacy predominated, especially in the Senate. George F. Hoar remarked:

> The most eminent Senators . . . would have received as a personal affront a private message from the White House expressing a desire that they adopt any course in the discharge of their legislative duties that they did not approve. If they visited the White House, it was to give,

not to receive advice. . . . Each of these stars kept his own orbit and
shone in his sphere within which he tolerated no intrusion from the
president or from anybody else.[18]

The president's functions and duties were limited and hemmed in on all sides.
As Lord Bryce put it: "A president need not be a man of brilliant intellectual
gifts. . . . Four-fifths of his work is the same in kind as that which devolved on
the chairman of a commercial company or manager of a railway."[19] Disputes
between Republican presidents and factions within their party turned on
questions of appointments, patronage, and organizational matters.

The great battles of the Hayes, Garfield, and Arthur administrations were
waged against the Stalwart faction led by New York Senator Roscoe Conkling.
Unaffiliated with a rival faction that was powerful in Congress, all three presidents alternated between direct confrontation and appeasement because they
could rely on the support of the other two party factions. Most often at issue
was whether powerful senators, who doubled as party bosses, should control
patronage in their states. To weaken senatorial control, the alternatives were to
give the president greater authority to appoint men loyal to him or to constrain
the number of discretionary positions altogether by reforming the civil service.
For Hayes, Garfield, and Arthur, their positions on public employment issues
were central to their presidencies. Stalwart vociferousness on party policy contrasted with Liberals, who preferred civil service reform, and Half-Breeds,
who tended to find presidential control of patronage congenial.

Hayes's difficulties with Stalwart Republicans began as soon as the 1876
national nominating convention ended.[20] Conkling was angry that neither
Hayes nor the vice-presidential nominee was beholden to him. At the New
York State Republican Convention in 1876, Conkling launched a savage attack
on reformers as the "man-milliners, the dilettantes and carpet knights of politics, [who] forget that parties are not built up by deportment, or by ladies' magazines, or gush." He concluded: "When Dr. Johnson defined patriotism as the
last refuge of a scoundrel, he was unconscious of the then underdeveloped capabilities and uses of the word Reform."[21] After the disputed 1876 general election, Conkling referred to Hayes as "Rutherfraud." For his part, Hayes chose to
side with Liberal Republicans and directly confront the Stalwarts by excluding
them from his cabinet and endorsing "thorough, radical, and complete" civil
service reform in his inaugural address. Liberal Republicans, of course, cheered
Hayes's address. In *Harper's Weekly*, George William Curtis wrote: "There have
been few inaugural addresses superior . . . in mingled wisdom, force, and moderation of statement." In *The Nation* E.L. Godkin pronounced the speech "a
clear, modest, and sensible document." It is no surprise that Hayes pleased reformers, as he had heeded Carl Schurz's advice on the substance of the speech.

Once in office, Hayes managed Stalwart power in three ways. First, he selected well-known Liberal Republicans—such as Schurz—to his cabinet, indicating his intent to align himself with reformers. This sent a powerful signal to Republicans in Congress that the *modus operandi* of the Grant administration would not continue. Reflecting on his appointment policy, Hayes wrote in his diary, "The end I have chiefly aimed at has been to break down Congressional patronage, especially Senatorial patronage. . . . It seemed to me that as executive I could advance the reform of civil service in no way so effectively as by rescuing the power of appointing to office from Congressional leaders."[22] Hayes sought to do away with what he called "Senatorial usurpation" and what Richard Henry Dana, Jr., called the "citadel of the Spoils System."[23] According to the president, "the claim of a single senator to control all nominations in his state" was "preposterous."[24] In particular, Hayes sought to break Conkling's grip on the New York State Republican Party, gain control of that state's Custom House (the largest source of federal government revenue), and forge a national party loyal to him. To that end, he removed Conkling's lieutenant Chester A. Arthur from his directorship. This move produced a dramatic conflict between Conkling and Hayes. In the fall of 1877, Hayes announced his appointments to the most important positions at the Port of New York. However, as chairman of the Senate Commerce Committee, Conkling rejected all the nominees except one. Hayes responded by filling the positions on a temporary basis during the congressional recess. He was then able to secure enough Republicans and Democrats to confirm the appointments in February 1879. This was a setback for the Stalwarts, revealing that even the domineering Conkling could not control federal appointments in his own state when faced with a determined president. Hayes's victory, however, rested largely on Democratic support because most Senate Republicans sided with Conkling.

Second, Hayes ended Reconstruction. Stalwarts saw their allies in the South abandoned in favor of a supposedly large number of "Southern Whigs" that Hayes believed could be drawn into the Republican Party. In 1876, Hayes wrote that: "by conciliating southern whites on the basis of obedience to law and equal rights . . . we may divide the southern whites, and so protect the colored people." Hayes believed that the Stalwarts' "bayonet policy" was no longer effective at protecting blacks. Stalwarts scoffed at the idea that Republicans could retain Southern elected offices without military occupation. Third, Hayes instituted new civil service rules by executive order that prevented federal employees from participating in political activity. Although Stalwarts were largely able to circumvent these provisions, the Hayes administration set an important precedent that other presidents would be inclined to follow.[25]

Similar battles played out between Garfield and Arthur and the Stalwarts. To aid Garfield in the delicate task of appointing a cabinet, Blaine wrote him a letter analyzing the party's structure. First, there was the "Blaine section," located in the West and strong in the House, on whose support Garfield could count. Second, there was "the Grant section, taking all of the South practically, with the machines in New York, Pennsylvania, and Illinois—and having the aid of rule or ruin leaders." These were, as Blaine colorfully put it, "all the desperate bad men of the party, bent on loot and booty. . . . These men are to be handled with skill, always remembering that they are harmless when out of power, and desperate when in possession of it." The last element, according to Blaine, was the "reformers by profession, the 'unco good.'" They were "to be treated with respect" but were "the worst possible political advisers." Blaine's letter demonstrated that governing entailed, first and possibly foremost, playing referee among party factions.

To secure a national Republican party loyal to the president, Garfield also directly confronted the Stalwarts on their own turf. To punish the forces that had voted against him at the convention, Garfield replaced the Custom House Collector with the leader of the anti-Conkling New York Republicans. A battle with Conkling over his confirmation ensued. Because Garfield was more popular than Hayes had been and some Republicans found refighting Conkling's battles distasteful, the president prevailed. In response, Conkling resigned his Senate seat in protest. The New York State legislature then refused to reinstate him, which undermined the Stalwart leadership and accelerated the faction's decline as a force inside the Republican Party. What Conkling hoped to gain from this strange tactical maneuver remains a mystery. Whatever the case, Garfield had taken an important step toward uniting the party behind presidential leadership.

Garfield's assassination by a deranged office seeker calling himself a Stalwart further eroded the faction's standing. Arthur assumed the presidency and signed the Pendleton Act, reforming the civil service. Not signing the act would have sullied the GOP's reputation. Republicans in Congress supported the Pendleton Act to keep Liberals (soon to be called Mugwumps) from deserting the party in 1884. In fact, a Liberal splinter movement was more of a concern than differences between Half-Breeds and Stalwarts. Stalwarts could support the act because it imposed few immediate costs, while also defusing the opposition of disgruntled Liberals. Stalwarts believed they could get around the law because growth of the American state would provide enough patronage positions to compensate for the technical positions covered by the new rules. Taking into account these factors, Arthur was able to sign a measure that a key faction of the party had long opposed.[26]

President Arthur asserted his independence from the Conkling machine in other ways as well. Although he gave Stalwarts plumb appointments, Conkling and Grant were disappointed by his patronage policies. Arthur also continued to pursue the Southern electoral strategy pioneered by Hayes that many Stalwarts opposed. These conflicts increased tensions between Congress and the White House, ultimately undermining Arthur's chances of being nominated for president in 1884.[27]

Presidential-congressional tensions during this period centered on questions of patronage and civil service reform. The federal government did far less then than it does today, and these areas, rather than the legislative creation of new federal programs, were the locus of policy activity. Yet, only the Stalwart faction in Congress really took action to block presidential policies. The Half-Breeds had better relationships with the presidents of the period, and the Liberals lacked sufficient numbers in Congress to take independent action. All three presidents of the period—including Arthur who emerged from the New York machine—chose direct confrontation with the Stalwart faction and relied on the support of Half-Breeds and Liberals. They were able to do this because upon entering office none had substantial debts to the faction. Ultimately, these presidents' management of factionalism helped prepare the ground for the increased Republican Party unity of the 1890s. And, of course, in the days of the premodern presidency none of these presidents took significant steps to go over the head of Congress and appeal directly to the people to support their initiatives.

Roosevelt, Taft, and the Progressive Republicans

During both the Roosevelt and Taft presidencies, GOP party factions were a major force in presidential decision making. Presidential initiatives had to run a gauntlet to secure support among competing factions within the party, which meant dealing with the Old Guard that exercised control of the nomination process and was dominant in Congress. Only weakly affiliated with that faction, Roosevelt held the Republican Party together by privately siding with the Old Guard on the details of legislation but publicly offering Progressives compelling rhetoric. As Robert La Follette put it in his *Autobiography*:

> While Theodore Roosevelt was President, his public utterances through state papers, addresses, and the press were highly coloured with rhetorical radicalism. One trait was always pronounced. His most savage assault upon special interests was invariably offset with an equally drastic attack upon those who were seeking to reform abuses. These were indiscriminately classed as demagogues and dangerous persons. In this way he sought to win approval, both from the radicals and the conservatives.[28]

The Rough Rider also kept divisive issues, especially the tariff, off the public agenda. According to one biographer, the President "found the tariff boring; he never really understood it as a policy."[29] On the other hand, Taft divided the GOP by personally alienating Progressives, publicly affiliating himself with the Old Guard, and putting the tariff on the agenda, which split the party.

Although he owed the Old Guard little for his ascension to power, Roosevelt alternated between confrontation and cooperation in his dealings with the faction in Congress. The President understood that unless he cooperated with Senator Nelson Aldrich (R-RI) and his allies, little legislation could be passed. Roosevelt wrote to one of the "Senate Four," John Spooner of Wisconsin: "I suppose it is hardly necessary for me to say that during the coming three years I hope to keep in closest touch with you and to profit from your advice in the future as I have profited in the past."[30] He also wrote to Taft:

> My experience for the past year and a half . . . has made me feel respect and regard for Aldrich as one other group of senators, including Allison, Hanna, Spooner, Platt of Connecticut, Lodge and one or two others, who together within men like the next speaker, Joe Cannon, are the most powerful factors in Congress . . . their intelligence and power . . . make them not only essential to work with but desirable to work with.[31]

As an unelected president in his first term, an open contest with the Old Guard Senate leadership would have jeopardized Roosevelt's nomination prospects in 1904. Therefore, the president consulted Mark Hanna, Thomas Platt, Matthew Quay, and others about appointments in 1901 and again in 1904 and kept the potentially explosive tariff issue off the table. "Roosevelt had managed to straddle [the parties'] factions," Sidney Milkis has written, "in no small part because he had been willing to forgo a fight on the tariff."[32] Rather than confront a faction by trying to mobilize public opinion, Roosevelt prioritized issues where there was already broad consensus in favor of action. Meanwhile, Aldrich scuttled Roosevelt's more controversial regulatory legislation. Intraparty tensions were thus held in abeyance.

On the other hand, Roosevelt was a catalyst in solidifying the policy goals of the Progressive faction. His expansive rhetoric between 1905 and his departure from office laid the foundation for the Progressive program. In December of 1905, Roosevelt delivered a series of bold messages to the Congress. He lambasted the "malefactors of great wealth," threatening the traditional powers of the business community. According to historian George Mowry, he proposed nearly every reform measure that became law during the Taft and Wilson administrations, calling for an increase in federal regulatory power, inheritance and income taxes, stricter regulation of the railroads, limitation on labor injunctions, and the extension of the eight-hour workday. "Congress does from a third to a half of what I think is the minimum it ought to do," Roosevelt wrote. By the time Roosevelt left the White House, his speeches helped consolidate the collective identity of the rising Progressive reformers.[33]

Conservatives, however, closed ranks in response to the Progressives' emergence, increasing friction between the president and the Senate leadership. Despite, or perhaps because of, the largest GOP electoral victories since the Civil War, the 1904 and 1906 elections solidified the fault lines between Progressives, the president, and the Old Guard. These elections brought some of the most famous Progressives into the House and Senate. The Old Guard response was to dig in their heels and defend the status quo against what they deemed radical change.

The Old Guard was not hostile to all federal regulatory expansion but only to the forms offered by Populist Democrats and Progressive Republicans. Conservatives were willing to accept business regulation, as long as it could accommodate rather than affront the interests of private enterprise. The Hepburn Act is a case in point. Hearings on bills to strengthen the Interstate Commerce Commission's powers were held in the House and Senate in 1904–1905, after President Roosevelt signaled his support for tougher legislation. Roosevelt had demonstrated his distrust of the railroad barons two years earlier when his administration blocked the formation of the Northern Securities holding company. Roosevelt wanted the locus of public control of these corporate entities to be within the executive branch, since he believed that Congress could not balance the need for corporate growth with consumer protection. Roosevelt was also aware that expert administration of railroad regulations was a means by which the president could respond to Progressive discontent within his own party, while enhancing his own institutional prerogatives.[34]

During the congressional hearings, farmers and small shippers were the advocates of increased regulation, while large shippers and railroad executives opposed regulatory expansion. The primary sticking point was the federal courts' power to review the commission's rate-setting decisions. The Old Guard faction favored a broad review power, while Progressives favored a narrowly tailored one. In the Senate, conservatives killed one bill (Esch-Townshend) in 1904. Aldrich's Interstate Commerce Committee held it up in hearings until the session adjourned. In 1905, a bill that embodied Roosevelt's approach, sponsored by William Hepburn (R-IA) was reported nearly unanimously out of the House.[35]

In the Senate, Aldrich's parliamentary tactics offended Progressives. He deprived Progressive Jonathan Dolliver (R-IA) of the opportunity to claim credit for introducing the bill. Instead, he selected Benjamin Tillman (D-SC) to be the bill's sponsor. Aldrich's aim was to ensure that federal courts had the final say on the ICC's rates. When the bill made it out of committee, Aldrich and his allies refused to support it. When the bill stalled in the Senate, garnering support primarily from Democrats, Roosevelt returned to Allison to craft a compromise, which granted broad court review of ICC decisions. The Old Guard then assented to the commission's rate-making powers. Supporters of the legislation still found it an improvement over the status quo, which then passed the Senate by a large margin in 1906, with only radical Progressives (Robert La Follette (R-WI)) and staunch conservatives (Joseph Foraker (R-OH)) opposing it. The result was the Hepburn Act. President Roosevelt claimed that it marked a "noteworthy advance in the policy of securing Federal supervision and control over corporations."[36]

President Roosevelt's approach to party factions in the passage of the Pure Food Act and the Meat Inspection Act followed similar patterns. The Old Guard stood against broad regulatory change that empowered executive agencies and threatened the interests of business, while Progressives and Populist Democrats formed an alliance in favor of more dramatic reform. Roosevelt's arbitration strategy was to try to bring the Old Guard along in private discussions, while publicly endorsing the aims of reformers. In the end, the Old Guard was able to shape these laws in ways that satisfied their policy preferences but could still be deemed an improvement over the status quo by supporters of reform.

Overall, Roosevelt worked to moderate the GOP's image by employing a "triangulation" strategy between the two factions within his party. The president believed this was the only way to pass legislation and slowly nudge the party in a progressive direction. Although Roosevelt became increasingly associated with the Progressive faction, his essential governing strategy was to act as an arbiter between factions.

To the extent that Roosevelt articulated what many Progressives were for, Taft clarified what they were against. In Progressives' eyes, conservatives such as Aldrich and Cannon led Taft by the nose. Progressive Iowa Senator Jonathan Dolliver described Taft as "an amiable island surrounded by men who know exactly what they want."[37] Taft chose to adopt the Old Guard faction's concerns as his own. His cabinet appointments, his handling of the move against Speaker Cannon, his intervention into tariff reform, and the Ballinger-Pinchot affair united the Progressive faction in opposition to him. Historian Arthur S. Link argues that, "in order to prevent the disruption of the Republican Party, Taft had to facilitate the shift in party control from the Old Guard to the Insurgents—but instead aligned himself with the reactionaries."[38] The campaign of 1910 sealed the factional split between the Old Guard faction and the Taft administration on one side and the Progressives on the other.

Historians have judged Taft's presidency harshly for his supposed ineptitude at managing GOP factions. As Lewis Gould put it: "Because he did not act in mold of a presidential activist and instead pursued moderate ends, he pleased neither faction of his own party."[39] But given the Old Guard's power in Congress and its hold on the nomination process, the strategy adopted by Taft is understandable.

Little did Old Guard conservatives know in 1908 that Taft's nomination handed the presidency to one of their own, as Roosevelt had claimed his successor would carry out "my policies." To maintain control over party policy priorities in the face of Roosevelt's rhetorical onslaught, conservatives rewrote the party platform to their specifications. Aldrich, along with Winthrop Murray Crane (R-MA) and James Van Cleave (president of the American Manufacturers Association) wrote the controversial labor and tariff planks. Instead of limiting injunctions as the original platform approved by Roosevelt and Taft did, the party pledged to "uphold at all times the authority and integrity of the courts."[40] And the platform only said that tariff reform was in order, not that the tariff should be revised downward as Taft requested.

Taft's presidential leadership quickly affiliated him with the Old Guard and alienated Progressives. As one historian put it, "Taft's relations with the progressive faction began badly, deteriorated rapidly, and reached open hostility within a year of his inauguration."[41] Taft was more intellectually conservative than Roosevelt and did not share the Rough Rider's confidence in the efficacy of state action or the speed with which social change could be affected. Nor did he hold Roosevelt's expansive view of executive power. Taft thought the president should be more of an executor of law than a policy initiator. Moreover, he was suspicious about the rights of organized labor and disposed to respect judicial injunctions. Socially, Taft remained a strictly establishment figure, who "scarcely corresponded or . . . mingled with a person of . . . progressive tendencies." He preferred men like Senator Crane, an organization man who distrusted reformers, especially those in his own party. Taft personally disliked or lacked confidence in many Progressives.[42]

Taft's handling of a series of separate but overlapping issues solidified the perception among Progressives that he was opposed to them and was strengthening the Old Guard. The president's appointment policies, especially his hastily formed cabinet, which included five corporate lawyers, left Progressives without patronage. In particular, his decision not to reappoint Roosevelt's Progressive friends, James R. Garfield and Luke E. Wright, disillusioned Progressives. Taft even went so far in some cases as to use patronage in an effort to discipline Progressive faction members. These symbolic personnel policies underscored the competing conceptions of the GOP's identity.[43]

Taft's maladroit handling of the insurgency against Speaker Joseph Cannon further disappointed Progressives. Under threat, Cannon became increasingly aggressive in his parliamentary tactics, blocking Progressive and Democratic measures in the last two years of the Roosevelt administration. The frustration of Progressive Republicans, and some Democrats, culminated in a rebellion. Taft encouraged the movement against the Speaker until Cannon, Aldrich, and Chairman of the Ways and Means Committee Sereno Payne (R-NY) informed him that tariff revision would be off the table unless he supported the speaker. Rather than imperil his legislative program, Taft sided with Cannon and the Old Guard. While Progressives, in league with Populist Democrats, eventually succeeded in weakening the speaker, Taft's intransigence enraged them.

By seeking tariff reform, Taft opened a Pandora's Box.[44] The president's frequent meetings with Aldrich and Cannon—champions of high tariffs—alienated Progressives who sought lower rates. The final bill was also disappointing for Progressives because its net effect was not to substantially reduce tariffs. Taft's excessive praise of the Payne-Aldrich tariff added insult to injury. Progressives assailed the president for not supporting further reductions in tariff schedules and adopting a personal income tax to raise revenue. They also attacked Cannon and Aldrich as being the representatives of big business. The entire process soured Taft on Progressives and reformers.

In the Ballinger-Pinchot affair, Taft once again managed to offend Roosevelt and the Progressives. A complex bureaucratic battle came to symbolize the struggle between Progressive and Old Guard factions for control of the GOP. By siding with his secretary of the interior, Richard Ballinger, against Roosevelt's friend, Chief Forester Gifford Pinchot, Taft associated himself with the Old Guard. The crack in the two men's friendship widened into a chasm when Roosevelt learned of Pinchot's firing.

In the last two years of Taft's presidency, he undertook more progressive measures on railroads and the trusts, but this did little to repair factional divisions within the party. Nonetheless, Taft had many advantages going into the 1912 election: The GOP had not denied an incumbent renomination since Chester Arthur, Taft had real accomplishments in the areas of trusts and social legislation, and a peaceful international scene allowed the economy to grow unimpeded. Although Taft had alienated Progressives, he might have regained his position and healed the wounds within the party, even as late as 1911. Unfortunately for him, his vigorous trust busting weakened the attachment of the Old Guard without scoring points with Progressives. The result was a badly divided party where one faction opposed the president and the other supported him only as the best choice among bad alternatives.

Woodrow Wilson and the Populist Democrats

Woodrow Wilson adopted an appeasement strategy to deal with the Populist faction because of its importance in securing him the nomination and its power in Congress. Harmony between Wilson and Populists was evidenced by the extraordinary cooperation between the White House and Congress during the first two years of his presidency. This derived in part from Wilson's theory of government, which held that Congress should behave more like the British Parliament and the president like the prime minister. Much of the legislation during Wilson's first term derived not only from his forceful leadership but also from the agenda Democratic reformers in Congress already had in hand. Indeed, legislators who had better reform credentials than the president spearheaded many bills, sometimes over his opposition. From his perch in the State Department, Bryan encouraged Populists in Congress to push Wilson on issues such as antitrust, labor, banking, currency, farm credit, and Philippine independence. Like Taft, Wilson arrived in the presidential spotlight largely unaffiliated but quickly found himself connected to a faction and unsure how to deal with it.

Wilson's administration, if not the president himself, quickly set out to link the White House to the Populists. The first Democratic administration since Grover Cleveland used its appointment powers to favor faction affiliates. Despite Wilson's personal hostility to patronage, his southern and largely agrarian cabinet was not similarly disposed. At the State Department, Bryan's methods made him something of a spoilsman. Other cabinet members, such as Postmaster General Albert Burleson of Texas, used patronage to simultaneously promote Wilson's program and build up Populist faction affiliates in the states. The administration's patronage methods were designed to enhance Wilson's effectiveness as a leader of the Democrats in the House.[45]

Many details of the New Freedom legislative program also emerged from discussions between Wilson and Populists in his cabinet. The president listened to counsel from Bryan, Louis D. Brandeis, and William Gibbs McAdoo. Wilson's governing strategy reflected his willingness to make the reformers' program his own. He wrote to a friend early in his administration, "Congress is made up of thinking men who want the party to succeed as much as I do, and who wish to serve the country effectively and intelligently. They . . . accept my guidance because they see that I am attempting only to mediate their own thoughts and purposes . . . I am not driving them."[46] A new cadre of reform-oriented congressmen that had taken their seats with the new Democratic majorities assisted Wilson in this endeavor. Among them were Joseph T. Robinson of Arkansas, Thomas J. Walsh of Montana, Robert L. Owen of Oklahoma, and Altee Pomerene of Ohio. Wilson's task in his first two years in office was to back reform measures by cajoling, pressuring, and otherwise inducing older conservative Democrats—such as Furnifold M. Simmons of North Carolina, Thomas S. Martin of Virginia, and William Stone of Missouri—to follow him.

The progressive spirit introduced and advocated by the Populists would, however, wane within Democratic presidential politics after Wilson's presidency. Wilson even declared the Progressive movement fulfilled as early as 1914. In a public letter to McAdoo he wrote: "We have only to look back ten years or so to realize the deep perplexities and dangerous ill-humors out of which we have at last issued, as if from a bewildering fog, a noxious miasma."[47] The passage of the New Freedom had apparently righted the deep wrongs that had scarred the country.[48]

Over the next two years, however, the Populist faction forced Wilson to reverse course on a number of policy issues. Initially, the President had blocked child labor legislation, stymied efforts to pass a farm credits bill, and been uninterested in proposals for workman's compensation. In 1915 and 1916, the administration reversed course on all of these initiatives. Early alignment with Populists had thus forced Wilson to later accede to their demands. Populists' cooperation meant that if Wilson wanted to be reelected in 1916, he had debts to pay. Wilson's first term showed that a strategy of alignment and cooperation with a faction can push a president further down a path laid out by that faction. How Wilson would have dealt with Populists in his second term is a mystery, because World War I overshadowed their domestically oriented partnership. After the War, the Democratic Party lay in shambles, passing through one of its weakest periods of national electoral strength in the 1920s.

Southern Democrats, Liberal-Labor Democrats, and Presidential Governance

Southern Democrats powerfully shaped the American presidency at mid-century. While weakened in presidential nomination contests by the abolition in 1936 of the Democratic Party's famous two-thirds rule, the faction's power in Congress ensured that it would profoundly shape the governing strategies of presidents from Franklin Roosevelt to Lyndon Johnson. The formulation of Roosevelt's so-called Third New Deal, announced in 1942, Truman's Fair Deal, Kennedy's New Frontier, and Johnson's Great Society all took into account the fact that passing domestic legislation was a three-cornered struggle between Republicans and the bi-factionalized Democratic Party. Historian William T. Leuchtenburg has written that three of the four Democratic presidents of the period all had "one foot below the Mason-Dixon line."[49]

By altering the balance of power in Congress, Southern Democrats forced presidents to reckon with them at every step of the legislative process. Powerful Southern committee barons shaped presidents' perception of what was politically possible. To govern, the president had to alternately appease, massage, confront, attack, and cajole the Southern Democratic faction. Roosevelt and Truman oscillated between publicly attacking and privately working with Southerners in hopes of implementing the New and Fair Deals. Both presidents understood that Southern Democrats were not completely opposed to their domestic programs but that they had incentives to join with Republicans against more liberal measures. Roosevelt and Truman were thus forced into a compensatory strategy of trying to lure Southerners to support their social policies. For instance, the Roosevelt administration steered defense industry contracts to the region in exchange for Southern support. This strategy often boiled down to trying to buy off the faction with federal assistance.[50]

In the 1950s and 1960s, the majority party in the House and Senate was split. The Liberal-Labor faction was the countervailing force to the Southerners in Congress. Not surprisingly, Kennedy and Johnson tried to enlist its resources. Upon Kennedy's election, Liberal-Labor found itself in a new position, aligned with a president who had run on a program that they had helped craft. Liberal-Labor became instrumental in trying to mobilize coalitions in favor of the president's legislative agenda and supported him against Southern Democrats who threatened to block the New Frontier. Rather than try to build up the faction's strength within the party, Kennedy chose to employ the resources it could offer him without much of a quid pro quo. His strategy was to use Liberal-Labor to spearhead his legislative program with the expectation that he would resort to spending his own political capital when necessary.

For nearly a thousand days, however, Southern Democrats were able to frustrate the enactment of key measures. Kennedy entered office with no coattails. Indeed, twenty-one liberal Democrats lost their House seats in 1960. In addition, he faced men occupying key committee chairmanships that possessed, as one analyst put it: "little more than a sentimental attachment to the national party and who were hostile to much or all of the party's program."[51] To put the machinery of Congress in the hands of those who supported him, Kennedy had three options: a frontal attack on the seniority system and the committee barons, lesser reforms in congressional organization, or simply relying on pressure and persuasion. Kennedy ruled out the possibility of a direct assault as hopeless, settling for a combination of lesser reforms, particularly the expansion of the Rules Committee, and intense pressure and persuasion. Although Kennedy did manage to reform the Rules Committee to weaken the power of Chairman Howard W. Smith (D-VA), his legislative program still foundered.[52] James L. Sundquist has shown that of the eleven major proposals in Kennedy's program, only three became law during the first two years of his administration.

In the early weeks of his administration, Kennedy forged ahead with his policy program. He had some successes, notably on his "depressed areas" bill, housing legislation, the Manpower Development and Training Act, and an increase in Social Security benefits. But in other areas he secured only pyrrhic victories or suffered defeats. After tough negotiations between the House and Senate, Kennedy won a victory of sorts on raising the minimum wage. But Kennedy's proposals to improve education faced even greater obstacles. Although the Senate passed the education bill, the House Rules Committee killed it. The administration then used a parliamentary move to circumvent the committee. But it died on the floor with eighty-two Southern Democrats voting in opposition. Medical insurance for the aged suffered a similar fate in the Senate, when Southern Democrats voted to table it. The defeat led Kennedy to complain that "he couldn't get a Mother's Day resolution through the goddamn Congress."[53] By late 1962, the Americans for Democratic Action complained about a "failure of leadership."[54]

It was not until after Kennedy's assassination, Johnson's destruction of Goldwater in the 1964 election, and the Democratic electoral landslide that year that the liberal agenda that had been percolating for nearly a decade came to fruition.[55] Congressional reform, a national tragedy, and a massive Democratic electoral victory put the Southern Democrats on the defensive, weakened their Republican allies, and ensured that Medicare, aid to elementary and secondary education, and the other elements of the party's program would pass. Johnson's intimate knowledge of Congress and forceful leadership no doubt also contributed to his ability to overawe a faction that had been weakened.

Johnson's strategy for dealing with the Southern Democrats differed from Kennedy's because he benefited from a double mandate composed of Kennedy's death and his massive electoral victory in 1964. Therefore, he boldly proclaimed his policies and began promoting them on Capitol Hill. In 1964, the administration pushed strongly for the Civil Rights Bill and announced the "war on poverty." According to Milton Eisenhower, "There was no question that when Johnson became president, he became the most militant civil rights leader in the country."[56] In his first state of the Union Address, Johnson said: "Let this session of Congress be known as the session which did more for civil rights than the last hundred sessions combined."[57] This immediately linked him to the Liberal-Labor faction. Johnson enlisted Hubert Humphrey to court pivotal Republican Senator Everett Dirksen of Illinois. With the faction's help, Johnson deftly drove the Civil Rights Act and the Economic Opportunity Act through the Congress.[58] According to aide Joseph Califano, Johnson "devoted a staggering amount of his time, energy, and political capital to breaking the Senate filibuster and passing the act."[59]

Under the second mandate, the strategy of applying powerful pressure on the committee barons worked. Johnson advised his aide Jack Valenti, "The most important people you talk to are senators and congressmen. You treat them as if they were president. Answer their calls immediately. Give them respect . . . they are your most important clients."[60] Eric Goldman counted the number of days it took to pass major legislation: 87 for education, 204 for Medicare, and 142 for the Voting Rights Act.[61] To realize the Great Society, Johnson used labor's network to outmaneuver the Southern committee barons whom he feared would block his legislative agenda.[62] This meant, for instance, getting around Rules Committee Chairman Smith and his "No Rules for Schools" motto to pass the Elementary and Secondary Education Act. Johnson's record of legislative successes is breathtaking. In 1964 fifty-eight bills passed, in 1965 sixty-nine passed, in 1966 fifty-six passed, in 1967 forty-eight passed, and in 1968 fifty-six passed.[63]

While adding his own innovations such as the Model Cities program, President Johnson essentially adopted the Liberal-Labor program of reform of unemployment insurance, health care for the aged, and aid to education. The Johnson presidency marked the high point of the faction's influence with executive branch. Union leaders and their congressional allies had regular access to the White House. The genesis of much of the Great Society legislative program and the way Johnson enlisted factional affiliates was the task force. These task forces included academics, activists, unionists, business leaders, government officials, and others. These task forces sped legislative draftsmanship, and their secrecy allowed conflict within the liberal coalition to be quietly managed.[64]

Labor provided an effective organizational apparatus for affiliated faction members in Congress; pressuring wavering members, collecting political intelligence, and coordinating legislative strategy. Labor leaders became the vanguard of liberal forces in Congress.[65] *Congressional Quarterly* concluded, "The lawmakers' action in the fields of civil rights, anti-poverty, education, and other social welfare areas under Mr. Johnson's energetic and experienced leadership generally followed the unions' longstanding stance on social legislation."[66] On civil rights, Medicare, and the administration's "War on Poverty," the Liberal-Labor faction assisted in producing dramatic new legislation.

Eisenhower and Modern Liberal Republicans

On election night in 1956, Dwight Eisenhower gave his most ringing endorsement of Modern (or Liberal) Republicanism. He told a national television audience: "I think that modern Republicanism has now proved itself. And America has approved of modern Republicanism. . . . Modern Republicanism looks to the future."[67] Although modern Liberal Republicans hoped Eisenhower would be their champion, the General did little to align himself the faction's few representatives in Congress. Given the fragility of the GOP's standing in Congress in the 1950s, however, that is not surprising. In addition, the Liberals lacked a comprehensive governing agenda that Eisenhower could sign onto. In the 1950s, Liberal Republican senator Jacob Javits said: "when a composite of our Party is taken, the thinking is Eisenhower [modern] thinking."[68] Javits's statement revealed the lack of defining issues and dependence on Eisenhower's personal vision. Even more importantly, their ranks in Congress were too thin, disorganized, and housed in the minority party for Eisenhower to pay them much heed. As a politician significantly more popular than his party, Eisenhower could legitimately claim to be above his party. Consequently, Eisenhower entered the White House with few commitments to the faction that had worked hardest to place him there.

Eisenhower has traditionally been portrayed as a president who basically ignored Republican Party affairs. More recently, however, scholars have portrayed Eisenhower as a more active and skilled president.[69] Cornelius Cotter argues that President Eisenhower "exerted considerable influence over the Republican Party and pursued a well-informed and sustained program to strengthen it."[70] To a large extent, then, Eisenhower's efforts at party leadership consisted of maintaining unity and massaging internal differences. According to Nicol Rae, his desire to maintain party unity restrained any desire he might have had to popularize Liberal Republicanism.[71] Eisenhower's overall attitude toward Liberals was, therefore, one of benign neglect, since the realization of his policy goals did not depend on them.

Even when Eisenhower did work to advance the Liberal cause, his actions often backfired. He tried to build the Republican Party up from the grassroots in a way that would infuse modern and liberal ideas into it. Yet, Daniel Galvin has argued that the General's party-building efforts had the unintended consequence, especially in the South, of empowering conservatives within the party.[72] While improving the party's recruitment capacities improved the party, they also opened the door to the recruitment of more conservative candidates. Galvin claims that Eisenhower's experience reveals that presidential efforts to "[bring] about ideological change require[s] more than successful organizational ventures."[73] The more Eisenhower built up the GOP organization, the more conservative that organization became.

The Eisenhower administration's policy choices did little to recast the GOP in a Liberal mold. For instance, after announcing a liberal budget proposal in 1957, Eisenhower and his administration quickly backtracked to the right and endorsed a more austere spending program. Generally, Ike cultivated the image of being above the political fray, and much of his influence was exercised behind the scenes. Therefore, his factional supporters could not claim much credit for his actions. This may have satisfied Eisenhower personally, but it did little to market the Liberal brand of Republicanism. Moreover, it was difficult for a president who championed slow change in public policy to burnish his image as someone working from a set of principles.[74]

Traditional GOP loyalists came from safe districts, while Liberals in Congress were often from hotly contested, and thus insecure, states and districts. Therefore, Eisenhower began his administration by satisfying the regulars. He ended all wage and price controls imposed during the Korean War; allowed the Reconstruction Finance Corporation to go out of business; and, in 1953, received congressional authorization to sell state-run rubber plants to private industry. A year later, the administration secured an amendment to the Atomic Energy Act that expanded the participation of private industry in the development of atomic materials and facilities. Eisenhower's dedication to balanced budgets reassured GOP regulars. Finally, the General had Vice President Richard Nixon act on Capitol Hill as a broker between Liberal internationalists and the isolationist majority. According to journalist Samuel Lubell, "Nixon [did] yeoman work on Capitol Hill in tempering the opposition of all but the most extreme Republicans to some of Eisenhower's foreign policy measures."[75] Each of these policy moves placed the president squarely in the mainstream of his party. The logic of the political situation dictated that the president favor the mainstream of his party rather than a faction.

On the other hand, some of Eisenhower's choices irked conservative Republicans. For instance, he did not try to dismantle the social welfare programs of the New Deal. In 1954 and again in 1956 he agreed to increases in Social Security benefits and in the number of workers included in the program. In 1955, he signed a bill increasing the minimum wage. In housing, slum clearance, and health care the administration maintained continuity. Moreover, his "hidden-hand" style of leadership allowed others to form their own, often incorrect, impressions of his motives, intentions, and views. Even his increased conservatism on budgetary matters in his second term went unrecognized and unrewarded by many on the right.[76] Indeed, the increased spending of the 1957 budget sparked a conservative revolt, with Goldwater charging that the president had been beguiled by the "Siren song of socialism."[77] In other areas, Eisenhower's public positions frustrated conservative Republicans. For instance, Eisenhower was committed to a strong national defense but was not shy about calling for arms control. Conservative Republicans were dismayed that the president did not try to "roll back" communism. Instead, Eisenhower continued Truman's containment approach.[78] Overall, the Eisenhower administration's continuity with past Democratic presidents left conservative Republicans deeply frustrated.

If Eisenhower's approach had proved more successful for the Republican Party generally, he might have persuaded conservative critics of the merits of his views. Yet, his style of governance sought simply to compensate Liberals and ignore the conservatives. Indeed, the GOP suffered three consecutive losses in congressional elections following Ike's ascendancy to the presidency (1954, 1956, and 1958). Liberals in the Northeast faced steep challenges. Eisenhower didn't do much to satisfy Liberals, but neither did he do much that benefited conservatives. Forced to deal with an increasingly assertive Democratic Congress, the president often neglected factional politics within the GOP.

Carter and the New Politics Democrats

In the wake of Watergate, Jimmy Carter emerged from obscurity to win the presidency. Carter's main appeal was less ideological than personal. Carter famously pledged never to tell a lie and to reflect "the high moral character of the American people." His campaign themes elicited some skepticism from the triumphant New Politics Democrats whose congressional ranks had expanded with the election of the "Watergate babies" in 1974.[79] While the faction was relatively weak as a force in Congress, its galaxy of "public interest" groups created by New Politics Democrats displaced organized labor's coordinating role among liberal members. Connecticut Senator Abraham Ribicoff observed in 1976: "instead of big lobbies from major corporations dominating the hearings process, you have had practically every committee in Congress according 'equal time' to public interest people." Illinois Representative Abner Mikva noted that New Politics public interest groups represented "the biggest change I've seen in Congress since I first came.... Instead of anti-establishment groups handing out leaflets on a street corner we have people working very effectively in the halls of Congress."[80] Common Cause and Naderite groups helped affiliates obtain information, collate research results, refine legislation, mobilize attentive publics, and publicize issues. The new form of political combat that resulted revolved around congressional subcommittees' knowledge about program detail, federal courts, and administrative agencies.[81]

In spite of its initial skepticism about a Southern peanut farmer, Carter's outsider quality, populist streak, and faith in technocratic expertise endeared him to New Politics Democrats. Once in office, his appointments affirmed the political power of the public interest groups and squared with the New Politics emphasis on racial and gender diversity.[82] His chief pollster, Patrick Caddell, had worked for the McGovern campaign upon graduation from Harvard and shared much of the New Politics Democrats' vision of America. According to

David Vogel, more than sixty public interest activists, hailing from organizations such as the National Resources Defense Council and Congress Watch, were awarded positions.[83] *Fortune* magazine noted: "Now public-interest organizations have the kind of access to the departments and the White House once enjoyed by national labor unions and large corporations working through highly paid Washington lobbyists."[84] Carter also increased the number of minorities and women in senior government positions and among his advisors. Congressman Andrew Young, previously an aide to Martin Luther King, Jr., became ambassador to the United Nations. Juanita Kreps and Patricia Roberts Harris, both black women, were named to cabinet posts. The president also appointed a large number of women to the federal courts.

However, conflict between the New Politics faction and an assertive president quickly emerged. While elements of Carter's expansive agenda hewed closely to the faction's preferences, Carter chose to assert his personal convictions on many occasions. To New Politics Democrats exasperation, Carter remained committed to fighting inflation as the chief cause of the country's economic difficulties. As a Southerner, Carter tended to view lobbyists and interest groups as corrupt parasites on government. He wanted to make government more efficient, rational, and responsive to the public, which to New Politics Democrats sounded like a plan to neglect the truly disadvantaged. Carter's fiscal prudence and his suspicion of social reform programs did not endear him to New Politics Democrats. This was evident in his first budget, where the president proposed cutting social programs, especially those serving urban areas, to fund a $25 billion dollar tax cut. Carter's relationship with Edward Kennedy over a national health insurance program began poorly, deteriorated quickly, and collapsed in 1978, when Kennedy accused Carter of "a failure of leadership."

On issues of race and gender, Carter also embittered the New Politics Democrats. The administration's muddled response to the Supreme Court's *The Regents of the University of California v. Bakke* (1978) decision sparked a heated debate over the constitutionality of affirmative action inside the White House that leaked to the press. While Carter had firmly endorsed the Equal Rights Amendment (ERA) by signing a bill to extend the time that the states could consider it, some feminist leaders accused the president of dragging his feet. Feminist organizations also attacked him for not supporting federal funding for abortion, despite the fact that he had made his opposition clear during the campaign.[85] The costs of these battles were high for the administration because, as Sean Wilentz has written, "Just when Carter became embattled over civil rights and cultural issues with blacks and feminists on his left, a resounding attack on both him and the left arose from hard-line conservatives" on the political right.[86] Carter's efforts to find a middle ground failed. The president's efforts to follow his own convictions or those of a powerful faction badly divided American government and ended in ashes.

By 1980, New Politics Democrats were lining up behind Edward Kennedy to challenge Carter for the Democratic nomination. By that point, the administration's inability to secure the passage of labor law reform, its support for oil price deregulation and regulatory reform, had deeply offended the New Politics faction. Other factors played a role, to be sure, but it was partly Carter's management of a party faction that elicited a strong challenge to a sitting president from within his own party. Neither the primary season nor the general election proved smooth sailing for President Carter.

Reagan, Bush, and the New Right

During the 1970s, the New Right developed its organizational apparatus and critical capabilities. Unlike Richard Nixon and Gerald Ford, who had tried to keep the New Right at arm's length, Ronald Reagan embraced it. The Reagan administration, especially in its first term, was a powerful experience for New Right activists. They had one of their own in the White House and were treated accordingly. Reagan gave keynote addresses at New Right fundraisers, such as Terry Dolan's annual CPAC conference. In addition to a cadre of appointees, New Right think tanks—such as the American Enterprise Institute, the Heritage Foundation, and the Cato Institute—placed conservative ideas at the center of the administration's policy debates. Indeed, the Heritage Foundation's 1,000-page book, *Mandate for Leadership*, became the policy bible of the incoming administration.

Reagan's election also coincided with Republicans' takeover of the Senate for the first time in a quarter century. The cohort of Republicans in the Senate included a number of conservatives and built on significant New Right affiliated victories in the 1978 midterm elections, which also saw the defeat of many Liberal Republicans.[87] Governing with a faction in his corner presented Reagan with new opportunities. Yet, it also had drawbacks. Whenever Reagan was seen as deviating from the conservative position on a subject—which frequently occurred since the New Right was a faction within the minority party in the House—the president could expect vociferous criticism from his allies. These occasions exposed the president to criticism in the press for violating his "principles."

Nonetheless, the buildup of New Right forces in Congress received a significant push from the President. Reagan was a "party man" who was genuinely concerned about the long-term health of the GOP. His efforts to institutionalize the national Republican Party paid dividends by smoothing his relations

with congressional Republicans in general and New Right affiliates in particular. As Galvin argues, the lack of solid GOP congressional majorities constrained Reagan's policy program. Therefore, he had a strong incentive to build
up the party to forge a new conservative Republican majority.[88] Reagan's objectives and those of New Right legislators were closely aligned: to remake the
party's image into that of a conservative party. He was aided in these efforts by
the organizational skills of William Brock. After 1976, the Republican National Committee and the other two national Republican campaign bodies,
the National Republican Senatorial and Congressional Committees, greatly
expanded their efforts to raise funds and provide services for GOP candidates.
In order to enhance cooperation between the White House, the National
Committee, and the congressional campaign organizations, in January 1983
Reagan chose his close personal friend, Nevada Senator Paul Laxalt to be the
new general chairman of the GOP. After replacing ineffective National
Chairman Richard Richards, the administration also replaced Senator Bob
Packwood with Richard Lugar as head of the Senate Republican Committee.
These moves represented a significant strengthening of the national Republican Party. While Reagan did remake the GOP as a solidly right-of-center party,
serious disagreements between ardent conservatives intent upon forging a
unified national party and those who favored a more incremental approach
continued to divide congressional Republicans during his presidency.

Reagan arrived in office with a clear set of conservative principles that dictated his approach to core issues. However, he showed himself to be a pragma-
tist who was willing to compromise to achieve some aspects of his program.
This was immediately apparent in his cabinet appointments, which blended
conservative loyalists with experienced hands. According to historian Donald
Crichtlow, "[Reagan's] nominations reveal[ed] a president confident in his
ability to reconcile factional differences within the party."[89] In addition, the
president's desire for legislative accomplishment led him, through his Chief of
Staff James Baker, to cultivate a strong relationship with Senate Majority
Leader Howard Baker (R-TN).

Nonetheless, Reagan's relations with Senate Republicans were not always
smooth. Senate Budget Chairman Peter Domenici (R-NM) was skeptical
about balancing the budget when the administration had called for deep tax
cuts and increased defense expenditures. Eventually the administration's efforts on Capitol Hill paid dividends and brought along even Domenici in support of the Economic Recovery Tax Act that cut income taxes, reduced capital
gains taxes, and indexed tax rates for inflation. The result was the largest tax
cut in American history. The administration also won plaudits for its deregula-
tory efforts in the federal bureaucracy, most of which were accomplished
through executive orders.

Only two short years later, however, faced with an economic recession and rising interest rates, the administration came under pressure from Senate Republicans to raise taxes. In 1982, Reagan bowed to the pressure for a tax increase and signed the Tax Equity and Fiscal Responsibility Act, which was one of the largest tax increases in American history. The New Right, led by activists such as Richard Viguerie and Paul Weyrich, erupted in a chorus of criticism. To garner conservative support for the tax bill, the administration had also been forced to expend precious political capital to secure Jesse Helms's (R-NC) support for the measure.

In foreign affairs, Reagan pursued the New Right's strategy of peace through strength. The idea was to challenge the Soviet Union on a number of fronts—including Africa, Latin America, Europe, the Caribbean, and even outer space—while simultaneously pursuing arms reduction. To carry out the first part of this policy, Reagan launched a major arms buildup, doubling the defense budget from $158 billion to $304 billion. The New Right was generally supportive of these measures. In Nicaragua, however, where the administration assisted the Contra rebels in their efforts to overthrow the Cuban-backed Sandinista government, a conflagration broke out when a CIA operation to mine the bay of Managua sank a Soviet freighter in 1983. Even Barry Goldwater distanced himself from the administration's policy in Central America.

In cultural politics, the Reagan administration was less successful. It was unable to win passage of antiabortion and voluntary school prayer bills. Acutely conscious of antiabortion groups' value to the Republican cause, Reagan sent letters to the national Right to Life Committee endorsing their cause. The White House also coordinated their efforts on one of the antiabortion bills with grassroots New Right activists. After the defeat of these bills, Reagan sought to appoint antiabortion judges to the federal bench using a tough screening process. He followed this up with the appointment of C. Everett Koop, an evangelical Christian, as Surgeon General.

Overall, Reagan's relaunching of the Cold War through tough anticommunist policies and his conservative economic program of tax cuts facilitated alliances with New Right affiliates in Congress and kept their critical energies in check. Ultimately, New Right affiliates were reluctant to oppose Reagan publicly.

The nomination and election of George H.W. Bush, however, left many New Right affiliates cold. Of course, Reagan, a conservative icon, was a tough act to follow. The arrival of a president not affiliated with the New Right made it seem as though the faction took over the party only to then to relinquish control. Bush was forced to govern in a complex situation where his party was factionalized but lacked control of either house of Congress. Indeed, Bush entered the White House facing a larger opposition majority in Congress than any other first-term president. The results were frustrating for Bush and the New Right faction.

During the Bush presidency (1989–1993), conservatives in the House hoped that he would pursue a bold agenda and put Democrats on the defensive, thereby creating opportunities for Republicans to attack Democrats in the 1990 and 1992 campaigns. Bush, however, pursued a moderate course that did not provide New Right legislators the targets they desired.[90] This course was in large measure dictated by circumstances. Without debts to the faction for his nomination and a Democratic majority in Congress, Bush had little room to maneuver. The budget deficit tightly restricted his ability to undertake new initiatives. He could not free up dollars by cutting domestic spending because Reagan had already done that. Nor could he cut defense. To cap off Bush's problems, issues from the Reagan years, such as the savings and loan scandals, cleaning up nuclear power plants, and corruption at HUD, still dominated the agenda.

Bush did not intend to openly confront the faction, but his course often veered close to doing so. His rhetoric also appeared to cast Reagan and the New Right in a bad light. His call for a "kinder, gentler nation" appeared to endorse Democratic criticism.[91] His desire to be the environmental president suggested that Reagan was a tool of industry indifferent to the fate of the planet. His praise for government service rankled Reaganite believers in the inefficiencies of big government. Finally, major domestic legislation passed under Bush—such as the Clean Air Act and the Americans with Disabilities Act—alienated the New Right. Rather than reduce the size of government, those laws expanded it. From the point of view of the New Right, Democrats in Congress too often set the government agenda during the Bush presidency.[92] The best the New Right could hope for was inaction. John Sununu, half-jokingly, told a conservative group in the fall of 1990, "There's not a single piece of legislation that needs to be passed in the next two years for this president. In fact, if Congress wants to come together, adjourn, and leave, it's all right with us."[93]

The classic battle between Bush and the rising New Right forces behind Gingrich came in the budget battle in the summer of 1990. After pledging "no new taxes" during the campaign to satisfy conservatives, the White House proposed a budget package that raised taxes over the next ten years. The Administration felt that this was the only way to reduce the deficit, which would put a long-term drag on the economy. The president gambled that Gingrich's minions would fall in line behind his program. The package was defeated in the House, however, with 105 Gingrichites voting against it. This spectacular defeat highlighted the divisions within the party between older moderates and New Right conservatives staunchly opposing any increase.

The Bush presidency is indicative of the problems presidents confront when they run up against a faction. These issues came to a head when Bush had to face a bitter primary battle for renomination in 1992 against more conservative candidates. Confronted with little room to maneuver and little desire for bold policy initiatives, Bush found himself locked in combat with the New Right, which ultimately cast a pall over his presidency.

Clinton and the New Democrats

Bill Clinton's victories in the nominating contest and the general election in 1992 along with the composition of the new Congress did not favor New Democrats. Clinton had not won more than 50 percent of the popular vote and had no coattails. In fact, Republicans gained ten seats in the House. While the congressional Democrats would obviously be better off with a Democratic president, they did not feel indebted to the man from Hope. The manner of Clinton's victory thus boded ill for New Democrats. His first two years in office, when he was closely tied to the Democratic Leadership Council (DLC) and seen as the faction's champion, sent several incorrect messages. Despite being the faction's champion, he did not consistently try to put its imprint on the party. Rather, the president either proposed "Old" Democratic politics or offered New Democratic policies in old-fashioned Democratic rhetoric. Clinton's mixed record would become a key stumbling block in the faction's effort to transform the party. However, his inability (or unwillingness) to fully pursue New Democrat policies is understandable, insofar as doing so would have entailed a governing strategy that alienated the majority of his party in favor of a minority faction.[94]

The course Clinton pursued in his first two years in office on the federal budget, appointments, and policy priorities demoralized New Democrats. The battle over Clinton's first budget in the spring and summer of 1993 raised serious questions about his commitment to their economic and policy solutions. The administration's budget, despite promising to reduce the deficit, included a number of old-school liberal taxes and social programs. After a tough legislative battle, with Senate Republicans filibustering the budget, Congress did pass a modified version of the budget, voting along strictly partisan lines. Clinton was only able to secure the support of New Democrats and moderates by promising a package of spending cuts in the fall. When this never materialized, it reinforced perceptions among New Democrats that Clinton had betrayed the cause. The era of Big Government seemed far from over.

Despite his campaign pledge to "end welfare as we know it," Clinton appointed Donna Shalala to direct the Department of Health and Human Services, even though she had not expressed any support for welfare reform. Many

New Democrats suspected, rightly it turned out, that she was opposed to their ideas. The DLC had well-developed policy prescriptions for welfare, which they argued should be the first agenda item to demonstrate that Clinton really was a "different kind of Democrat." Clinton, however, sided with the party's majority, choosing to push the Health Security Act (HSA) as his first piece of major legislation.

HSA was a complicated plan designed by a commission headed by First Lady Hillary Clinton. It aimed to guarantee all Americans access to health insurance while controlling costs and leaving the private sector to provide most of the coverage. While elements of the proposed bill had aspects that appealed to New Democrats—particularly the market-based incentives— the plan was too big and unwieldy. It was attacked from all sides. Republicans claimed it would create "socialized medicine," and liberal Democrats said it relied too heavily on the private sector.[95] Clinton was thus unable to build the necessary legislative coalitions to pass HSA.[96] The defeat contributed to the Republican landslide in the congressional elections two months later, when they recaptured control of the House for the first time in forty years.

In the first two years of his presidency, Clinton did not follow the DLC's counsel of moderation on cultural issues and was rudderless in foreign affairs. Gays-in-the-military, abortion, gun control, and controversial appointments plagued the administration's first days in office. According to veteran New Democrats Al From and Will Marshall, the values that elected Clinton "were not always front and center" in the administration's first weeks in power.[97] In foreign affairs, which did not deeply interest Clinton, the administration was indecisive in the Balkans and stumbled into a debacle in Somalia.

By the time Republicans took over Congress in 1994, New Democrats were disheartened. Yet, a major change in the partisan balance of the Congress forced Clinton to take up the New Democrat mantle again. The president renewed his New Democrat credentials in time to win reelection in 1996. He accomplished this by winning a tough budget battle with the Republican Congress and signing a Republican-crafted welfare reform bill, fulfilling his promise to "end welfare as we know it." The welfare legislation came, however, at a heavy cost: Clinton only signed after two vetoes and over the strong objections of a majority of his party. It endeared Clinton to New Democrats but outraged liberals. New Democrats in Congress were key negotiators for the Democratic Party in working with the Republican House majority to craft the welfare legislation.[98] Clinton used them to spearhead his initiatives and priorities in Congress. Armed with DLC policy studies, congressional New Democrats were prepared to compete and negotiate with the Republican majority and their think tank supporters.

Most New Democrats encouraged the president to sign the final bill. Not doing so would destroy Clinton's claim to be a "different kind of Democrat." Yet, a host of the president's policy advisors opposed the measure. Half of the Democratic House Caucus opposed the bill (ninety-eight members), including most black, Hispanic, and female representatives. Finally, pollster Dick Morris argued that a veto could cost Clinton reelection. Although the final legislation had been produced by a Republican-controlled Congress and contained measures that Clinton was skeptical about (or opposed to), the president signed the bill and took credit for the legislation.

In economic policy, Clinton stayed roughly true to his factional commitments. He rejected traditional fiscal stimulus in favor of economic restraint and deficit reduction. He also managed to move a free trade agenda forward, getting both the North American Free Trade Agreement (NAFTA) and the latest round of the General Agreement on Tariff and Trade (GATT) passed over the staunch opposition from within his own party.

Clinton's second term was not particularly fulfilling for New Democrats. Rather than continue the struggle to transform the party's reputation, Clinton adopted a governing strategy dubbed "triangulation." This put the president in a sense above and outside his party. He became a powerbroker between Democrats and Republicans. This opened him up to charges from left-leaning Democrats that New Democrat policies were the product of cynical calculation. As Richard Gephardt put it in 1997, "New Democrats [are those] who talk about the political center, but fail to understand that if it is defined by others, it lacks core values."[99] Clinton's last years in office proved a major missed opportunity, as scandals consumed his presidency. However, by signing welfare reform, passing both NAFTA and GATT, and balancing the budget, Clinton achieved much of the DLC agenda. Clinton's personal problems, however, obscured his New Democratic achievements and handicapped the faction's future prospects. His policy achievements did not penetrate the broader image or ideology of the party.[100] The Clinton presidency reveals the difficulties of tying a factional program to a leader who must be the head of his entire party as well as the representative of the nation. To some extent, judgments of Clinton's presidency have thus far turned on his management of a factionalized party.

Conclusion

As the above examples attest, the relationship between factions and presidents turns on the strategy the latter adopt to deal with the former. Much hinges on appointments, legislative initiatives, and governing style. Presidents have four governing strategies for dealing with factions. One is rhetorical: Presidents publicly embrace a faction, without necessarily taking steps to pass its preferred policies. The second is appeasement: adopting some of the faction's program and appointing some of its affiliates. The third is triangulation, or brokerage, wherein the president places himself between the parties (or factions within his own party), playing factions off one party or another. The final strategy is more or less direct confrontation. Which of these strategies presidents adopt depends on their relation to the existing factions and often varies over the course of their presidency as the balance of power changes and different issues appear on the agenda.

Presidents' solicitousness for their reputation has led scholars to assess their individual abilities to win policy battles and forge legacies for the history books.[101] Following Richard Neustadt many scholars have seen the president's skill at influencing other political insiders as the key to programmatic accomplishment.[102] However, because the policy choices confronting any president are often highly constrained by the environment in which he governs, much less may depend on the individual characteristics of the president. Confronted with a limited set of options, the vices and virtues of the president may be much less relevant. This behooves analysts to pay more attention to the political context and how it structures presidents' choices. Such a change of focus will reorient research away from explanations that hinge on the biographies of individual presidents and toward contextual factors in explaining presidential behavior.[103] This chapter has identified and traced party factions as a persistent element of the political contexts that shape presidents choices.

Analysis of presidents and factions reveals that presidents in America are unable to take their party's support for granted. Indeed, they are confronted with a kaleidoscopic set of shifting factional alliances and positions to which they must adapt. Presidents must negotiate with party factions at nearly every stage of the legislative process. It is often the case that only by crafting various compromises and bargains can the president bring a faction to heel. America's lack of unified parties shifts the contest for command from a battle between opposing parties to a swirling multifront engagement of presidents, factions, and other party members that occur beneath the party labels. This circumstance provides both opportunities and constraints for presidents.

CHAPTER 8

Factions and American State Building

The trajectory of state building since the Civil War has often been the result of factional struggles within the major parties rather than the result of conflict between the two parties.[1] Sometimes factions have thrust wholly new initiatives onto the national agenda, providing the critical jolt needed to enact institutional reforms that had long been considered but not acted upon. On the other hand, some factions have sought to preserve the status quo or dismantle existing government programs. Their aim was to block, dilute, or otherwise modify initiatives proposed by others or, going further, to roll back pieces of the state. Whether as catalysts for change or as an impediment to it, factions have consistently played an important state-building role. This chapter treats the conditions under which factions have had a powerful influence on the development of the American state.[2]

Factions have been at the center of debates over the state's size and character. There have been two main flash points in these debates. The first is over the size of American government and its power to intervene in the economy and society. In this context, factions' objectives can be grouped into three major groups: those that seek to increase government power, those that seek to roll that power back, and those that seek to manage that power (Table 1). It is interesting to note that with the exception of the Stalwarts and Progressive Republicans all of the interventionist factions emerged from the Democratic Party, while with the exception of the Southern Democrats all the factions seeking to restrain government growth were Republicans. Not all factions are equal in the degree to which they sought to shape the state-building process. Some factions have had much more influence on the character of the American state than others.

The second debate is over the *means* of state intervention. The central issue here is where power is allocated across institutions and levels of government. Factions have sought to affect how power is distributed: among the three branches of the federal government; between the national, state, and local governments; and between the bureaucracy, the political parties, and the people.[3] Some factions have favored concentrating power in Washington in the hands

Table 8.1 **Factions' Role in State Building**

Interventionist Factions	Restraintist Factions	Caretaker Factions
Stalwart Republicans	Liberal Republicans (Gilded Age)	Half-Breed Republicans
Progressive Republicans	Old Guard Republicans	Liberal Republicans (Modern)
Populist Democrats	Southern Democrats	New Democrats
Liberal-Labor Democrats	New Right Republicans	
New Politics Democrats		

of a strong president who would supervise bureaucratic experts. Others have favored a predominant role for Congress and the greater decentralization of power to the states. Still others have held that party loyalists should staff the bureaucracy and implement government policy. Finally, some have wanted to grant expert administrators greater discretion to formulate policy, while others argued that administrative agents should be constrained by detailed laws written by Congress. At least one faction oscillated between support for bureaucratic discretion and greater popular participation in bureaucratic decision making. In each case, the faction acted upon a distinct set of preferences regarding the allocation of political power. The analysis here therefore addresses both issues of government structure as well as the substantive content of public policies, including both regulatory and redistributive measures.

The Conditions for Factions' Importance

The principal objective of this chapter is to identify the conditions under which factions are likely to matter most. I argue that key shifts in the process of state building are only intelligible if one adopts a faction-based analysis. There are important moments in American state building that are explicable only if we analyze the activity of factions. That means that we are able to specify the conditions under which the attributes and strategies of factions enter with particular force in the state-building process. The conditions under which factions matter are determined by four factors that establish the weight of factions in the state-building process.

1. For factions to matter, the dynamics of internal competition and alliances across party lines need to be as significant as the dynamics of interparty

competition. In circumstances where factions can operate as "swing votes" or "veto players," their power to shape state building is at its peak. In this sense, the archetypal state-shaping faction is the Southern Democrats. They were profoundly important both because they had antagonistic relations with the northern elements of their party, and because they could ally with the Republican Party. Similarly, the Mugwumps and Progressive Republicans competed with the Stalwarts and Half-Breeds within the GOP, and were willing to align (or threaten to align) with Democrats, which gave them influence far beyond their numbers. Playing this type of power politics gives these factions a political impact that is not reducible to their influence over their party.

2. Factions need a kind of fragmentation of power—particularly in their own parties. Power must be dispersed and obscurely allocated. Factions can then find niches to exploit their resources. Examples of this on the American political scene are multiple and are a result, primarily, of the Constitution's dispersion of power.

3. Factions are more likely to be influential in the state-building process when they are rooted in the legislature, because a president can more easily cast a faction's agenda aside. Congress remains the keystone in the domestic policy-making establishment. There, factions draw together like-minded legislators for mutual protection and, if possible, to increase their influence over legislation. Therefore, factions command votes. They play a central role in the legislative bargaining process. In contrast, presidents are more often preoccupied with managing factions than pushing them in one direction or another. In addition, presidents that campaign on a faction's program may be unfaithful to it once in office. Dwight Eisenhower, Ronald Reagan, and Bill Clinton were all accused of such disloyalty.

4. Factions with social bases and specific constituencies—those that are concentrated in one geographic region or demographic group, or that can marshal particular resources—are often able to exercise greater influence. This is especially the case when it comes to the Electoral College. Liberals/Mugwumps were especially powerful in state building because they were concentrated in key swing states such as New York, which led both parties to compete for their allegiance. As Scott C. James has shown, electoral competition channeled through the Electoral College led to the creation of key pieces of the regulatory state.[4] In another mode, Elizabeth Sanders has argued that Populist Democrats created a political coalition of Midwestern and Southern farmers that could not be ignored.[5] Factions press networks of individuals from universities, professional associations, campaign organizations, and private enterprise into service for their cause. Many changes in state capacity turn on the factions' ability to mobilize networks into party politics.

These four conditions are important in setting off the factions that mattered more from those that mattered less. I find that six factions—Liberal/Mugwump Republicans, Progressive Republicans, Populist Democrats, Southern Democrats, New Politics Democrats, and New Right Republicans—were deeply important to American state building. The other six factions impacted state development in various ways, but they were much less consequential.

The analysis provided here locates factional dynamics at the core of American political development. This means something very particular: It is not just that the ideas that factions have matter; it is, rather, that the dynamics of factional competition are essential for developing those ideas. Oftentimes, political programs are essentially about winning a factional struggle—because moving the state in one direction or another is a way of preserving or expanding a faction's powers or undercutting those of its rivals. Without factional combat, politics conflict may be less pointed, and factions may never adopt the positions they do.[6] It is the result of such strife that determines the parties' positions and reputation on the Left-Right spectrum.

In addition, factional analysis accents aspects of the state-building process that analysts operating with other perspectives are likely to underplay or miss altogether. Attention to factions means paying greater heed to forces in American politics that have sought to stop, retard, and even roll back the growth of the national state. Much of the state-building literature traces out the causes of state expansion, producing a portrait where the accent is on growth in an upward direction. While such an approach is valuable, there is a tendency to downplay how those *opposed* to state enlargement shaped the final arrangement of institutions, distribution of power, and capacity of the state. By shining a spotlight on factions—such as the Liberal/Mugwumps, Southern Democrats, and New Right Republicans—this chapter brings out the role of factions dedicated to the restraining government growth.

Studying state building through the lens of factions also takes us beyond the stale debates over whether it is a process that is "state-centered" or "society-centered" and whether it is "executive-led" or "congressionally-driven."[7] Factions cut through these artificial distinctions because they mediate between the state and society and thus reveal how they are inextricably entangled. Factional analysis forces a consideration of links between executive and legislative process. One of the central properties of factions is that they are networks that connect actors across institutional venues.

Finally, the factional perspective helps explain the degree of coherence or incoherence and fragmentation or unification of the American state. Factions pull in both directions on the coherence/incoherence or fragmentation/unification spectrums. Some aim to increase state coherence by creating clear lines of authority and chains of command. Others aim to dismantle state capacity, fragmenting it and giving greater responsibility to private or semiprivate actors. Looking at factions clarifies what outcomes are most relevant to state building and the historical moments at which the American state developed some of its exceptional features.

The Character of the American State

According to Alexis de Tocqueville, the decentralization of administration in the United States distinguished it from European nations. U.S. government, for all of the nineteenth and much of the twentieth century, simply did far less than its European counterparts. Hence the United States has often been considered a "laggard" in creating *un état* in the French sense.[8] Indeed, the growth of the power of the American *national* state was comparatively slow. And American government programs for retirees, the poor, and the unemployed remain, generally speaking, less generous than those in Europe. Nonetheless, despite the constitutional barriers to the creation of a large European-style national state, America developed one.[9]

There are three principal debates in the scholarly literature on American state building. The first debate turns on the *timing* of state growth. One group of analysts holds that the administrative state was born during the economic crisis of the 1930s. The Great Depression and unified Democratic Party control led the government to undertake a vast new array of programs to regulate economic activity, improve the nation's infrastructure, and stabilize the agricultural and extractive industries. However, few of the policies from the New Deal state building endured past 1950, which complicates the picture of the period as the major surge in state growth.

Another group of scholars argues that the key steps in American state building occurred before the stock market crash of 1929. Based on the work of Stephen Skowronek, Richard Bensel, Elizabeth Sanders, Theda Skocpol, Daniel Carpenter, and Scott C. James, there is now broad agreement that major construction of the American state occurred between the 1870s and the 1920s. These writers detail how the national government gained new powers to tax, regulate industry, and provide pensions to veterans and widows. A new civil service code restricted patronage and increased job security and professionalism in the federal bureaucracy. During this period, the military was also transformed from a state-based militia to a centralized bureaucracy. My analysis extends existing accounts by showing how factions provide a thread that links the pre– and post–New Deal periods.

The second major debate turns on the *process* by which the state developed. The "state theory" school argues that wars, natural disasters, class conflict, and economic change drive state growth. These are usually functionalist and Marxist accounts that treat politics as the epiphenomena of larger forces in society and the economy. Other scholars, however, have argued for "state autonomy" from the economic or sociological base. Their aim is to treat *politics* as a distinct realm of thought and action. They claim that the politics of state building is not simply the product of larger economic, sociological, or military forces; rather, political actors retain an important degree of independence.

The third debate turns on the *institutional locus* of state development. Scholars disagree about where the action is. Separation of powers has created something of a division of scholarly attention between those who concentrate on the executive branch versus those who focus on the legislative branch. For the most part, the focus has been on the executive branch and bureaucratic agencies. A few scholars, however, such as Richard Bensel and Elizabeth Sanders, have paid greater attention to Congress and legislative processes in state development. Still other scholars have sought the sources of state development in social movements, political parties, and federal courts. Again, attention to factions bridges these divides.

Interventionist Factions

Five factions have sought to increase the size and power of the national state in order to intervene more effectively in the economy and society. Three of these five operated under conditions that made them the most consequential factions. In each case, however, the faction promoted different ends, employed different means, and achieved varying degrees of success in increasing state capacities. It is to these cases that we now turn.

STALWART REPUBLICANS: RECONSTRUCTION AND PATRONAGE

Martin Shefter has argued that stronger parties can extract patronage from the state because weaker public agencies are especially liable to being captured by parties.[10] Without access to the state, parties must find alternative means for mobilizing support. From the other side, stronger and more autonomous bureaucracies can develop greater administrative capacity. Stalwarts' objectives were to support the Republican governments in the South, retain allegiance in the North, and prevent tariff reduction and civil service reform to ensure the growth of patronage positions.[11] The Stalwart faction shaped state development by creating powerful party organizations that could extract resources from state and national governments. The consequence was weaker bureaucratic capacity and more fragmented lines of political authority. The power of the Stalwart-dominated state parties and the decentralization of authority they produced lasted into the twentieth century. Given the slow implementation of civil service reform, the Republican Party was able to remain powerful even as the patronage well was running dry.

During the Civil War and Reconstruction, the American state grew rapidly. New relationships between business and government emerged. To manage these interconnections, parties became big employers. Stalwart Republicans encouraged the growth of the business-government nexus. They protected the cooperative relationships they enjoyed with elements of the business community. The faction represented business, but also extorted kickbacks to line the party's pockets. In response to reformers' complaints about Stalwart practices, Kansas Senator John J. Ingalls said: "This modern cant about the corruption of politics is fatiguing in the extreme. It proceeds from the tea-custard and syllabub dilettantism, the frivolous and desultory sentimentalism of epicenes."[12] The faction increased the number of offices available for appointment while enforcing fragmented lines of control over those offices to ensure party dominance of them.

Four conditions enabled Stalwarts to shape state building. One was their control of jobs. Theda Skocpol has remarked that patronage was the "meat and potatoes" of late nineteenth-century politics.[13] The second was their ability to influence key industrial states and the South in presidential nomination contests and the Electoral College. Third, they championed the system of veterans' pensions that helped sustain the Republican Party.[14] Finally, they skillfully exploited the fragmentation of power in the Senate. Control of state party machines created powerful senators in an institution without a hierarchical structure.[15] Their control of federal patronage lubricated state parties, which wove together newspaper editors, postal workers, and local revenue collectors.[16]

To protect the resources needed for government growth, Stalwarts from the Northeast and Great Lakes regions combined with Midwestern Half-Breeds to support higher tariffs. As Richard Bensel has shown, the tariff knitted together the factional coalition of the Republican Party into a workable majority.[17] Indeed, it was tariff revenues that were used to fund veterans' pensions and forge a workable majority comprised of Stalwarts and Half-Breeds. The precise balancing of tariff schedules was central in bringing factions together, promoting northern industrialization, and providing revenues for the vast system of veterans' pensions that tied non-Southern regions together.[18] Bensel concludes that "protectionism was always more important politically than economically" because it smoothed factional conflict.[19]

The linchpin in this arrangement was New York Senator Roscoe Conkling's control of the New York Customs House, at the time the largest source of federal government revenue and the largest patronage operation in the country. Its control meant that Stalwarts could exercise significant influence over state development. By 1873, they dominated the Senate Committee on Committees and chose the working committees' staff. In 1875, Conkling arranged his own appointment to chair the Commerce Committee. All presidential appointments to ports or harbors ran through this committee, which gave Conkling veto power over those he disliked. Conkling's power led presidents to try to bring the appointment process under their command. In response to calls for civil service reform, Conkling delivered a forceful rebuke, saying that reformers were "the dilettanti and carpet knights of politics, whose efforts have been expended in denouncing and ridiculing and accusing honest men who, in storm and sun, in war and peace, have clung to the Republican flag and defended it against those who have tried to trail and trample it in the dust."[20]

The Stalwarts' effect on state development was a combination of expanding state growth, fragmenting lines of authority, and decentralizing decision-making structures, which could be captured by party machines. Stalwarts ingeniously forced the state to create new policy by distributing funding widely and carefully. Perpetuating the power of state party machines directly resulted in power for senators well into the twentieth century, when a new faction, Progressive Republicans, arose to confront them.

PROGRESSIVE REPUBLICANS AND THE ADMINISTRATIVE STATE

Progressive Republicans held that the policies promoted by Old Guard Republicans—who were tied to party machines of the nineteenth century—were corrupt, irrational, and inimical to the public interest. As the Progressive Party's 1912 platform put it: "Instead of instruments to promote the general welfare, [the old parties] have become the tools of corrupt interests which use them impartially to serve their selfish purposes."[21] The reformers' ultimate goal was an administrative establishment under the control of the president that stood above and outside the hurly-burly of partisan competition. Only such an arrangement, they held, could advance the national interest. It would make the state more coherent by rationalizing the policy process and creating clear lines of authority.

To weaken their Old Guard opponents, enhance democracy, and provide the public with the fruits of scientific administration, Progressives sought to reduce the number of executive offices open for election, constrict the franchise with literacy tests and citizenship requirements, institute examinations for government jobs, and replace party conventions with primaries to nomi-nate candidates for office. Like the Liberal/Mugwumps before them, Progres-sives sought to shift power towards the national bureaucracy and away from the parties, defeating rival factions within the party. Unlike the Liberal/ Mugwumps, however, the Progressives were much more successful.

All four key conditions that empower factions assisted the Progressives in shaping these developments in the American state. First, they were able to forge cross-party alliances with Democrats. This was evident in the votes in the House both to remove Speaker Joseph Cannon and to decide a series of important laws between 1905 and 1914. The power to confront their own party by creating alliances across the aisle became the central mechanism for passing "progressive" legislation on railroads, food and drug safety, economic regula-tion, and banking. Second, the faction had a solid presence in both houses of Congress. Third, Progressives could draw on intellectual talent in universities and the private sector. The most obvious connection was with the University of Wisconsin, Madison, which produced such figures as Richard T. Ely. In addition, the Progressives could claim a broad constituency in both the rural Midwest and the urban Northeast. Finally, the fragmentation of the American state allowed the faction to enact many of its policy ideas at the state and local levels, creating a logic whereby some of those ideas would eventually be adopted at the national level. Without this window of opportunity, Progres-sives would not have been able to make such important changes to the character of the state.

The effects of Progressive Republican state-building efforts were nothing short of profound. First, they greatly enhanced the power of executive bureau-cracies at the expense of the parties. Rather than patronage appointments and party work, the bureaucracy came to be governed not by personal connections but by rationalized techniques of job-classification plans, salary schedules, promotion rules, and so on. Second, these interconnected reforms made the executive branch in general, and the president in particular, the new locus of power at Congress's expense. Third, new avenues to government service other than the parties opened up. Talent began to arrive from corporate business, universities, and major law firms. Finally, the Progressives' reforms increased capacities by providing greater technical competence and organizational rationality.

POPULIST DEMOCRATS AND THE STATUTORY STATE

The Populist Democrat faction sparked a battle within the Democratic Party over how to reconcile "Jeffersonian doctrine" with a modern industrial economy. Many Cleveland Democrats and Southern Bourbons clung to the old faith in states' rights, strict constitutionalism, and economy in govern-ment.[22] Yet, Populists extolled a vision of greater state intervention into the economy and society. Unlike many Progressive Republicans, they did not look up to bureaucratic experts or federal courts. Rather, the Populist faction sought to craft a national state that reduced the discretion of bureaucrats and judges by writing detailed laws. The Populist faction was particularly suc-cessful in achieving many of its objectives because all four of the conditions that make factions matter in state development were in effect. In Congress, Populists' significant numbers enabled them to forge cross-party coalitions with Progressive Republicans. In addition, with the fall of Speaker Cannon, they were able to exploit a moment of fragmentation in legislative lines of authority to create new structures of party government in 1912. Also, the fac-tion could mobilize a major coalition of Midwestern and Southern farmers, small shippers, and laborers. Finally, President Woodrow Wilson proved amenable to the faction's policy thrust.

For instance, railroad regulation raised the question of how far the na-tional government should intervene in the economy. Greater government control served Populists' ideological proclivities and electoral interests, since they represented shippers in the Midwest and South. The Democratic plat-forms in 1896, 1900, and 1904 all called for expanding the power of the Inter-state Commerce Commission (ICC) to regulate railroads. Since its creation in 1887, the commission had been weakened by the actions of courts and rail-roads. In the legislative battles to further regulate railroads that produced the Hepburn Act (1905) and the Mann-Elkins Act (1910), Populist Democrats consistently favored tougher regulatory measures. In the battle for the Hepburn Act, Populists, though comprising slightly less than a third of the Senate membership, forced the bill out of committee, helped attach strength-ening amendments, and claimed credit for it on final passage. Their ability to move such bills in Congress relied on their willingness to forge cross-party coalitions with Progressive Republicans. The Hepburn Act, however, left a thorn in the side of reformers and their constituents: the power of federal courts to suspend the ICC's rates while they were being appealed by the rail-roads, which meant that shippers had to continue to pay the old rates for years while the appeals process worked itself out. In 1910, Populist Demo-crats and Progressive Republicans again set out to weaken the judicial review process. The result was the Mann-Elkins Act.[23] The Populist Democratic fac-tion was thus a key factor in expanding state power to regulate the private economy.

Populists also sought to reign in the rent-seeking capitalism of big business. Between 1909 and 1912 Populist Democrats again formed a coalition with Progressive Republicans in an effort to block President Taft's tariff policies.

Populists attacked high tariffs because, in their view, they contributed to both corporate consolidation—or the "trusts"—and increased the cost of living. They argued that tariffs were a hidden (and regressive) tax on consumers and that an income tax would be more open, honest, and fair. Tariff reform would also obviously benefit their agrarian constituents by allowing them to buy cheaper foreign-manufactured goods. Although the bipartisan coalition was unable to stop the passage of the Payne-Aldrich tariff, the experience in these heated debates provided them with an opportunity to develop the measures that eventually became the Underwood tariff. In the 63rd Congress (1913–1915), the Populist faction provided the muscle for Democrats to pass the Underwood tariff, which constituted the largest rate reduction in American history. Because the tariff had been the principal source of federal revenue, a significant reduction in rates would mean that lost revenue would have to come from elsewhere. Therefore, the law also included a strong income tax provision, which would be paid by wealthy individuals.

Reforming the nation's banking system provided Populist Democrats with another opportunity to show that the party was on the side of "the people," against powerful bankers and speculators. William Jennings Bryan argued that "the right to coin and issue money is a function of government, a part of sovereignty, and can no more safely be delegated to private individuals than we could afford to delegate to private individuals the power to make penal statues or levy taxes."[24] Before 1912, corporate and financial leaders, represented in the Senate by Nelson Aldrich (R-RI), had spearheaded the drive for a national bank. Populist Democrats actively opposed the Aldrich plan. The debate over the central bank hinged on whether the bank would be a public or a private institution and the degree of centralization. Eastern bankers favored a highly centralized private institution, but Populists favored a more decentralized publicly controlled one. Ultimately, the Federal Reserve Act became law in December 1913.

When McKinley's election in 1896 gave business the green light to embark on an impressive number of corporate consolidations, Bryan Democrats responded with a platform plank in 1900 that pledged the party into waging "unceasing warfare" against private monopoly. Although Roosevelt and Taft both demonstrated that the Sherman Antitrust Act could be used effectively, their approach remained highly executive-centered, opaque, and discretionary. By 1908, Populist Democrats had developed a very different program. Under the influence of reformers, the party platform called for a more transparent, legalistic, and punitive approach that prohibited price discrimination and interlocking directorates. The severity and specificity of these legal proposals would also permit greater decentralization of enforcement and would not require extensive executive administration. Indeed, the faction believed that a discretionary bureaucracy controlled by the president would condone more anticompetitive agreements and mergers.[25] In early 1914, antitrust policy finally became the party's number-one agenda priority. However, the outbreak of World War I and President Wilson's shift of support to an executive commission weakened reformers' drive.[26] Under the circumstances, Populist Democrats chose to compromise with the administration on moderately strengthening legislation. The result was the Clayton Act.

Overall, the Populist Democratic faction sought to pressure the Wilson administration to expand regulatory and social welfare aspects of the American state. Wilson had obstructed child labor measures, halted efforts to extend farm credits, and ignored workman's compensation proposals. In 1915 and 1916, the administration reversed course on all of these measures. By the fall of 1916, Wilson and the Democratic Congress had enacted much of the Progressive Party platform of 1912. The overarching thrust of these measures was a Congress-dominated legalism that tried to reign in the growing power of the president and the bureaucracy, without handing power back to the political parties and the patronage system. The Populist faction helped build an American state that was more powerful, more transparent, and more unified in its lines of governing authority.

LIBERAL-LABOR DEMOCRATS: PREPARING THE GROUND

Liberal-Labor Democrats sought to "complete" the New Deal, pressing for greater rights for African-Americans and unions, national health care, urban renewal, and macroeconomic intervention. Only a centralized government could manage a modern economy and equitably distribute the benefits of a comprehensive welfare state. Liberal-Labor rejected the Southern Democrats' vision of a welfare state that relied on means-tested state programs and private charity. The faction sought a more efficient national state that would be able to bypass the states or use the states for its own purposes. It held that this was the only way to ensure that social policy could be equitable and efficient.

However, the Liberal-Labor faction was largely unsuccessful in expanding the American state throughout the 1950s. While it could occasionally form winning cross-party congressional coalitions with modern Liberal Republicans from the Northeast and Midwest, the number of such congressional Liberals was small. The fragmented structure of Congress also worked against Liberal-Labor, as its Southern rivals held most of the important positions in Congress. Finally, while the faction did have a powerful set of constituencies with ties to labor unions, the unions' geographic concentration weakened their ability to exercise national power.

Consequently, the faction's major contribution was to develop a policy program, which, under prevailing conditions, was unable to pass Congress. That program later proved enormously influential, preparing the ground for Lyndon Johnson's Great Society legislative program. The Great Society focused on poverty, health care, education, and civil rights. It expanded regulation of individuals, businesses, and organizations; it also created new bureaucracies and committed the American state to major long-term financial expenditures. The War on Poverty was overlaid on existing programs, including social security, welfare, and veterans' benefits. In the Johnson years, total social-welfare spending increased from $67 billion to $127 billion. The government's share of health care expenditures, with the passage of Medicare and Medicaid, surged from $8.5 billion to $24 billion.[27] The Elementary and Secondary Education Act vastly increased the federal government's role in funding education. The federal share of education spending grew from 14.9 percent in 1960 to 19.1 percent in 1968.[28] The Civil Rights Act dramatically changed the practices of businesses and governments in the South, and the Voting Rights Act made a huge difference in the number of black Americans registered to vote in the Southern states. In sum, the Liberal-Labor faction honed in on President Johnson's task forces and enacted new agendas under the Great Society banner, drastically increasing the functions of the American federal government.

In the longer term, however, the faction's consensus on ideological and policy priorities unraveled. First, the arrival of Democratic presidents and large Democratic majorities in Congress in the 1960s meant that the unity provided by being in the opposition began to fray as the faction gained power and prominence. Indeed, the large number of ADA members and former members of the Kennedy administration meant that faction affiliates had to take some responsibility for governing the country. Second, the passing of the 1964 Civil Rights Act and the Elementary and Secondary School Act and the creation of Medicare and Medicaid took some of the faction's central priorities off the agenda. The consequence was that there was simply less consensus on the smaller issues further down the faction's agenda. Third, the escalation of American involvement in the Vietnam War shattered the Cold War foreign-policy consensus within the faction. As a result, the faction began to unravel by the end of the 1960s.

NEW POLITICS DEMOCRATS AND THE "NEW" POLICY-MAKING PROCESS

The New Politics faction initiated another major effort in state aggrandizement that centered on shifting the balance of power between parties and the bureaucracy. Their principle aim was to expand the size, competence, and power of the national government to address issues of business regulation, racism, poverty, and alienation. To secure these ends, they had three priorities: to alter the procedures by which parties selected their candidates for office; to change the way administrative officials were recruited, hired, and promoted; and to shine light on the way elected officials, bureaucrats, and private interests interacted.

Conditions were ripe for New Politics Democrats' objectives. The New Politics faction was able to shape American state development because they exploited the fragmentation of legislative, bureaucratic, and judicial processes of American institutions, mobilized a new constituency of upper class suburbanites, and had a strong presence in Congress, especially in the wake of the Watergate scandal.

The political developments in the American state affected by the New Politics faction came in two phases. The first phase was during the Democratic presidencies of John F. Kennedy and Lyndon Johnson (1961–1969), when the power of "professional reformers" inside the policy-making apparatus grew. This group of nascent New Politics liberals was composed of academics, foundation officers, senior civil servants, and interest-group leaders. They took up important policy positions on presidential "task forces." Federal laws and regulations emerging from those bodies created a vast new array of agencies that launched the federal government into largely uncharted areas of social policy, consumer protection, the environment, women's rights, poverty relief, and occupational health and safety. These upper-middle-class New Politics types sought to enlist the national state in an effort to bring local governments, especially large municipal governments, under their thumb. To do this, they proposed increases in federal-grants-in-aid to ameliorate the living conditions of poor urban blacks.

The second phase of political developments influenced by the New Politics Democrats was in response to the Vietnam War. The war drove New Politics Democrats into direct conflict with the rest of the Democratic Party, the bureaucracies that delivered social programs, and the national-security establishment. Conflict within the party came to a head in the reforms proposed in the presidential nominating system and the selection of George McGovern as the party's standard-bearer in 1972. In addition, organizations such as Common Cause promoted a number of campaign finance reforms, including public funding of elections, limiting individual campaign contributions, and greater transparency in campaign financing. The aim of New Politics reforms was to destroy the remnants of the large urban machines and their labor union allies in favor of aiding the groups they claimed to represent, namely blacks, women, youth, and intellectuals.

The New Politics faction brought about major changes in the operation of administrative agencies. It made the bureaucracy more transparent, subjected it to greater judicial scrutiny, and provided more avenues of public participation in agency decision-making. The aim was to halt what they believed to be corrupt practices, such as agency capture by regulated interests and elitist policy-making processes. The result was an altogether new system of public policymaking.

Prior to the 1960s and 1970s, the policy process had unabashedly favored particular interests. In the old policy process, "iron triangles" predominated, wherein a few key congressional committees, the regulated interests, and relevant administrative agencies were the centers of action. The old system sought to manage rent-seeking behavior by allotting tangible benefits to powerful interests. In the new system, congressional subcommittees and their staff, courts, and public interest organizations and their foundation allies became the key sources of policy development in many areas. The way the political game was scored also changed. In the past, political victory meant winning material rewards, such as funds, government contracts, or land. In the new system, it came to be defined as obtaining new rules, procedures, or implanting new symbols.[29]

The result of the faction's efforts was a major increase in environmental, consumer, and other social regulatory legislation. Policy activism in these areas began late in the Johnson administration and continued through the early Carter years. Between 1966 and 1975, Congress passed the National Traffic and Motor Vehicle Act, the Fair Packaging and Labeling Act, the Federal Hazardous Substances Act, the Truth in Lending Act, the Child Protection Act, the National Environmental Policy Act, major amendments to the Clean Air Act, the Federal Environmental Pesticide Control Act, Federal Water Pollution Control Act amendments, and the Occupational Safety and Health Act. Such regulatory legislation was appealing to members of Congress because it did not cost much, as the costs of the laws would be passed on to business, and ultimately consumers. It also created a number of new regulatory agencies with broad powers to enforce those statues, including the Environmental Protection Agency (EPA), the Occupational Safety and Health Administration (OSHA), and the Consumer Product Safety Commission (CPSC). David Vogel found: "Between 1970 and 1975, expenditures by federal social regulatory agencies increased from $1.5 billion to $4.3 billion, and the number of pages in the *Federal Register* rose from 20,000 to 60,000."[30] This new sort of social regulation built state capacity in a variety of areas.

New Politics Democrats also contributed decisively to making the policy process more national, more adversarial, and more judicial.[31] This ensured that, as James Q. Wilson put it, "the legislative fight over [a program's] purpose and power [could] be restaged in court by the allies of the congressional faction that initially did battle."[32] The New Politics faction contributed to Congress's paradoxical delegation of more power to administrative agencies with provisions that expanded judicial review of administrative decisions.[33] These provisions facilitated a host of legal innovations, such as class action lawsuits; recognizing individuals as private attorneys general; and empowering judges to supervise schools, prisons, mental hospitals, environmental regulations, and various forms of social provision.[34] By creating a series of procedural rights allowing for individual citizens to help craft federal programs, New Politics Democrats in Congress invited courts to play a permanent role in policy development. This encouraged those affected by federal programs to shape them, giving birth to a variety of "citizen lawsuits" against federal agencies administering various programs.[35] In 1975, New Politics Democrats in Congress intensified their efforts to enhance citizen participation in federal programs. This time citizen participation was not defined simply as procedural rights that allowed individuals to sue administrative agencies. Rather, public interest groups were considered adequate stand-ins. Congress authorized the financing of public interest organizations in specific regulatory decisions of the Federal Trade Commission, the Consumer Product Safety Commission, and the Environmental Protection Agency.[36]

The congressionally created procedural and programmatic rights with orders for public participation were infused with an antibureaucratic ethos. Paradoxically, by trying to give citizens and their public-interest-group representatives greater say in administrative decision making, which was supposed to be more transparent, the faction created the opposite effect, spawning the rise of adversarial legalism and pushing more policy decisions out of the hands of administrators and into the federal courts.[37] Thus, the New Politics faction contributed to an expansion of state authority but simultaneously fragmented that authority.

New Politics Democrats helped reshuffle the institutions and individuals empowered to make decisions. The form of partisan and institutional combat that resulted—revolving around congressional subcommittees, federal courts, and administrative agencies—made partisan competition increasingly an elite activity without substantial connections to the mass public.[38] The faction enhanced its power by extending national government control over state and local bureaucracies to the exclusion of party machines and labor unions. Conversely, the New Politics faction empowered public interest groups with which they were allied by directing public resources to key groups.[39] The result was expanded central state authority but a fragmentation of that authority that undermined the ability of specialized bureaucrats to implement any decision.

Factions and the Restraint of State Expansion

In different ways and to serve different ends, three party factions have, on the whole, sought to restrain the growth of the American state and limit its power to intervene in the economy and society.

THE GILDED AGE LIBERAL REPUBLICANS:
RECONSTRUCTION AND CIVIL SERVICE REFORM

Among the most important institutional changes to occur in the United States in the post–Civil War period was the shift in authority first to political parties, and then from the parties to bureaucracies. These shifts had major consequences for the organization of political parties and their electoral strategies and mobilization techniques. The Liberal Republican faction was a key agent in speeding the shift in authority from the party to a more specialized bureaucracy with clearer lines of authority. This, they hoped, would reduce the size of the state, leave more decisions to market forces, and put what remained of state functions in the hands of educated elites. For example, Thomas Jenckes (R-RI) argued on behalf of the earliest civil service reforms in terms of state retrenchment: "Let us seek to obtain skill, ability, fidelity, zeal and integrity in the public service, and we shall not be called upon to increase salaries or the number of offices. It is safe to assert that the number of offices may be diminished by one-third, and the efficiency of the whole civil service increased by one-half, with a corresponding reduction of salaries for discontinued offices."[40] According to the Liberals/Mugwumps, the patronage system was the problem. As George Curtis put it, "The difficulty is not the abuse of patronage but the patronage itself."[41] Ultimately, the Liberals' efforts produced modest steps to reduce in the size of the American state and simultaneously make it more coherent, unified, and efficient.

The Liberal/Mugwump faction was influential in the state-building process because it was willing to threaten to bolt the party in presidential elections. Liberal influence hinged on the concentration of their constituency of highly educated men in key swing states, especially New York. In 1872, they bolted the Republican Party and joined with Democrats to nominate Horace Greeley for president; in 1876, Rutherford B. Hayes won the Electoral College but lost the popular vote; in 1880, a switch of a few thousand votes in New York would have handed the state and the election to the Democrats; and in 1882, Republicans suffered congressional losses in states where Liberals/Mugwumps were the strongest. Liberals felt that the influence they exercised had led President Hayes to declare the "paramount public necessity of reform in our civil service—a reform not merely as to certain abuses and practices of our so-called official patronage . . . but a change in the system of appointment itself; a reform that shall be thorough, radical, and complete."[42] In 1881, Garfield also declared in his inaugural address that "the civil service can never be placed on a satisfactory basis until it is regulated by law."[43]

The other major source of Liberals/Mugwumps' influence came from the constituency from which they were drawn. Highly educated and in command of key newspaper outlets and prominent professional associations, the constituency possessed power greater than its numbers indicated. In state after state, however, party development had sidelined men who had considered themselves the natural leaders of the GOP. These Republicans became the Liberals/Mugwumps that began to object to patronage practices that were building the professionalized party. They wanted a lean and efficient state, not an expansive and transformative one—the word *liberal* then referred to a classical liberalism that privileged free markets. It is not surprising then that Liberals and Mugwumps became the leading advocates of civil service reform in 1870s and 1880s. Civil service reform was the way to undercut the power of the two other GOP factions. Again, George Curtis argued: "The great officers of government [are] constrained to become mere office-brokers."[44] Henry Adams claimed that reform would bring back "that class of men who had gradually been driven from politics" by the spoilsmen.[45] Depriving the Stalwarts and Half-Breeds of patronage would, Liberals hoped, destroy the foundation of their dominance in Congress. The "best men" could replace men like Roscoe Conking. They were patricians, journalists, and professionals who were the moral salt of the nation. Without the demand for patronage, there would also be less of an incentive for the state to expand in inefficient, irrational, and corrupt ways.

To achieve their aims, Liberals/Mugwumps founded one of the first public interest groups in the history of America, the National Civil Service Reform League. Like modern public interest groups, it endorsed candidates on the basis of their position on this single issue. In addition, Liberals/Mugwumps advocated bipartisan representation on congressional commissions and government boards to prevent corruption. Other Republican factions, therefore, were leveraged into supporting the Pendleton Civil Service Act in order to prevent Liberal/Mugwump defections to Democrat Grover Cleveland in the 1884 presidential contest. Stalwarts and Half-Breeds were willing to go along with civil service reform on the basis of short- and long-term calculations. In the short term, they believed President Chester A. Arthur could use the new civil service rules to lock in some Republican appointments and make them impervious to Democratic spoilsmen even if a Democrat won the presidency. In the long term, only a few positions would be protected by the new rules and therefore would not jeopardize the organizational structure of the GOP. Stalwarts and Half-Breeds also calculated that the American state was in a period of expansion and therefore the number of federal jobs would increase faster than the number of positions in the newly classified civil service. Most of the positions covered under the new rules were technical and required skill, which reduced their relevance for party patronage activity. Nor would civil service reform touch state and local operations, the real bread and butter for the Stalwarts and the Half-Breeds in late nineteenth-century politics. Finally, supporting the Pendleton Act would provide symbolic cover for a party in need of a makeover. Shefter neatly summarizes the logic of the situation: "The very reason the parties were prepared to live with civil service reform was that it imposed no present costs on them, while it enabled the government to respond to technological change and defused the opposition of some disgruntled elites."[46]

The Pendleton Act was thus only a small first step toward shifting authority from parties to public bureaucracies. Liberal/Mugwumps did not enjoy greater success, and the law was less effective than they hoped. The Liberal/Mugwump faction was ultimately limited in how much it could reshape the American state, since it lacked strong roots in Congress. Nonetheless, the activity of a party faction was essential in passing an important law. The ultimate aim of the Liberal/Mugwump faction was to reduce the demand for patronage posts by covering more administrative positions under civil service protections. Factional conflict thus shaped the depth and the timing of the shift from partisan to bureaucratic authority.

OLD GUARD REPUBLICANS, THE COURTS, AND BIG BUSINESS

President Theodore Roosevelt, in December of 1905, delivered a series of bold reform messages to Congress. He called for a change in railroad rates, an end to overcapitalization of corporations, supervision of interstate insurance transactions, prohibition of corporate campaign contributions, and a halt to interstate shipment of adulterated and misbranded goods. To top it off, he also indicted judges for the misuse of injunctions. This overall message challenged the three traditional powers of the business community defended by GOP conservatives: the freedom to set their own prices, to keep their books secret, and to negotiate labor contracts independently.

The Old Guard response was to dig in their heels to defend the status quo against what they deemed to be radical change. The faction vetoed social welfare laws and the facilitation of unionism, which they believed would hurt business. The legislative histories of the period, however, show that conservatives were willing to accept business regulation, as long as it could be made to accommodate rather than directly confront the interests of business. Conservatives were thus not hostile to all federal regulatory expansion in principle—only to the forms offered by Democrats and Progressive Republicans.[47]

The source of the Old Guard's power was not its ability to craft cross-party alliances, even if it could occasionally draw in some Democratic Southern Bourbons. Rather, it was its ability to exploit the fragmentation the Senate in order to concentrate power in the hands of the Senate Four. They in turn could draw on campaign funds from their eastern business constituency. Domination of the Senate by Nelson Aldrich and his allies, which rested on their control of state party machines and their links to Eastern capital, proved a formidable restraint on state expansion.

The Hepburn Act is a case in point.[48] Hearings began on bills to strengthen the Interstate Commerce Commission's powers and were held in the House and Senate in 1904 to 1905, after President Roosevelt signaled his support for tougher legislation. "The government," the president wrote, "must in increasing degree supervise and regulate the workings of the railways engaged in interstate commerce."[49] Roosevelt's distrust of the railroad barons had been demonstrated two years earlier when his administration went to court to block the formation of the Northern Securities holding company. Roosevelt wanted executive-branch control over these large corporate entities. In his view, Congress could not be trusted to balance the need for corporate growth and the demands of consumers.[50] Roosevelt was also aware that expert administration of railroad regulations was a means by which the president could respond to Progressive discontent within his own party while simultaneously enhancing the president's institutional prerogatives.

During the congressional hearings, the primary sticking point was the extent of the courts' power to review decisions made by the commission to regulate rates. The Old Guard faction favored broad court review power, while Progressives favored a narrowly tailored one. In the Senate, Aldrich's stalling tactics enraged Progressives, especially when he deprived Progressive Jonathan Dolliver (R-IA) of the opportunity to claim credit for introducing the bill. Instead, Aldrich selected "Pitchfork" Benjamin Tillman (D-SC) to be the bill's sponsor. Aldrich's aim was to ensure that federal courts had the last say on railroad rates set by the ICC. When the bill finally made it out of committee, Aldrich and his allies refused to support it and tried to amend it to death. With the bill stalled in the Senate and garnering support primarily from Democrats, Roosevelt was forced to return to Old Guard leader William Allison (R-IA) to craft a compromise. The compromise granted broad court review of ICC decisions. With unrestricted court review, the Old Guard faction conceded to commission rate-making powers. The supporters of the legislation still found it to be an improvement over the status quo. The result was the Hepburn Act.

The legislative histories of the Pure Food Act and the Meat Inspection Act followed similar patterns. The Old Guard faction stood against broad regulatory reform that empowered executive agencies and threatened the interests of business, while Progressives and Populist Democrats formed an alliance in favor of more expansive reform. In the end, the Old Guard was able to shape the laws in ways that satisfied their preferences but could still be deemed by reformers to be an improvement over the status quo.

These patterns reveal that the object, and often the effect, of the Old Guard faction was to protect business from expansive regulation and state intrusion. The faction sought to limit the size and capabilities of the state by making the federal courts the chief umpire of regulatory decisions. By shifting the distribution of power in Congress in their favor, they could claim significant policy achievements, from the Dingley and Payne-Aldrich tariffs to broad powers of judicial supervision of regulatory agency decisions. For much of Roosevelt's second term they exercised a powerful veto on legislative initiatives with which they disagreed. Nonetheless, they were forced into taking rearguard actions—such as empowering courts to rein in regulatory agencies— to achieve legislative outcomes they could stomach.

SOUTHERN DEMOCRATS: RACE, LABOR, AND THE WELFARE STATE

The fundamental debate of the 1940s and 1950s was over the welfare state. Northern Democrats favored a comprehensive, racially integrated, "cradle to grave" welfare state. Southern Democrats sought a decentralized welfare state based on means-tested programs and private charity.[51] Yet, Southern Democrats did find some redistribution programs congenial—this was especially the case because the South was the poorest region in the country and stood to benefit.[52] The shift of the Southern Democrats against the New Deal after 1936 and efforts to expand the welfare state thereafter reflected concern for the racial status quo in the region combined with adherence to the Jeffersonian tradition of states' rights and limited government. "The South," wrote Carter Glass (D-VA) in 1938, "would better consider whether to cast its . . . votes according to the memories of the Reconstruction era of 1865 . . . or will have the spirit and courage enough to face the new Reconstruction era that northern so-called Democrats are menacing us with."[53]

All four of the conditions that make factions powerful shapers of the American state existed for the Southern Democrats. First, they could act as swing voters and veto players by forging alliances with the Republican Party. Second, they were able to thrive inside a highly fragmented Democratic Party and a set of congressional rules that favored decentralization and dispersion of power. Third, while Southerners were never successful at capturing the presidency for one of their own, they were firmly rooted in Congress. Finally, they could draw upon vast resources of an entire region, especially from upper-class whites in the South.

The faction's ability to shape the trajectory of welfare state development hinged above all on its privileged position within the national legislature. In 1952, Southern Democrats controlled 66 percent of the Democratic Senate seats and 54 percent of the party's seats in the House of Representatives, compared to 44 percent in the Senate and 46 percent in the House for the Midwest, Northeast, and Pacific coast combined. All senators and 94 percent of congressmen from the South were Democrats.[54] The power and positioning of Southern Democrats in the Congress provided ample incentives for the maintenance of a factional network to pursue its goals. The fragmentation and decentralization of Congress in the 1940s and 1950s gave Southern conservatives abundant opportunities to block or shape legislation in their favor.

Hailing from rural districts in a one-party region, Southern Democrats were selected by an electorate that excluded blacks and most poor whites. Consequently, most Southern Democrats held their seats for extremely long periods. Between 1937 and 1946, they used the seniority rule to take control of committee process in the House of Representatives.[55] From 1933 to 1950, Southern Democrats controlled 51 percent of the House committees, including most of the most important and most powerful committees.[56] This empowered them to design, hone, and refine measures to fit their preferences.

The committee system dominated by the Southern Democrats faction was complex. Formal rules and informal norms empowered committee chairs. A host of factors, such as committees' secret deliberations, the campaign process, district boundaries, and legislators' relationships with external institutions all conspired to Southerners' advantage.[57] The fact that power in the House was highly decentralized among the committee chairs—each with extensive policy expertise—meant that policy making also took a long time, which favored conservative Southerners' preferences.

The Senate was the strongest bastion of Southern Democrats' power in the federal government. In the 1950s, analysts agreed that "southern culture" had come to define the folkways of the institution. The civilities, deference, and traditions were products of southern mores. As William S. White put it, "[the southerner] is preeminently *the* 'Senate man' and this is his great home. It is not so much that he is so like the Institution as that the Institution is, in its fundamentals, so like him."[58] As in the House, Southern Democrats dominated the committee chairmanships. Southern Democrats like Richard Russell (Armed Services), Harry Byrd (Finance), James Eastland (Judiciary), and A. Willis Robertson (Banking and Currency) controlled the most powerful committees, committee assignments, and transfers within the system.[59] Senate rules benefited Southern Democrats also. The filibuster was a powerful weapon for blocking antithetical legislation. With a few allies from other regions of the country, Southern Democrats could assemble enough members to block a cloture vote to end debate on a measure. White wrote: "The Senate might be described without too much violence to fact as the South's unending revenge upon the North for Gettysburg."

In addition, Southern Democrats were able to create one of the most powerful cross-party alliances in American history: the so-called Conservative
Coalition. Southern Democrats' skepticism regarding government's role in the
economy and social welfare policy often placed their policy preferences closer
to Republicans. Joining hands with the GOP was, in part, a response to the
Southern Democrats' social base. As Morris Fiorina has pointed out, the
Southern Democrats in the House who voted with Republicans were from particularly safe rural and agrarian Democratic districts, the makeup of which
closely resembled those of many Midwestern Republicans.[60] The "marriage of
corn and cotton" during the New Deal enhanced "[t]he impact of the southern
bloc in Congress [which] was augmented considerably by the implementation
of a strategic voting alliance with Midwesterners."[61] Constituency pressures
thus drove Southern Democrats in the House to create temporary alliances
with Republicans on certain issues.[62] In the Senate, Southern Democrats
aligned with the powerful "inner club" of conservative Republicans, including
William Knowland, Barry Goldwater, Eugene Millikin, and Robert Taft.[63]
When Southern and non-Southern Democrats both approved policies, they
were passed into law; when Southerners dissented, measures failed or were
recast in cooperation with Republicans.[64]

The Southern Democrat faction, in concert with Republicans, sought to
restrain the size of the federal government.[65] The conservative coalition rested
on an unstated quid pro quo: Republicans would vote against civil rights legislation and Southern Democrats would vote against liberal economic legislation. Republican House Minority Leader Joseph Martin (R-MA) recalled:
"When an issue of spending or new powers for the president came along, I
would go to see Representative Howard Smith of Virginia, for example, and
say, 'Howard, see if you can't get me a few Democratic votes here.' Or I would
seek out Representative Eugene Cox of Georgia, and ask, 'Gene, why don't you
and John Rankin (D-MS) and some of your men get me some votes on this?'"[66]
Through such informal means, conservatives opposed the creation of a comprehensive welfare state and the extension of regulatory reforms.[67] Despite the
Democratic majority in name, the Coalition's power made it appear that there
was actually a conservative or even Republican majority in the Congress.[68]

From the late 1930s through the 1960s, the Conservative Coalition was a
major force in national policy making, whose existence created a triangular
struggle between Republicans, Southern Democrats, and liberal Democrats.
With liberal Democrats advocating expansion of the welfare state's size and
scope and Republicans opposing such measures, Southern Democrats could
play one off the other.[69] In this arrangement, Southern Democrats positioned
themselves to be power brokers, offering a distinct vision of the welfare state
from their Liberal-Labor colleagues as well as the Republicans with whom

they often voted. If welfare state measures proposed by northern Democrats threatened the racial status quo, Southern Democrats would join Republicans to block them. If northern Democrats could design their measures to ease Southern concerns on the race issue, Republicans could still drive Southerners into their corner by using nondiscrimination riders as a tool to block measures they opposed. Federal aid to education provides an example of this strategy. In 1943, Democrats introduced a $200 million proposal of federal aid to schools that had strong support among Southerners. However, when Republicans offered an amendment stipulating that the funds must be equally distributed among black and white schools the measure failed. Yet, Southerners still wanted federal dollars to industrialize their region and could, therefore, often be drawn into alliance with their northern colleagues to support liberal measures.

Southern Democrats thus shaped the New Deal and Fair Deal legislation and its implementation—including the Social Security system, unemployment compensation, the minimum wage, and the G.I. Bill of Rights—in ways that discriminated against blacks. Black Americans therefore received significantly fewer benefits from federal programs than whites.[70] Southern Democrats also sought to circumscribe labor legislation so as to keep agricultural labor unregulated by the central state. Robert Lieberman has argued that the occupational exclusions in the Social Security Act of 1935 were inserted at Southern insistence, entwining racial considerations in the centerpiece of the American welfare state.[71] This was affected primarily by excluding agricultural and domestic workers from the 1935 Social Security bill. "Across the nation," Ira Katznelson has written, "fully 65 percent of African Americans fell outside the reach of the new program; between 70 and 80 percent in different parts of the South."[72]

A host of issues centered on race and class created by the New Deal and World War II gave Southern Democrats incentives to block the expansion of the labor movement and changes in the racial status quo. By the 1940s, it was obvious to Southern Democrats that labor markets, union power, and race relations were deeply intertwined. In the wake of the New Deal, Southern Democrats set up a legislative system that decentralized control over most federal programs in order to exclude many African-Americans from government programs, privileges, and protections.[73] As the *New Republic* put it, "a solid phalanx, Democratic in name, reactionary in principle, and with influence far beyond that of the states it represents, has been constructed in the halls of Congress, . . . national economic and social reform is being hampered by a narrow, undemocratic clique of politicos from the poll tax states, permanently vested in office by spoon-fed machines."[74] By rigging the committee system in their favor, southern congressmen sought to maintain the inexpensive labor

pool that segregation provided. The best way to do this was to maintain fragmented and incoherent lines of authority that could be exploited and adapted
to local purposes.

During FDR's third term and throughout the Truman years, Southern
Democrats worked to stop the expansion of the labor movement after its rapid
growth during the New Deal and World War II. Edward Cox (D-GA) voiced
the view of many Southern Democrats when he described the Wagner Act as "a
vicious law that is wrapped up in high-sounding language to conceal its wicked
intent. It is one-sided and had been administered in a one-sided way."[75] In
1946, the CIO launched "Operation Dixie," an organizing drive in many
southern states to ameliorate the condition of the southern industrial worker.[76]
Thus, after supporting labor legislation during the Depression, Southern Democrats aligned with Republicans to dismantle the laws that had facilitated
labor's expansion. The effect was to constrict labor's territorial extension and
political power. As Congressman James Mark Wilcox (D-FL) explained:

> [There] is the problem of Negro labor. There has always been a differ-
> ence in the wage scale of white and colored labor. So long as Florida
> people are permitted to handle the matter, the delicate and perplexing
> problem can be adjusted; but the Federal government knows no color
> line and of necessity it cannot make any distinction between the races.[77]

Moreover, stopping labor's expansion preserved the faction's bargaining position within the party. Southern conservatives could then strike compromises
with other Democrats in exchange for regional favors.

On the heels of the most powerful wave of strikes in the nation's history,
Republicans secured a majority in both houses of Congress in the 1946 elections and placed legislation to weaken unions at the top of their agenda. President Truman's veto threat meant that Republicans needed a large number of
Democrats to join with them if they were to secure labor law retrenchment.[78]
Southern Democrats were therefore well positioned to determine the fate of
New Deal labor policy. Yet, they had powerful reasons to join with Republicans against labor. After the passage of the Wagner Act, unions had grown rapidly, especially in the South, where the number of unionized workers had
doubled from 500,000 to roughly 1 million. Joining Republicans in an assault
on labor laws and unions, Southern Democrats were crucial to passage in 1947
of the Labor-Management Relations Act (Taft-Hartley) over President Truman's veto and to the changes in the enforcement of minimum wages and
maximum hours, weakening the Fair Labor Standards Act.[79]

The move was a direct assault on the one power source that Southern
Democrats realized could challenge them within the Democratic Party. By

dramatically slowing the growth of the labor movement, Southern Democrats temporarily defeated the one force in the country with the potential to challenge the racial status quo. After Taft-Hartley, labor's organizing efforts in the South withered.[80] Ultimately, the defection of the Southern faction from the Democratic Party on labor policy was bad for labor and especially bad for black workers. If a powerful labor movement is a key source of welfare state development, the Southern Democratic faction helps explain America's peculiar developmental trajectory.

In sum, the Southern Democratic faction shaped the policy development of the welfare state, national labor policy, and the slow advancement of racial politics. The ways the faction changed the trajectory of state intervention in society—by slowing it in some areas, while accelerating it others—had deep and lasting consequences for the character and development of the American state. Some of these consequences would require massive political mobilization in the future to alter.

New Right Republicans and the Welfare State: "Starve the Beast"[81]

A central thrust of New Right doctrine from Goldwater to Reagan and beyond was antistatism. "It is my intention to curb the size and influence of the Federal establishment," Reagan stated in his first Inaugural Address.[82] Eight years later, Reagan sought to remind the American people that ". . . man is not free unless government is limited. There is a clear cause and effect here that is as neat and predictable as a law of physics: As government expands, liberty contracts."[83] Conservatives viewed the welfare state as a major cause of society's ills. They argued that social programs created perverse incentives and financing them required levels of taxation the destroyed entrepreneurship and increased budget deficits. Once in power, the faction thus aimed to reduce the size and scope of the welfare state. The major achievements in this regard were, first, a series of tax and spending cuts under the administration of Ronald Reagan; second, a drive to transform welfare from an entitlement into a block grant workfare program in the 1990s, under the direction of Newt Gingrich; and third, another round of tax cuts under George W. Bush.

The New Right faction was less powerful because not all conditions for factional importance applied. It was unable to ever forge any durable cross-party alliances. But it could capitalize on the fragmentation of power within the GOP, which had long been the minority party in Congress. Its position in Congress began modestly and expanded until 1994 when Republicans took over the House for the first time in forty years. The New Right could also draw on important constituencies in the South and Southwest, especially a growing cadre of conservative religious groups. In addition, contrary to most factions, it managed to have one of its own elected president, who remained roughly in tune with the faction's agenda.

When Ronald Reagan assumed the presidency in 1981, he inherited a situation in which the public was rebelling against government growth. Backed by the New Right faction, Reagan was elected on a platform crafted to counter the build-up of domestic social spending. And the amount of government social spending did slow dramatically under Reagan. Reducing taxes was a way for the New Right faction to promote an economic and fiscal policy that deprived the state of funds needed for expansion.

Tax policy lay at the heart of Ronald Reagan's domestic agenda.[84] Fiscally conservative Republicans held that returning more money to individuals and businesses would spur economic growth, enhance efficiency, and retard the growth of government social programs. Reagan made large individual tax cuts the centerpiece of his fiscal policy. Economist Eugene Steurele called the 1980s the "tax decade." The big political battles were fought over a series of major laws that cut, then raised, and then reformed federal taxes.[85]

The Reagan administration's two biggest moves to roll back government growth were the 1981 Omnibus Budget and Reconciliation Act and the Economic Recovery and Tax Act. The former made significant cuts in domestic spending, expanded military spending, and changed a number of programs from categorical grants to block grants for the states. The latter "indexed" tax rates and reduced rates for individuals and corporations. However, the administration's victories had to be modified (taxes were raised in 1982 and again in 1984) as Democrats regained their footing after the 1980 elections and alarm increased among moderate Republicans about massive budget deficits. Nonetheless, these two policy initiatives fundamentally reshaped the national debate over the size and scope of government. As Newt Gingrich put it, "From January to August of 1981, it [the nation] lived through a truly revolutionary period in the tradition of the New Deal. We conservatives began to change the direction of federal spending, we changed the direction of national defense, we changed the pattern of the regulatory bureaucracy, and we changed the pattern of taxation."[86] By reducing federal revenue, the laws put government on a path whereby it would be very difficult down the line to enact new domestic social programs. Rather, groups would have to fight to maintain existing benefits. Indeed, the 1990s might be characterized as the decade of "budget deficits," insofar as the central policy-making thrust was a set of packages that slightly increased taxes (which conservatives hated) and slightly reduced spending (which liberals deplored).

However, despite significant spending cuts in social programs (specifically AFDC and food stamps), the administration was unable to alter the basic structure of these programs. As one commentator has written, "Watching conservatives try to reduce the welfare state after 1980 was like looking at people trying to walk down an up escalator."[87] Primarily this was because the Republican Party in general and New Right affiliates in particular lacked sufficient numbers in Congress, especially the House. The Reagan administration was only able to force through its tax and spending package because they used the budget reconciliation process rather than voting on each piece of tax and spending legislation separately. Nonetheless, the administration failed in its efforts to enact further cuts in 1982 as a recession took hold. Thus, although tax policy had reduced the possibility of program growth, the New Right and its allies in the Reagan administration were less successful in reducing overall government spending in the short term.

The other major push for welfare state retrenchment was the Reagan administration's New Federalism proposals announced in the president's State of the Union Address in 1982. The President said that the country's "next major undertaking must be a program . . . to make our system of federalism work again."[88] The proposal would have strongly reinforced the decentralized character of the American state, reduced social spending, and reversed the trend toward centralization of power in Washington. After negotiations with members of Congress and the National Governor's Association in the spring of 1982, the New Federalism proposal failed to garner enough support to be even introduced into Congress.[89]

With New Federalism dead on arrival, tax policy remained the primary tool for shrinking the American state after the 1980s. The issue of taxes, deficits, national debt, and government revenue continued to configure partisan identification, the nature of electoral campaigns, and legislative agendas into the twenty-first century. This shift in the operation of the American state, which greatly constrained the growth of nonmilitary domestic spending, is a legacy of the New Right.

George W. Bush, who made tax cuts the centerpiece of his domestic agenda, extended this legacy. In the 2000 presidential campaign, both Bush and Al Gore offered tax reduction plans. Bush's proposed cuts were substantially larger than Gore's more targeted approach. But both candidates increased the size of their plans over the course of campaign as the federal surplus continued to grow. Following up on its campaign proposals, the Bush administration developed a tax reduction package estimated to cost $1.6 trillion over ten years. The total cost of these rate reductions was estimated at $724 billion over ten years. A highly partisan process in the House and an unevenly bipartisan approach in the Senate characterized the legislative politics of tax cuts in 2001.

Conservative House Majority Leader Tom DeLay's tactics ultimately destroyed any hopes for bipartisanship in the House.[90] After more bipartisan negotiations in the Senate, the final legislation contained most of the major features of the president's proposal. Two years later the administration sought another round of major tax cuts. The centerpiece of the 2003 proposal was a plan to eliminate the taxation of corporate dividends.

The consequence of the two tax cuts, the 2001 recession, and higher discretionary spending on defense and homeland security was ballooning deficits. By the end of 2004, federal tax receipts as a percentage of net national income had plummeted to 16.3 percent of GDP, the lowest level since 1959. Further tax reduction became increasingly hard to justify or sustain. But deficits and the low revenue percentage from taxes made it difficult for Democrats to propose new government programs.

Despite the signature achievement of the New Right under Bush, the underlying commitment to a policy of lower taxes appears vulnerable. Although some tax cuts were part of a stimulus package to combat the recession of 2008–2009, future federal tax increases of some kind appear to be inevitable, barring a major decline in demand for government services. The structural fiscal imbalance of an aging society and escalating health care costs is poised to unleash a fiscal emergency within the next decade.

The other major area of achievement of the New Right faction in limiting the growth of the American state and changing its nature is the area of welfare for the poor. The initial movement was the slight expansion of AFDC in 1988, when the Reagan administration pushed for changes in the program to require participants to work. "Workfare" gained steam in Congress in the 1980s as the New Right faction, under Newt Gingrich's direction, increased in strength. In 1982, Gingrich founded the Conservative Opportunity Society in the House, which emphasized the economic libertarianism of the New Right faction.[91] The takeover of the House Republican Party by New Right–affiliated conservatives was cemented with Gingrich's election as minority whip in 1988, which accelerated the process of bringing the House Republican Conference under conservative control.

After engineering a stunning victory in the 1994 elections—bringing in a Republican majority in the House for the first time in forty years—Gingrich and the other leaders of the House had a menu of policy options they wanted to put on the agenda and pass into law. Many of these policies dealt with economic and regulatory issues. Representatives of the New Right faction in the House were more attached to the free-market, small-government libertarian ideas than Republican's moral traditionalism. The number two in the House Republican leadership, Dick Armey, was a consistent advocate of supply-side economics. As a key architect of the Contract with America, Armey was responsible for many of the economic provisions.[92] The overall thrust of the Contract was to reduce the size of government.

A major change in the configuration of the American state driven by the New Right faction was to change the welfare entitlement Aid to Families with Dependent Children (AFDC) into a block grant program called Temporary Assistance for Needy Families (TANF). Gingrich had promised welfare reform as a way to reduce the dependency of individuals on the state and promote work. Changing welfare from an entitlement to a block grant would allow for funding cuts and other savings, which conservatives hoped could help finance tax cuts and deficit reduction. After an intense series of policy-making rounds, President Bill Clinton signed the Personal Responsibility and Work Opportunity Reconciliation Act of 1996 (PRWORA).[93]

The overall objective of the New Right was a smaller federal government that allocated more power and functions to the states and organizations that contract with the government. State governments could adapt better to local conditions, and private organizations would deliver government services more efficiently. Although the New Right's aims were never fully realized, the faction did contribute to constraints on state growth, as Democrats were unable to pass major new programs. Moreover, the New Right was highly effective in changing the nature of the public debate over the size of the state. Bill Clinton's declaration that "the era of big government" was over signaled a profound change in attitudes for a Democratic president.

Factions as Caretakers

Three other factions—the Half-Breed Republicans, Modern Liberal Republicans, and New Democrats—did not try to either expand the state or restrain its growth. Rather, they took on an important third role in state development: that of caretakers. They tried to craft a "centrist" approach, so to speak, between working for or against state expansion. Consequently, these factions did much less to shape state development. Nonetheless, by blocking efforts coming from the left and the right to either increase the size of the state or dismantle parts of it, they played an important role in temporizing state development.

HALF-BREED REPUBLICANS

Between 1870 and 1880, the Half-Breed faction did not seek to reduce state growth, like the Liberals, nor did they try to expand the patronage system that fuelled that growth, like the Stalwarts.[94] Historians have described the Half-Breeds as more moderate on Reconstruction policy and in their pursuit of patronage than the Stalwarts. Mark Hirsch characterized the Half-Breeds as in between the Stalwarts and reformers, advocating protectionism and hard money, while opposing tough Reconstruction.[95] In general, Half-Breeds' differences on policy questions with the other party factions were differences of degree rather than principle. While usually closer to the Stalwarts ideologically, they were more inclined to make rhetorical gestures in the direction of positions favored by Liberal reformers. Because other factions within the party shared many of these views, this made Half-Breeds the broad middle swath of the party. They pursued a cooperative strategy, navigating between and playing off the other factions.[96]

Whatever their policy preferences, Half-Breeds could not forge cross-party alliances, and their numbers in the Senate were thin and their constituencies dispersed. Their coalition was based on prosperous farmers, tariff-protected workers, and businessmen tired of bare-knuckled Stalwart governance. This electoral base was broad but thin and rested on support in Midwestern states such as Ohio and northeastern states like New Hampshire. Consequently, none of the four conditions that enable factions to shape the state-building process applied to the Half-Breeds.

MODERN LIBERAL REPUBLICANS

The Modern Liberal Republican faction of the 1950s did not seek to roll back the achievements of the New Deal. Rather they sought to streamline and accommodate it to the postwar political economy. To move the GOP to the political center, however, Liberal Republicans had to defend the status quo of government's role in society. This was a paradoxical position for affiliated Republicans, insofar as the status quo they defended just happened to be the New Deal, including rights for organized labor and a welfare state created by Democrats. Liberals sought to create a more efficient and effective welfare state, one shorn of graft, corruption, and incompetence. Although President Dwight Eisenhower, the Liberals champion, was deeply suspicious of elements of the New Deal, he believed that widespread public support for many measures made a direct assault on the welfare state politically suicidal. As he told his brother: "Should any political party attempt to abolish social security and eliminate labor laws and farm programs, you would not hear from that party again in our history."[97]

Liberal Republicans' distinct constituency made them the closest thing to an "establishment" in the European sense.[98] These men emerged from the new managerial occupations and retained close ties with the manufacturing and business communities of the old cities. They were willing to accept greater state involvement in the economy, the expansion of federal power over the states, and were more attuned to the GOP's civil rights heritage. On the other hand, the regular GOP had close ties to small business, came from the plains states and the West Coast, and believed that the New Deal represented a revolutionary change that should be rolled back when Republicans regained power.

The new managerial class, college educated and economically secure, was the milieu from which Liberal Republicans were drawn and where they found support. Derisively called "organization men," Liberal Republicans were the product of the new white-collar jobs created by the explosive growth of corporate entities in the 1940s and 1950s.[99] Liberal Republicans' former corporate employers became their chief source of funds for campaign and party activities. Accustomed to dealing with government and unions, corporate leaders were willing to accommodate organized labor and state economic intervention.[100] But even this constituency was relatively thin electorally speaking and was not strategically placed to enhance its importance in the Electoral College.

However, Liberals were successful in winning important governorships. It was at the state level that they exercised their greatest influence. This was most evident on a central domestic-policy issue of the 1940s and 1950s: labor management relations. Because they came from corporate headquarters where they met organized labor at the bargaining table, they accepted unions as a part of the political and economic landscape. Unlike others in the GOP, who denied the legitimacy of unions, Liberals sought only to constrain labor's power by ensuring that the rules of corporate-labor relations did not privilege unions. Indeed, Liberal Republicanism—concentrated geographically in the Northeast, industrial Midwest, and West Coast—derived from the same regions in which union membership was highest. These states were places where sentiment was strongest in favor of the New Deal welfare state. Therefore, electoral incentives dictated a move to the center and acceptance of the welfare state. The Liberal Republican doctrine was to contain the costs of welfare state programs without threatening their legitimacy or directly attacking their beneficiaries.

The limited contribution of Modern Liberal Republicans to state development was not to discourage unions in those states where the Liberals were often governors, nor to attempt to roll back major provisions of the national welfare state; their ability to forge cross-party alliances with Liberal-Labor Democrats from the North enhanced this power in Congress. However, they ultimately had very limited effects on state development because their numbers in Congress, especially the House, were too small.

NEW DEMOCRATS

The New Democratic prescription for winning the White House, retaining Democratic congressional majorities, and remaking the party became limiting state expansion, encouraging market-driven growth, and demonstrating cultural moderation. According to New Democrats, New Politics Democrats' institutional reforms and policy positions had distorted state development with both their defenses of affirmative action, "the right to be different," and rights to clean air, water, and welfare, as well as their beliefs that large social and economic forces were the "root causes" of crime, racism, and poverty. The New Democratic faction argued that a shift in power in favor of elected officials and away from interest groups and activists was needed. Such a strategy entailed a direct confrontation with the Rainbow Coalition, labor unions, public interest groups, and feminist organizations. New Democrats saw this mosaic as creating unsustainable rigidities that blocked forward-looking policies and reinforced a party image that emphasized minority rights and individual entitlements.

The New Democratic faction did not seek to encourage state involvement in the economy. Nor did it seek to drastically reduce the existing role of the state. Rather, the New Democrats' economic program sought to modestly reduce state intervention through fiscal discipline, using market mechanisms in policy areas such as health care and environmental regulation, and increasing bureaucratic efficiency. According to New Democrats, the best ways to spur economic growth were free trade and deficit reduction, underpinned by educational opportunity and job training. As their "credo" put it: "We believe that economic growth generated in the private sector is the prerequisite for opportunity, and that government's role is to promote growth and to equip Americans with the tools they need to prosper in the New Economy."[101]

New Democrats' problems were that that they had a limited presence in Congress, were reluctant to forge alliances with conservative Republicans, and chose a leader, Bill Clinton, who was not a consistent advocate for their ideas. After running as a New Democrat, Arkansas Governor Bill Clinton's victory in the 1992 presidential election did not result in an administration that favored the faction's policy prescriptions. Once in the White House, in New Democrats eyes, Clinton proposed "old" Democratic policies or offered New Democratic policies dressed up in "old" Democratic rhetoric. The course Clinton pursued in his first two years in office on the federal budget, appointments, and policy priorities actually demoralized New Democrats. As Kenneth Baer has written, the Clinton administration, in its first two years, "continued to send an Old Democratic, liberal message to the public."[102]

The choice to launch a major health care reform initiative before dealing with welfare also outraged New Democrats. The DLC had specific ideas about how to reform welfare, which it argued should have been the first big-ticket agenda item. Instead, Clinton sided with the party's majority and decided to push health care reform as his first major piece of legislation. However, Clinton's unwillingness to prioritize New Democratic policies was understandable, since doing so would have alienated the majority of his party in favor of a faction.

After the Republican takeover of Congress in 1994, however, Clinton was forced to change course in order to shore up his centrist credentials for the 1996 election. He accomplished this by winning a tough budget battle and, after two vetoes, signing a Republican-crafted welfare reform bill. New Democrats, who were key negotiators with the Republican majority, cheered the welfare legislation. But the law elicited vociferous protest from liberals. Half of the Democratic House Caucus (98 members) opposed the bill. A few of Clinton's advisors resigned in protest. In economic policy, Clinton also pushed many New Democratic ideas. He advanced the free trade agenda, getting the North American Free Trade Agreement (NAFTA) and the latest round of the General Agreement on Tariffs and Trade (GATT) through Congress, over opposition from his own party.

New Democrats' limited effect on state development was due to the fact that conditions did not favor them. They couldn't openly seek alliances with Republicans, had a dispersed constituency that offered little leverage in the Electoral College or in presidential-nominating politics, and lacked large numbers in the Congress. Declaring war on liberals within their own party was also counterproductive, as they lacked the resources in Congress to win such a fight. Under such conditions, they turned their energies to more efficient management of the existing state. The result was a relatively limited number of major policy departures in the 1990s.[103]

Conclusion

Factions have been the driving elements behind three elements in the configuration of the American state. First, Liberal Republicans, Progressive Republicans, and New Politics Democrats all sought to shift power away from the political parties in favor of the bureaucracy. On the other hand, Stalwarts and Liberal Republicans tried to maintain or increase the power of the parties in relation to competing power centers. Second, some factions have been involved in recalibrating the relationship of the federal government to the states. Old Guard Republicans tried to maintain local control over many government operations in the face of challenges from Progressive Republicans and Populist Democrats. Southern Democrats sought to retain the decentralized republic of states' rights, while Liberal-Labor Democrats and New Politics Democrats after them tried to centralize power in Washington. Finally, New Right Republicans and New Democrats helped craft a welfare reform policy that converted an entitlement into a block grant, giving the states much more flexibility in program design and implementation. Factions have shaped the degree of coherence or incoherence and fragmentation or unification of the American state. They are at the root of why power in many public programs remains diffuse and obscurely assigned.

Given the dispersion of power in the design of the American Constitution, which works against responsible parties, it is perhaps not surprising that the way state building has occurred has been through a kaleidoscopic process of factional competition beneath the party labels rather than through direct party battles. Insofar as factions control votes in Congress and they can act as swing votes in committee or on the floor, they can force major changes in state development. As the dean of American political journalism David Broder has written, "The clear lesson is that the factions command votes—and cannot be ignored."[104]

CHAPTER 9

Factions, Party Responsibility, and American Institutions

This book has argued that parties rarely, if ever, act as wholes. Neither are they simply the product of free-floating individuals who are their members. Much of the time, the most important actors are subunits within the parties that have a self-conscious identity and a certain organizational form. These are factions, which often constitute a basic element of American political parties. They are the spirit that animates the partisan body. Party decisions are often either the decision of a dominant faction, or they represent an accommodation of the interactions of factions.

A number of interesting conclusions follow from viewing factions as primary actors within parties. One is that factions' organizational power and cohesion make American political parties more vibrant and less diffuse than they are normally depicted. If there is not always a purpose to parties, there is often a purpose to factions. Factions acting within parties coordinate disparate actors to rationalize the public agenda and the policy process. Factions do not merely respond to existing public preferences but bring new ideas onto the agenda, hone these ideas into workable policies, and take concerted action to promote their adoption. It has often been the case that when analysts speak of one of the parties, what they really have in mind is a party faction.

Another conclusion is that factions complicate the applicability of Duverger's law to the American party system.[1] This law, named after the great French analyst of parties, holds that plurality elections systems automatically produce two-party politics where the major parties tend toward the political center. In the strict sense the law has held—with the exception of the Republican Party, no third party has ever won a national election. The study of factions reveals that despite a nominal two-party system, at certain periods, such as the early twentieth-century Republican Party or the Democratic Party of the 1950s, parties can be so divided by factions as to nearly constitute distinct parties traveling under a common label. At such moments, there is often as much ideo-logical diversity within parties as between them.[2] A first-past-the post electoral system, in tandem with the Electoral College, discourages third parties, but it provides incentives for factions to form and room for them to act.

Finally, the courses of action that parties adopt are not simply the products of exogenous factors—such as the electorate, the economy, or the behavior of the other party—but are also induced by conflict between factions. Factional conflict among party elites produces much party change.[3] This proposition is a valuable corrective to recent scholarly literatures that diminish parties' roles in American politics. One school attacks critical realignment and the notion that parties are constitutive of electoral eras in favor of other factors.[4] Another holds that elites—such as political entrepreneurs, activists, and experts em-bedded in interest groups, think tanks, and social movements—are respon-sible for political change.[5] In contrast, the argument here is that factions give parties a certain unity and energy, and elite actors are often part of larger intra-party factional networks. The study of factions brings the parties back in.

Factions and American Institutions

Working in presidential and congressional arenas, factions' efforts to gain office and reshape their respective party's character have a powerful effect on the operations of America's governing institutions. Factions operate in Con-gress to secure both symbolic benefits, such as enhancing their reputations as reformers, and substantive benefits, such as being able to pass laws they have been fighting for. Factions change the distribution of power in two ways: by creating new communications networks and organizations or by changing congressional rules. Networks such as the "Senate Four" around 1900 and the "Liberal bloc" in the Senate in the 1950s and 1960s performed key legislative functions. Formal organizations, such as the Democratic Study Group, the Wednesday Group, and the Conservative Opportunity Society, were crucial in coordinating the activity of legislators. They also linked affiliated legislators to sympathetic interest groups, think tanks, and journalists. These networks and organizations became primary sources of policy promotion and effective in-struments to coordinate legislative strategy, tactics, and voting. They are also points on political elites' mental maps indicating the sources of activity and the balance of forces.

Changing congressional rules can empower factions to pass legislation that would otherwise be blocked, enhance their reputations as reformers, or both. Some factions sought more substantive gains, others more symbolic ones. Progressive Republicans were catalysts in the reforms of House rules that weakened the power of Speaker Joseph Cannon; Liberal-Labor Democrats sparked the expansion of the House Rules Committee to secure their policy objectives; New Politics Democrats instituted new "sunshine" rules and other procedural innovations; and New Right Republicans instituted changes in the GOP House Conference. Each of these rules changes involved a combination of interest and principle, as faction affiliates sought to facilitate the passage of their policies and enhance their reputation with the public.

In presidential politics, the type of men nominated for the nation's highest office and the debts they accumulated during their campaigns were often decided by factional contestation. Candidate selection and platform craftsmanship can be the means to leverage the party because they determine the character of the candidate and the program to be presented to voters. Liberal Republicans, Populist Democrats, modern Liberal Republicans, the New Right, New Politics Democrats, and New Democrats all adopted a strategy centered on securing the nomination for one of their own and crafting a platform to their specifications as the means to take over the party. The most extreme cases involve a faction forcing an "irrational" or "anti-Downsian" candidate or electoral strategy on the rest of the party. New Right Republicans saddled the GOP with Barry Goldwater in 1964, and New Politics Democrats handed their party George McGovern in 1972. In contrast, in the name of moving their party to the center, Liberal Republicans encouraged the Republican Party to abandon Reconstruction, even though this did not produce the electoral gains in the South that their "centrist" electoral strategy promised.

Presidents' debts to, affiliations with, or distance from factions shaped their governing tactics. As presidents survey the political and institutional context in which they must govern, factions add additional layers of complexity to the situation of divided government. The traditional analysis takes as its starting point whether there is unified (one party controls all three elected institutions), divided (one party controls the presidency the other the House and Senate), or mixed (one party controls the presidency and one chamber of Congress but the other party commands the other chamber) control of government. The implicit assumption is that unified government is the most "responsible" and the best at producing legislation. But the study of factions provides evidence that this assumption has only limited applicability. For instance, because of factions, divided government in the Eisenhower era proved more effective at producing legislation than unified government in the Kennedy years. The presence of factions can alter individual and partisan calculations of policy makers as they seek a course of action on a given issue.

Presidents have four choices when dealing with factions in their own party: They can try to ignore them, cooperate with them, champion them, or confront them. For instance, William H. Taft first ignored and then confronted

Progressive Republicans. Franklin Roosevelt and Harry Truman both confronted Southern Democrats. Affiliated with the Liberal-Labor faction, Kennedy cooperated with it. As the New Right's champion, Reagan put its networks to work on his behalf. Sometimes presidents combine these tactics, by rhetorically confronting a faction but quietly working with it behind the scenes. Theodore Roosevelt and Richard Nixon both employed this governing technique. Gaining the implicit or explicit recognition of a president demonstrates to the attentive public a faction's power and influence. To the extent that factions shape the governing tactics of presidents, they can consider their investment of political capital as contributing to their long-term objectives.

Ultimately, if one accepted the idea that parties direct American government, one would expect that party dominance would produce more policy change. But if one looks at factions, one can understand why this has not been the case. That is, one gets a better understanding of American politics by looking for, and at, party factions.

Factions and Party Responsibility

Factions in American politics are closest to Burke's original definition of political parties as "a body of men united, for promoting by their joint endeavors the national interest, upon some particular principal in which they are all agreed."[6] Therefore, as factions develop coherent programs they are the best approximation of "responsible parties." Writing in 1950, the Committee on Political Parties of the American Political Science Association, headed by E.E. Schattschneider, asserted that: "an effective party system requires . . . that the parties bring forth programs to which they can commit themselves."[7] Many scholars have subsequently argued that America's large, diffuse parties are not, and cannot be expect to be, responsible in this way because they cannot do what the APSA committee said they should do.[8] Yet, the previous pages have shown repeated examples of factions doing just the things the committee suggested. They have developed programs, publicly committed themselves to them, and acted on them after winning office. These activities are not the result of a party acting as a monolithic bloc, but rather of factions behaving like "proto-parties." Factions seek to gain control of national governing institutions to show that their views can win over a national majority.

Of course, some factions are more "responsible" than others. Change factions, such as the Liberal Republicans of the Gilded Age, New Right Republicans, as well as Populist, Liberal-Labor, and New Politics Democrats come closest to the APSA Committee model. Status quo factions, such as the Stalwarts, Old Guard Republicans, and Southern Democrats target their messages to particular constituencies. Their accountability is more narrowly tailored. Mixed cases, such as the Half-Breeds or the modern Liberal Republicans, are the least dependable, since they often lack a fully developed program and behave expediently, splitting differences within their party or between it and the other party.

These differences in factional "responsibility" are partly related to factions' attitude toward ideas. Because ideas can and often do structure how party elites determine strategy, isolating the terms of ideational conflict to clarify factions' decision making. Change factions are usually deeply committed to a public philosophy. Their idealistic attitude means that beliefs, values, and aspirations are central to politics, insofar as they seek to determine the overall character of the regime. Status quo factions tend to adopt a utilitarian (or functional) attitude concerning ideas. That is, ideas are necessary and useful in rallying the faithful but aren't where the real action is. For them, politics is more about power, positioning, and coercion than deliberation and persuasion. Mixed-case factions often esteem ideas but pay them little heed, settling instead for pragmatism. Paradoxically, these factions recognize the value of ideas but don't try to advance a truly distinctive vision. Rather, they strive to prove their realism by adjusting to contemporary circumstances.

Another way to gauge factions' "responsibility" is to evaluate their "success" at doing what they set out to do. Change factions define success as the extent to which they can take over the party and implement their policy menu. The comparison of change factions yields a general rule: To be successful they must plant their flag in both the presidential and congressional arenas. Populist, Liberal-Labor, New Politics Democrats, and the New Right all managed to take their case into both institutional venues. The most striking cases of this phenomenon are when a faction begins in the minority, commandeers the party, and leads it to win a national majority. Change factions that did not have as much success remaking their respective party, such as Liberal Republicans, Progressive Republicans, and New Democrats, were only able to establish their presence in presidential politics or to gain a foothold in Congress.

Status quo factions define success as staving off other factions' reform efforts. By this criterion, all three of the status quo factions achieved considerable success. Stalwarts slowed the collapse of Reconstruction and, for more than a decade, retarded the implementation of civil service reforms that threatened the patronage system. Old Guard Republicans stymied attempts by Progressive Republicans to transform the party. Southern Democrats kept civil rights for African-Americans off the agenda and shaped the welfare state to fit their preferences. Status quo factions also improve their fortunes if they can get out of their congressional refuge, where status quo factions tend to build their base of operations, and impact presidential elections. Stalwarts

were greatly aided by Grant's victory in 1872, the Old Guard by Taft's renomination in 1912, and Stevenson's nomination didn't threaten Southern Democrats in 1952 and 1956. To defeat status quo factions, major changes in the
structure and operation of American government are required.

Mixed-case factions' definition of success is more fluid because they aim to
retain elements of the past as well as adjust to new circumstances. For them,
success means securing a position from which to manage intraparty conflict to
maintain the right balance of old and new. They are driven by a confidence in
their own competence to perform these tasks. Without a fully coherent vision
for the future of the nation, they act as arbiters, rarely presenting bold new
measures and programs. Instead, they split the difference between the parties
and call that innovation. Such expedient factions try to secure outcomes
through negotiation and cooperation. Their willingness to work with a variety
of partners on an issue-by-issue basis exposes them to accusations that they
lack political scruples. These centrist factions have difficulty establishing a
grassroots base and mobilizing a cadre of activists. Mixed-case factions have
often been successful at the presidential level but unable to carve out a niche in
Congress or exploit the power they had.

Factions and Contemporary Polarization

The factional cycle of boom and bust since World War II has reshuffled the
parties' coalitions, transformed the programs the parties offer to voters, and
registered a shift in the affiliations that define party membership. The working
out of factional politics is at the root of contemporary interparty polarization.
The nearly complete disappearance of durable factions in the first decade of the
new century increased polarization. Political parties in the United States Congress have sharply diverged over the last generation. The Republican Party has
become more conservative and the Democratic Party more liberal on nearly
all policy issues. Divergences between the parties occur across social, economic, and foreign policy dimensions. The percentage of congressional votes
pitting most Democrats against most Republicans has increased markedly
since the 1970s.[9]

Contemporary divisions appear all the more insidious, coming as they
have on the heels of a high point in intraparty factionalism that reduced interparty tensions. According to many pundits, increased polarization is a threat
to the maintenance of American constitutional democracy. They claim that
partisan rancor has the potential to undermine American institutions and so
thoroughly alienate citizens so as to destroy key habits of citizenship.[10] Yet,
most analysts came of age in a highly distinct factional period that muted

polarization. What they take to be the norm is in fact atypical. Placed in the broad sweep of American political history, contemporary polarization seems milder than some have made out.[11]

In fact, government is returning to levels of polarization, at least as measured by congressional roll call votes, that prevailed from the 1870s through the 1920s.[12] Mid-century factions reduced polarization, and with their departure it has returned. There does not, therefore, appear to be a rule that holds that the decline of factions increases polarization. Factions existed within the GOP during the 1870s and 1880s, and within both parties from the turn of the century into Wilson's first term, without reducing polarization. It is nonetheless true that over the past half-century, this has been the case. Factional history is a key source of today's distinct ideological visions, feelings of moral superiority (which exist on both sides of the aisle), and the networks that sustain them.

The decline of factionalism has coincided with two major regional partisan realignments, which have produced a situation where neither party today has an element within it that overlaps the center. On the right, the decline of modern Liberal Republicanism and the rise of the New Right have coincided with a decline of the Republican Party in New England, once a GOP stronghold, and its rise in the South and Southwest. Republicans have also disappeared from many American cities and old-line suburbs. Today's Republican Party is rightly described as the party of exurban, rural, and small-town America. The retreat from New England and from major cities has transformed the party. The takeover of the party by the New Right has helped usher in a new era, where the value of ideas has increased exponentially. The entrenchment of the "counter-establishment" in Washington anchors the Republican Party on the right. The electoral appeal of conservatism suggests solid ties to a broad swath of the American public.

However, just as factionalism seemed to have disappeared on the political right, a movement combining grassroots activists and big donors calling itself the Tea Party emerged in 2010 on the political right. The Tea Partiers' ideological thrust opposes federal control, more government spending, and the political establishment, is wrapped in a curious penchant for Jeffersonian constitutionalism.[13] The movement's unifying belief is that government and special interests have created an interlocking directorate to the detriment of average Americans. It quickly inserted itself into the 2010 elections, helping defeat a number of established Republicans in primary elections and backing a number of conservative candidates for federal and state offices. Minnesota Congresswoman Michele Bachmann established a Tea Party Caucus in the House of Representatives. Its membership expanded with electoral victories in 2010, and the caucuses' members enforced a hard line in 2011 budget negotiations with President Obama.

To date, characterizations of the Tea Party have ranged from its affiliates being poor uneducated racists to dupes of corporate power to tight-fisted privileged whites to Republican conservatives rebranded.[14] Beyond such sociological characterizations, the fluidity of the Tea Party's organizational structure has flummoxed analysts. While the Tea Party has many of the trappings of a faction as analyzed here, it is too early to tell whether the movement will congeal into a durable faction. However, the perspective offered in this book provides a template for analyzing the Tea Party as it develops.

On the other side of the political spectrum, the inroads made by Liberal-Labor and New Politics Democrats in the Northeast have produced lopsided electoral results in favor of Democrats in the region. The disappearance of conservative Southern Democrats weakened the party in the South. Consequently, today's Democratic Party is based on the coasts and in the big cities. In the 1970s, New Politics Democrats brought new ideas, attitudes, and lifestyles onto the national stage. As the educated few have now become as numerous as to constitute a multitude within the Democratic Party, the gap between them and Republicans has widened. The Dean movement and the role of the 527 groups in the 2004 election, plus the Netroots cyberactivists and the power of public employees unions, pull the party to the left.

The purposeful action of factions on the right and the left is an unexpected source of contemporary polarization. The tone, style, and attitude toward politics initiated by factions have now taken over the rest of their parties, pitting them against each other in fierce combat, where "one way of thinking about the world is assumed to be morally superior to any other way; [and] one set of political beliefs is considered to be entirely correct and a rival set wholly wrong."[15] Factions within both parties helped destroy the notion that politics was about brokering compromises. Rather, they held it to be a moral activity driven by lofty ideas. By the end of the 1970s, the older, more prosaic conception of American politics had been overthrown.[16] Factions thus increased the importance of ideological combat in American politics.[17]

The Persistence of Factions in American Politics

In concentrating on what factions do, this study has also cast some light on why they form. As "proto-parties," faction members derive a sense of satisfaction from contributing to the attainment of what they believe is a worthy cause. And politicians may be inclined to form factions when they feel that parts of their political personas—their ideas, interests, or associations—are being misrecognized or undervalued by the rest of the party. Likewise, factions often form when a group believes that the party is missing opportunities to win votes by neglecting some part of the electorate that has not been fully mobi-lized. Factional affiliation is thus a key part of the political identity of those involved in party politics because a faction's tone, style, posture, strategies, and tactics are adopted for the sake of changing or maintaining their respec-tive party's "brand name."

Therefore, using and modifying the scheme of analysis developed in this book can open new lines of scholarly inquiry. Some might focus on more con-ceptual and definitional issues, which, if pursued, would further explore the sort of networked links among politicians and activists. Other avenues of in-vestigations are of more historical interest, such the question of whether the New Dealers, for instance, should be considered a party faction as defined here. And still others are of contemporary relevance, such as the development and effects of the Tea Party.

Because factions are, for the most part, made up of elites and concerned with more subtle distinctions than the average voter, their audience is that slice of the population, perhaps 20 percent, that follows politics in Washington. An essential reason why savvy politicians choose to form or associate themselves with factions is that they are instruments of differentiation among other polit-ical elites. Factions help structure the public debate. They can provide a number of powerful shortcuts or cues for the politically active and informed. Factional affiliation can help associated politicians attract media attention, campaign funds, and a cadre of activists. By affiliating themselves with a fac-tion, politicians can also garner a degree of political cover, which can assist them in their eternal quest to claim credit and avoid blame.[18] Finally, Ameri-ca's parties are ill-equipped to act quickly and decisively, which provides in-centives for factional formation, because factions are more agile and adaptable to situations and events, allowing politicians to tie causal stories to their par-ticular affiliations. Major crises, such as economic depressions or environmen-tal disasters, that direct public attention to certain problems can serve as catalysts to form factions as politicians respond by jockeying for position among party elites.

Democratic theory holds that voters must be offered a genuine choice of alternative candidates, programs, and policies. Only by virtue of these alterna-tives is government responsive to the popular will. One-party government is not democratic. But as those on the extremes of the political spectrum enjoy pointing out, two like-minded parties are simply one party government in dis-guise. Downsian logic shows that parties competing for majority status will resemble each other. Yet, happily for America, factions often fragment the parties, offering more choice than a strictly two-party system. Factions offer a limited menu of options just beneath the binary alternatives provided by the two parties but above the teeming multitude of different, and occasionally contradictory, demands of interests and voters that support a party. The opportunity for political elites to form or support competing factions offers the public more variety than the choice between two parties, but not so many choices that the public is crushed under their weight. Factions' intermediate position, although it can complicate the picture of American parties and frustrate majority rule, forms part of the solution to the central problem of republicanism: how to endow the government with enough power to govern, while simultaneously constraining that power to protect rights.

Contemporary interparty polarization forms a hostile climate for factions, but the Tea Party shows their potential for rapid re-emergence. Barring a major regime change, savvy political operators will find reasons to form factions in the future. Therefore, they are certain to continue to play an important role in American party politics. The interplay of factions contributes to firm government while protecting and encouraging political liberty. American institutions are to factions what air is to fire, an element without which it instantly expires. Factions are sown in the nature of our republic, and, on balance, we are better off for it.

APPENDIX

Canvassing Multiple Sources

Following a technique developed by David Mayhew, this study has canvassed multiple sources to identify national intraparty factions in American political history. This meant making multiple sweeps though American history using different sources. Each sweep was roughly calibrated at a different level of generality. This allowed me to capture different properties of factions' makeup as well as their conspicuous actions. By looking at multiple sources I was better able to see the interconnections and links that constitute factional networks across their manifold dimensions. "Data collection" consisted of three sweeps though American political and party history.

I. Works by Historians

1. General period political histories of the United States
2. General histories of the major political parties
3. Histories of the specific factions
4. Biographies of major factional leaders

II. Primary Party Documents

1. Platforms
2. Speeches
3. Congressional votes

III. Newspapers, Magazines

The sweeps through the general political histories and the histories of the major political parties coded for the following elements: the composition, character, and social ties of a faction, combined with its conspicuous actions. To supplement these more general works, a selection of biographies of the relevant factional leaders also needed to be consulted, albeit in a less systematic way. This helped fill out picture of the strategic choices made by political actors in the face of uncertainty.

For a closer look at factions, another set of sweeps through American history was necessary. Party platforms and relevant speeches were then coded for the same characteristics as the history books: mentions of factions, their composition, character, role, and conspicuous actions. A final set of sweeps through newspapers and other contemporary documents was then made to fill out the picture. In the end, I folded these historical sweeps together. For example, if a factional action was captured in each sweep, it was most likely very important, but if it was only captured in one sweep, it may have been less significant. On any one subject, we are likely to see a "family" of overlapping treatments. Convergence will occur on certain items that are thought to be major, but divergence grows and comes to dominate as items are seen to be more peripheral—although the same kind of items may be identified in the peripheral range. The chief remedy for this divergence problem is plural sources. Below are the checklists for each faction.

Faction Checklist

1) Name:
   a) self-ascribed _____
   b) other-ascribed _____
   c) other-ascribed but adopted _____
   d) created by historians _____
2) Structure:
   a) organized _____
   b) fluid _____
   c) mixed _____
3) Approach:
   a) change _____
   b) status-quo _____

4) Identity:
   a) regional _____
      a1. Northeast _____
      a2. South_____
      a3. Midwest_____
      a4. Southwest_____
      a5. West_____
   b) social _____
      b1. education _____
      b2. profession _____
      b3. ethnicity _____
      b4. family_____
   c) values _____
      c1. religion/church _____
      c2. union_____
      c3. associations _____
      c4. periodical readership _____
5) Durability:
   a) long_____
   b) short _____
   c) unknown _____
6) Motivation:
   a) spoils—power group _____
   b) idea—promotional group _____
   c) both _____
   d) neither _____
   e) unknown _____
7) Attitude:
   a) ideological _____
   b) pragmatic _____
   c) both _____
   d) neither_____
   e) unknown _____
8) Positioning:
   a) leftist _____
   b) centrist _____
   c) rightist _____
   d) unknown_____
9) Composition:
   a) personalist _____

b) coalitionist _____
c) mixed _____

10) Cause:
   a) policy/fundamental issue _____
   b) election system/Electoral College_____
   c) crisis/war _____
   d) other _____

11) Objective:
   a) takeover _____
   b) cooperation _____
   c) splinter _____
   d) mix _____

12) Strategy:
   a) presidential _____
   b) congressional _____
   c) both _____

NOTES

Preface

1. Daniel DiSalvo, "The Politics of a Party Faction: The Liberal-Labor Alliance in the Democratic Party, 1948–1972," *Journal of Policy History* 22, no. 3 (Summer 2010).
2. James L. Sundquist, "Needed: A Political Theory of the New Era of Coalition Government in the United States," *Political Science Quarterly* 103 (Winter 1988–1989): 614.
3. Wilson quoted in Sundquist, "Needed," 618.
4. Woodrow Wilson, *Congressional Government: A Study in American Government* (Boston: Houghton Mifflin, 1913, original, 1885); Schattschneider, *Party Government*; APSA Report, "Toward a More Responsible Two-Party System: A Report of the Committee on Political Parties" *American Political Science Review* 44, no. 3 (1950).
5. Leon D. Epstein, "What Happened to the British Party Model," *American Political Science Review* 74 (March 1980): 9–22.
6. For example, see Marc K. Landy and Martin A. Levin, eds., *The New Politics of Public Policy* (Baltimore: Johns Hopkins University Press, 1995); Martin A. Levin, Marc K. Landy, and Martin Shapiro, eds., *Seeking the Center: Politics and Policymaking at the New Century* (Washington, DC: Georgetown University Press, 2001); Anthony King, ed., *The New American Political System* (Washington, DC: AEI Press, 1978). For other works on policy change produced by courts, subcommittees, and bureaucrats, see R. Shep Melnick, *Regulation and the Courts: The Case of the Clean Air Act* (Washington, DC: Brookings Institution, 1983); Melnick, *Between the Lines: Welfare Rights in Court* (Washington, DC: Brookings Institution, 1994); Peter Skerry, *Counting On the Census? Race, Group Identity, and the Evasion of Politics* (Washington, DC: Brookings Institution, 1999); Skerry, "The Charmed Life of Head Start," *The Public Interest* 73 (Fall 1983).
7. James Bryce, *The American Commonwealth*, vol. 2, *The Party System, Public Opinion, Illustrations and Reflections, Social Institutions* (New York: Macmillan & Co., 1888).
8. James Q. Wilson, *Political Organizations*, new ed. (Princeton: Princeton University Press, 1995): 95.
9. E.E. Schattschneider, *Party Government* (New York: Farrar & Rinehart, 1942); V.O. Key, *Southern Politics in State and Nation* (New York: Knopf, 1950); Schattschneider, *Politics, Parties, & Pressure Groups* (New York: Crowell, 1964); Anthony Downs, *An Economic Theory of Democracy* (New York: Harper & Row, 1957).
10. Schattschneider, *Party Government*, 60.
11. John H. Aldrich, *Why Parties? The Origin and Transformation of Political Parties in America* (Chicago: University of Chicago Press, 1995).

194   *Notes to Pages xiv–4*

12. Marty Cohen, David Karol, Hans Noel, and John, Zaller *The Party Decides: Presidential Nominations Before and After Reform* (Chicago: University of Chicago Press, 2008).
13. I thank Daniel Galvin for clarifying this point.
14. David R. Mayhew, *Electoral Realignments: A Critique of an American Genre* (New Haven: Yale University Press, 2002). For a recent defense of realignment, see James W. Ceaser and Andrew Busch, *Red Over Blue: The 2004 Elections and American Politics* (Lanham: Rowman & Littlefield Press, 2005), 21–30; Jeffrey M. Stonecash, Mark D. Brewer, and Mack Mariani, *Diverging Parties: Social Change, Realignment, and Party Polarization* (Boulder, CO: Westview Press, 2003); Mark D. Brewer and Jeffrey M. Stonecash, *Dynamics of American Political Parties* (New York: Cambridge University Press, 2009). The classics of realignment theory are V.O. Key, "A Theory of Critical Elections," *Journal of Politics* 17 (1955): 3–18; Walter Dean Burnham, "Party Systems and the Political process," in William N. Chambers and Burnham, eds., *The American Party Systems: Stages of Political Development* (New York: Oxford University Press, 1967); Burnham, *Critical Elections and the Mainsprings of American Politics* (New York: Norton, 1970); James L. Sundquist, *Dynamics of the Party System: Alignment and Realignment in the United States* (Washington, DC: Brookings Institution, 1973, rev. ed., 1983); Paul Allen Beck, "A Socialization Theory of Realignment," in Richard G. Niemi et al. eds., *The Future of Citizens* (San Francisco: Jossey-Bass, 1974); Burnham, "Critical Realignment: Dead or Alive?" in Byron Shafer ed., *The End of Realignment? Interpreting American Electoral Eras* (Madison: University of Wisconsin Press, 1991).
15. John Gerring, "The Mechanismic Worldview: Thinking Inside the Box," *British Journal of Political Science*, 37 (2007); "What Is a Case Study and What Is It Good for?" *American Political Science Review*, 98, no. 2 (May 2004); *Social Science Methodology: A Critical Framework* (New York: Cambridge University Press, 2001); Henry E. Brady and David Collier, *Rethinking Social Inquiry: Diverse Tools, Shared Standards* (Lanham, MD: Rowman & Littlefield, 2004); Alexander L. George and Andrew Bennett, *Case Studies and Theory Development* (Cambridge: MIT Press, 2005).

Chapter 1

1. Giovanni Sartori, "Guidelines for Concept Analysis," in *Social Science Concepts: A Systematic Analysis*, ed. Giovanni Sartori (Beverly Hills: Sage Publications, 1984); John Gerring, *Social Science Methodology: A Critical Framework* (New York: Cambridge University Press, 2001); "What Is a Case Study and What Is It Good for?" *American Political Science Review* 98 (May 2004): 341–354; Henry E. Brady and David Collier, *Rethinking Social Inquiry: Diverse Tools, Shared Standards* (Lanham, MD: Rowman & Littlefield, 2004), 105–156.
2. Alexis de Tocqueville, *Democracy in America*, trans. and ed. Harvey C. Mansfield and Delba Winthrop (Chicago: University of Chicago Press, 2000), 411.
3. Max Weber, *The Protestant Ethic and the Spirit of Capitalism*, trans. Talcott Parsons (New York: Scribner, 1930), 47–48.
4. Intraparty factions at the state level have been an object of study since V.O. Key's *Southern Politics in State and Nation* (New York: Alfred Knopf, 1949). For example, Allan P. Sindler, "Bifactional Rivalry as an Alternative to Two-Party Competition in Louisiana," *American Political Science Review* 49, no. 3 (September 1955): 641–662. At the national level, Howard L. Reiter has done some of the only systematic work on national factions by focusing on presidential nominating conventions. See Reiter, "Creating a Bifactional Structure: The Democrats in the 1940s," *Political Science Quarterly* 116, no. 1 (Spring 2001); Reiter, "Party Factionalism: National Conventions in the New Era," *American Politics Quarterly* 8(2) (July 1980); Reiter, "Why Did the Whigs Die (And Why Didn't the Democrats)? Evidence from National Nominating Conventions," *Studies in American Political Development*, 10, no. 2 (Fall 1996); Reiter, "The Bases of

Progressivism within the Major Parties: Evidence from the National Conventions," *Social Science History* 22, no. 2 (Spring 1998); Reiter, "Factional Persistence within Parties in the United States," *Party Politics* (May 2004). Nicol C. Rae has studied both the Southern Democrats and the Liberal Republicans; and Kenneth S. Baer has analyzed the New Democrats as an Intraparty faction. Rae, *The Decline and Fall of the Liberal Republicans* (Cambridge: Oxford University Press, 1989); Rae, *Southern Democrats* (New York: Oxford University Press, 1994); Baer, *Reinventing Democrats: The Politics of Liberalism from Reagan to Clinton* (Lawrence: University of Kansas Press, 2000). For a historical work that treats factions in the nineteenth and twentieth centuries, see Ralph M. Goldman, *The National Party Chairmen and Committees: Factionalism at the Top* (Armonk, NY: M.E. Sharpe, 1990). For work on contemporary party factions, see Gregory Koger, Seth Masket, and Hans Noel, "Cooperative Party Factions in American Politics," *American Politics Research* 38, no. 1 (January 2010).

5. Robert Michels, *Political Parties: A Sociological Study of the Oligrachical Tendencies of Modern Democracy*, intro. Seymour Martin Lipset (New York: Free Press, 1998); Moisei Ostrogorski, *Democracy and the Organization of Political Parties* (New Brunswick: Transaction Publishers, 1981).

6. John Gerring, *Party Ideologies in America, 1828–1996* (New York: Cambridge University Press 1998), 24.

7. David Hume, "Of Parties in General," in Eugene F. Miller ed., *David Hume, Essays: Moral, Political, and Literary*, rev. ed. (Indianapolis: Liberty Fund Press, 1985), 55.

8. In *The Federalist*, Madison defines a faction as a "number of citizens . . . who are united and actuated by some common impulse of passion, or of interest, adverse to the rights of other citizens, or to the permanent and aggregate interests of the community." Clinton Rossiter ed., *The Federalist Papers*, intro. Charles Kesler (New York: Mentor Book, 1999), 45.

9. Samuel P. Huntington, *Political Order in Changing Societies* (New Haven: Yale University Press, 1968); Frank P. Belloni and Dennis C. Beller, eds., *Faction Politics: Political Parties and Factionalism in Comparative Perspective* (Santa Barbara: CLIO Press, 1978); William N. Chambers, *Political Parties in a New Nation: 1776–1806* (New York: Oxford University Press, 1962).

10. Harold D. Lasswell writes, "a faction seems to subordinate the public good to private gain," in "Factions," *Encyclopedia of the Social Sciences*, 6:51, 51; Richard Hofstadter, *The Idea of a Party System* (Berkeley: University of California Press, 1969), 9–22; Giovanni Sartori, *Parties and Party Systems: A Framework for Analysis*, vol.1 (New York: Cambridge University Press, 1976), 4–9; Pierre Rosanvallon, "Factions et partis," in *Dictionnaire de philosophie politique*, eds. Philippe Raynaud and Stéphane Rials (Paris: PUF, 1996), 449–453.

11. For a further discussion of terminological issues, see Richard Rose, "Parties, Factions, and Tendencies in Britain," *Political Studies* 12 (February 1964): 33–46.

12. David Hine, "Factionalism in Western European Parties: A Framework for Analysis," *West European Politics* 5, no. 1 (1982); Richard W. Nicholas, "Factions: A Comparative Analysis," in S.W. Schmidt, ed., *Friends, Followers, and Factions* (Berkeley: University of California Press, 1977); Raphael Zariski, "Party Factions and Comparative Politics: Some Preliminary Observations," *Midwest Journal of Political Science* 4, no. 1 (February 1960): 27–51; Norman K. Nicholson, "The Factional Model and the Study of Politics," *Comparative Political Studies* 5, no. 3 (October 1972): 291–314.

13. Anthony Downs, *An Economic Theory of Democracy* (New York: Harper & Row, 1957), 25.

14. John H. Aldrich, *Why Parties? The Origin and Transformation of Political Parties in America* (Chicago: University of Chicago Press, 1995), 283–284.

15. Joseph A. Schlesinger, "On the Theory of Party Organization," *Journal of Politics* 46, no. 2 (1984): 379.

16. Marty Cohen, David Karol, Hans Noel, and John Zaller, *The Party Decides: Presidential Nominations Before and After Reform* (Chicago: University of Chicago Press, 2008), 88.

17. James A. Stimson, Michael B. MacKuen, Robert S. Erikson, "Dynamic representation" *American Political Science Review* 89 (1995): 543–565.

18. Bernard Grofman, "Downs and Two-Party Convergence," *Annual Review of Political Science* 7 (June 2004): 25–46; Donald Wittman, "Candidate Motivation: A Synthesis of Alternative Theories," *American Political Science Review* 77 (March 1983): 142–157. Philip Converse, "The Nature of Belief Systems in Mass Publics," in *Ideology and Discontent*, ed. David Apter (New York: Free Press, 1964); Michael Lewis-Beck et al., *The American Voter Revisited* (Ann Arbor: University of Michigan Press, 2008); John Zaller, *The Nature and Origins of Mass Opinion* (New York: Cambridge University Press, 1992).

19. Larry M. Bartels, "Uninformed Votes: Information Effects in Presidential Elections," *American Journal of Political Science* 40 (1996): 194–230.

20. V.O. Key, *Parties, Politics, and Pressure Groups*, 568. For an argument that the public pays closer attention to issues than previously thought, see William J.M. Claggett and Byron Shafer, *The American Public Mind: The Issue Structure of Mass Politics in the Postwar United States* (New York: Cambridge University Press, 2010).

21. Larry M. Bartels, *Unequal Democracy: The Political Economy of the New Gilded Age* (Princeton: Princeton University Press & Russell Sage Foundation, 2008), 287.

22. Steven Ansolabehere, Charles Stewart, and James Snyder, "Candidate Positioning in House Elections," *American Journal of Political Science* 45, no. 1 (2001); Brandice Canes-Wrone, David W. Brady, and John F. Cogan, "Out of Step, Out of Office: Electoral Accountability and House Members' Voting," *American Political Science Review* 96 (2002): 127–140; Morris Fiorina, *Culture War? The Myth of Polarized America* (New York: Pearson Longman, 2005).

23. Cohen et al., *The Party Decides*, 89–92; Keith Poole and Howard Rosenthal, "U.S. Presidential Elections, 1968–1980: A Spatial Analysis," *American Journal of Political Science* 28, no. 2 (1984): 283–312; Jacob Hacker and Paul Pierson, "Abandoning the Middle: The Bush Tax Cuts and the Limits of Democratic Control," *Perspectives on Politics* 3, no. 1 (2005): 33–53.

24. Norman Schofield, *The Spatial Model of Politics* (New York: Routledge, 2008), 164–165; Martin Levin, Daniel DiSalvo, and Martin Shapiro, *Building Coalitions, Making Policy* (Baltimore: Johns Hopkins University Press, 2012).

25. See Wilson Carey McWilliams, "The Two Tier Polity," and James Q. Wilson, "New Politics, New Policies, Old Publics," in Marc Landy, Martin Levin, and Martin Shapiro, eds., *The New Politics of Public Policy* (Baltimore: Johns Hopkins University Press, 1995).

26. Samuel Huntington, *American Politics: The Promise of Disharmony* (Cambridge: Harvard University Press, 1983).

27. David A. Horowitz, *Beyond Left & Right: Insurgents & the Establishment* (Urbana: University of Illinois Press, 1997), xi–xiii, 1–4.

28. R. Douglas Arnold, *The Logic of Congressional Action* (New Haven: Yale University Press, 1990); R. Kent Weaver, "The Politics of Blame Avoidance," *Journal of Public Policy* 6 (1986): 371–398.

29. On the notion of a public philosophy, see James W. Ceaser, *What Is the Public Philosophy? An Inaugural Lecture Delivered Before the University of Oxford* (Oxford: Cambridge University Press, 2000); Michael J. Sandel, *Democracy's Discontent: America in Search of a Public Philosophy* (Cambridge: Harvard University Press, 1998); Sandel, *Public Philosophy: Essays on Morality and Politics* (Cambridge: Harvard University Press, 2005); Samuel Beer, "In Search of a New Public Philosophy" in Anthony King, ed. *The New American Political System* (Washington, DC: AEI Press, 1978); Walter Lippmann, *Essays in the Public Philosophy* (Boston: Little, Brown, 1955). For a definition of the

nettlesome concept of ideology, see John Gerring, "Ideology: A Definitional Analysis," *Political Research Quarterly* 50, no. 4 (December 1997): 657–694.

30. E. E. Schattschneider, *The Semisovereign People: A Realist's View of Democracy in America* (New York: Holt, Rinehart and Winston, 1960), 62.

31. Samuel Lubell, *The Future of American Politics* (New York: Harper & Row, 1952).

32. Earle Dudley Ross, *The Liberal Republican Movement*, intro. John Sproat (Seattle: University of Washington Press, 1917, 1970); Matthew G. Downey, "Horace Greeley and the Politicians: The Liberal Republican Convention in 1872," *Journal of American History* 53 (March 1967): 727–750; William Gillette, "Election of 1872," in *The History of American Presidential Elections*, vol. 2, ed. Arthur M. Schlesinger Jr. (New York: Chelsea House Publishers, 1971), 1304, 1306; John M. Dobson, *Politics in the Gilded Age: A New Perspective on Reform* (New York: Praeger Publishers, 1972), 52, 57, 108–120; Gerald W. McFarland, "The Mugwumps and the Emergence of Modern America," in McFarland, ed., *Moralists or Pragmatists? The Mugwumps, 1884–1900* (New York: Simon and Schuster, 1975), 1–16; McFarland, *Mugwumps, Morals & Politics, 1884–1920* (Amherst: University of Massachusetts Press, 1975), 1–80; William Gillette, *Retreat from Reconstruction, 1869–1879* (Baton Rouge: Louisiana State University Press, 1979), 61; Michael Les Benedict, "The Politics of Reconstruction," in John F. Marszalek and Wilson D. Miscamble, eds., *American Political History: Essays on the State of the Discipline* (Notre Dame: University of Notre Dame Press, 1997), 89–90; Xi Wang, *The Trial of Democracy: Black Suffrage and Northern Republicans, 1860–1910* (Athens: University of Georgia Press, 1997), 86, 103–106, 138–140, 159, 183–184; David M. Tucker, *Mugwumps: Public Moralists of the Gilded Age* (Columbia: University of Missouri Press, 1998); Hans L. Trefousse, *Carl Schurz* (Knoxville: University of Tennessee Press, 1982); Ari Hoogenboom, "Civil Service Reform and Public Morality," in H. Wayne Morgan, ed., *The Gilded Age*, rev. ed. (Syracuse, NY: Syracuse University Press, 1970).

33. Elizabeth Sanders, *The Roots of Reform: Farmers, Workers, and the American State, 1877–1917* (Chicago: University of Chicago Press, 1999), 5, 389; David Sarasohn, *The Party of Reform: Democrats in the Progressive Era* (Jackson: University of Mississippi, 1989); R. Hal Williams, "'Dry Bones and Dead Language': The Democratic Party," in H. Wayne Morgan ed., *The Gilded Age*, rev. ed., (Syracuse, NY: Syracuse University Press); Robert Harrison, *Congress, Progressive Reform, and the New American State* (New York: Cambridge University Press, 2004); John J. Broesamle, "The Democrats from Bryan to Wilson," in Lewis L. Gould, ed., *The Progressive Era* (Syracuse, NY: Syracuse University Press, 1974), 83–113; J. Rogers Hollingsworth, *The Whirligig of Politics: Democracy from Cleveland to Bryan* (Chicago: University of Chicago Press, 1963); Gene Clanton, *Congressional Populism and the Crisis of the 1890s* (Lawrence: University of Kansas, 1998); John D. Hicks, *The Populist Revolt* (Minneapolis: University of Minnesota Press, 1931); Lawrence D. Goodwyn, *The Populist Moment: A Short History of Agrarian Revolt in America* (New York: Oxford University Press, 1978); Robert C. McMath, *American Populism: A Social History 1877–1898* (New York: Hill and Wang, 1990); Norman Pollack, *The Populist Response to Industrial America: Midwestern Political Thought* (Cambridge: Harvard University Press, 1962); Anne Fior Scott, "A Progressive Wind in the South," *Journal of Southern History* 29 (February 1963): 52–70; Dewey Grantham, *Southern Progressivism: The Reconciliation of Progress and Tradition* (Knoxville: University of Tennessee Press, 1983); Dewey W. Grantham, "Southern Congressional Leaders and the New Freedom, 1913–1917," *Journal of Southern History* 13 (November 1947): 439–459; Arthur S. Link, "The South and the 'New Freedom': An Interpretation," *American Scholar* 20 (Summer 1951): 314–324; Link, "Woodrow Wilson and the Democratic Party," *Review of Politics* 18 (April 1956); Richard M. Abrams, "Woodrow Wilson and the Southern Congressmen, 193–1916," *Journal of Southern History* 22 (November 1956): 417–437; Michael Kazin, *A Godly Hero: The Life of Williams Jennings Bryan* (New York: Knopf, 2006); Robert W. Cherny, *A Righteous Cause: The Life of*

William Jennings Bryan (Boston: Little, Brown & Co., 1985); Louis W. Koenig, *Bryan: A Political Biography of William Jennings Bryan* (New York: Putnam, 1917); Arthur S. Link, *Woodrow Wilson and the Progressive Era, 1910–1917* (New York: Harper Bros., 1954).

34. Nunn quoted in *CQ Weekly Report*, March 9, 1985. William Galston and Elaine Kamarck, *The Politics of Evasion: Democrats and the Presidency* (Washington, DC: Progressive Policy Institute, 1989); Galston, "Incomplete Victory," in *Varieties of Progressivism*, ed. Peter Berkowitz (Stanford: Hoover Institution Press, 2005); John F. Hale, "The Making of the New Democrats," *Political Science Quarterly* 110 (Summer 1995); Kenneth Baer, *Reinventing Democrats: The Politics of Liberalism from Reagan to Clinton* (Lawrence: University of Kansas Press, 2000); Philip Klinkner, "Democratic Party Ideology in the 1990s: New Democrats or Modern Republicans?" in John K. White and John C. Green, eds., *The Politics of Ideas: Intellectual Challenges Facing the American Political Parties* (Albany: State University of New York Press, 1999); Franklin Foer, "Center Forward? The Fate of the New Democrats," in Peter Berkowitz, ed., *Varieties of Progresssivism* (Stanford: Hoover Institution Press, 2005); Alex Waddan, *Clinton's Legacy? A New Democrat in Governance* (New York: Palgrave, 2002); Sidney M. Milkis, *Political Parties and Constitutional Government: Remaking American Democracy* (Baltimore: Johns Hopkins University Press, 1999); Colin Campbell and Bert Rockman, eds., *The Clinton Legacy* (New York: Chatham House, 2000).

35. Norman M. Wilensky, *Conservatives in the Progressive Era: The Taft Republicans of 1912* (Gainesville: University of Florida Press, 1965), 35.

36. George E. Mowry, "Election of 1912," in Arthur M. Schlesinger, Jr., ed., *The History of American Presidential Elections, 1789–1968*, vol. 3 (New York: Chelsea House Publishers, 1971), 2135–2166; George E. Mowry, *The Era of Theodore Roosevelt: 1900–1912* (New York: Harper & Brothers, 1958); Arthur A. Ekirch, Jr., *Progressivism in America: A Study of the Era from Theodore Roosevelt to Woodrow Wilson* (New York: New Viewpoints, 1974); Russel Nye, *Midwestern Progressive Politics: A Historical Study of Its Origins and Development, 1870–1958* (East Lansing: Michigan State University Press, 1959); Lewis L. Gould, "The Republicans Under Roosevelt and Taft," in Lewis L. Gould, ed. *The Progressive Era* (Syracuse, NY: Syracuse University Press, 1974); Robert Harrison, *Congress, Progressive Reform, and the New American State* (New York: Cambridge University Press, 2004); John M. Cooper, *The Warrior and the Priest* (Cambridge: Harvard University Press, 1983); Paolo E. Coletta, *The Presidency of William Howard Taft* (Lawrence: University of Kansas Press, 1973); Nathaniel W. Stephenson, *Nelson W. Aldrich: A Leader in American Politics* (New York: Scribner's, 1930); Leland Livingston Sage, *William Boyd Allison: A Study in Practical Politics* (Iowa City: State Historical Society of Iowa, 1956).

37. Ira Katznelson, *When Affirmative Action Was White: An Untold History of Racial Inequality in Twentieth Century America* (New York: W.W. Norton & Co., 2005); Ira Katznelson, Kim Geiger, and Daniel Kryder, "Limiting Liberalism: The Southern Veto in Congress, 1933–1950," *Political Science Quarterly* 108 (Summer 1993): 296–229; Sean Farhang and Ira Katznelson, "The Southern Imposition: Congress and Labor in the New and Fair Deals," *Studies in American Political Development* 19 (2005).

38. James T. Patterson, *Congressional Conservatism and the New Deal: The Growth of the Conservative Coalition in Congress, 1933–1939* (Lexington: University of Kentucky Press, 1967); Nicol C. Rae, *Southern Democrats* (New York: Oxford University Press, 1994); Herbert S. Parmet, *The Democrats: The Years After FDR* (New York: Macmillan Publishing Co., 1976); Bruce J. Schulman, *From Cotton Belt to Sunbelt: Federal Policy, Economic Development, and the Transformation of the South, 1938–1980* (Durham, NC: Duke University Press, 1994); Barbara Griffith, *The Crisis of American Labor: Operation Dixie and the Defeat of the CIO* (Philadelphia: Temple University Press, 1988).

39. Eric Foner, *Reconstruction, 1863–1877* (New York: Harper & Row, 1988); H. Wayne Morgan, "The Republican Party 1876–1893," in Arthur M. Schlesinger Jr., ed., *History of U. S. Political Parties*, vol. 2 (New York: Chatham House, 1972); David M. Jordan, *Roscoe Conkling of New York: Voice in the Senate* (Ithaca, NY: Cornell University Press, 1971); William G. Eidson, "Who Were the Stalwarts?" *Mid-America* 52 (October 1970); Allan Peskin, "Who Were the Stalwarts? Who Were Their Rivals? Republican Factions in the Gilded Age," *Political Science Quarterly* 99, no. 4 (Winter 1984–1985); Morton Keller, *Affairs of State: Public Life in Late Nineteenth-Century America* (Cambridge: Harvard University Press, 1977); Matthew Josephson, *The Politicos* (New York: Harcourt, Brace & World, 1966); H. Wayne Morgan, *From Hayes to McKinley: National Party Politics, 1877–1896* (Syracuse, NY: Syracuse University Press, 1969); Ralph M. Goldman, *The National Party Chairmen and Committees: Factionalism at the Top* (New York: M.E. Sharpe, 1990); Xi Wang, *The Trial of Democracy: Black Suffrage and Northern Republicans, 1860–1910* (Athens: University of Georgia Press, 1997).

40. Russel Nye, *Midwestern Progressive Politics: A Historical Study of Its Origins and Development, 1870–1958* (East Lansing: Michigan State University Press, 1959); James L. Sundquist, *Dynamics of the Party System: Alignment and Realignment of Political Parties in the United States* (Washington, DC: Brookings Institution, 1983); Sundquist, *Decline and Resurgence of Congress* (Washington, DC: Brookings Institution, 1982); Howard Reiter, "The Bases of Progressivism within the Major Parties: Evidence from the National Conventions," *Social Science History* 22, no. 2 (Spring 1998); Stephen Skowronek, *Building a New American State: The Expansion of National Administrative Capacities* (New York: Cambridge University Press, 1982); Robert Harrison, *Congress, Progressive Reform, and the New American State* (New York: Cambridge University Press, 2004); Richard Hofstadter, *The Age of Reform: From Bryan to F.D.R.* (New York: Random House, 1956); Richard L. McCormick, ed., *The Party Period and Public Policy: American Politics from the Age of Jackson to the Progressive Era* (New York: Oxford University Press, 1986); Claude G. Bowers, *Beveridge and the Progressive Era* (New York: Literary Guild, 1932).

41. James L. Sundquist, *Politics and Policy: The Eisenhower, Kennedy, and Johnson Years* (Washington, DC: Brookings Institution, 1968); J. David Greenstone, *Labor in American Politics* (Chicago: University of Chicago Press, 1969); Nelson Lichtenstein, *The Most Dangerous Man in Detroit: Walter Reuther and the Fate of the American Labor Movement* (New York: Basic Books, 1995); Julian E. Zelizer, *On Capitol Hill: The Struggle to Reform Congress and Its Consequences, 1948–2000* (New York: Cambridge University Press, 2004); Karen Orren, "Union Politics and Postwar Liberalism in the United States, 1946–1979," *Studies in American Political Development* 1 (1986): 219–228; Taylor Dark, *Labor and the Democratic Party: An Enduring Alliance* (Ithaca, NY: Cornell University Press, 1999); Steven M. Gillon, *Politics and Vision: The ADA and American Liberalism, 1947–1985* (New York: Oxford University Press, 1987); Kevin Boyle, ed., *Organized Labor and American Politics, 1894–1994: The Labor-Liberal Alliance* (Albany: State University of New York Press, 1998); Mark. F. Ferber, "The Formation of the Democratic Study Group," in Nelson Polsby, ed., *Congressional Behavior* (New York: Random House, 1971); Arthur G. Stevens et al., "Mobilization of Liberal Strength in the House, 1955–1970: The Democratic Study Group," *American Political Science Review* 68 (June 1974): 667–681; Michael Foley, *The New Senate: Liberal Influence on a Conservative Institution, 1959–1972* (New Haven: Yale University Press, 1980).

42. Paul Berman, *A Tale of Two Utopias: The Political Journey of the Generation of 1968* (New York: W.W. Norton, 1986); James W. Ceaser, *Presidential Selection: Theory and Development* (Princeton University Press, 1979); Byron E. Shafer, *Quiet Revolution: The Struggle for the Democratic Party and the Shaping of Post-Reform Politics* (New York: Russell Sage Foundation, 1983); Richard A. Harris and Sidney M. Milkis, *The Politics of Regulatory Change: A Tale of Two Agencies*, 2nd ed. (New York: Oxford University Press, 1996);

Jeffrey M. Berry, *The New Liberalism: The Rising Power of Citizen Groups* (Washington, DC: Brookings Institution, 1999); Berry, *Lobbying for the People: The Political Behavior of Public Interest Groups* (Princeton: Princeton University Press, 1977); Steve Fraser and Gary Gerstle, eds., *The Rise and Fall of the New Deal Order, 1930–1980* (Princeton: Princeton University Press, 1989); Byron Shafer, *The Two Majorities and the Puzzle of Modern American Politics* (Lawrence: University of Kansas Press, 2004), 157–169; Lawrence S. Rothenberg, *Linking Citizens to Government: Interest Group Politics at Common Cause* (New York: Cambridge University Press, 1992); Andrew McFarland, *Common Cause: Lobbying in the Public Interest* (New York: Chatham House, 1984); William M. Lunch, *The Nationalization of American Politics* (Berkeley: University of California Press, 1987), 24–30.

43. Dan Balz and Ronald Brownstein, *Storming the Gates: Protest Politics and the Republican Revival* (Boston: Little, Brown, 1996); Andrew E. Busch, *Reagan's Victory: The Presidential Election of 1980 and the Rise of the Right* (Lawrence: University of Kansas Press, 2005); William F. Connelly, Jr., and John J. Pitney, Jr., *Congress' Permanent Minority? Republicans in the U.S. House* (Lantham, MD: Rowman & Littlefield Publishers, 1994); Lisa McGirr, *Suburban Warriors: The Origins of the New American Right* (Princeton: Princeton University Press, 2001); John A. Andrew III, *The Other Side of the Sixties: Young Americans for Freedom and the Rise of Conservative Politics* (New Brunswick, NJ: Rutgers University Press, 1997); Rick Perlstein, *Before the Storm: Barry Goldwater and the Unmaking of the American Consensus* (New York: Hill and Wang, 2001); Jerome L. Himmelstein, *To The Right: The Transformation of American Conservatism* (Berkeley: University of California Press, 1990); Godfrey Hodgson, *The World Turned Right Side Up: A History of the Conservative Ascendancy in America* (Boston: Houghton-Mifflin, 1996); Douglas L. Koopman, *Hostile Takeover: The House Republican Party, 1980–1995* (Lanham, MD: Rowman & Littlefield, 1996); Jeffrey Hart, *The Making of the American Conservative Mind: The National Review and Its Times* (Wilmington, DE: ISI Books, 2005); Sidney Blumenthal, *The Rise of the Counter-Establishment: From Conservative Ideology to Political Power* (New York: Harper & Row, 1985); John Micklethwait and Adrian Wooldridge, *The Right Nation: Conservative Power in America* (New York: Penguin Press, 2004); Richard Viguerie, *The New Right: We're Ready to Lead* (Washington, DC: Viguerie, 1980); George H. Nash, *The Conservative Intellectual Movement in America Since 1945* (New York: Basic Books, 1976); Mary C. Brennan, *Turning Right in the Sixties: The Conservative Capture of the GOP* (Chapel Hill: University of North Carolina Press, 1995); Lee Edwards, *The Conservative Revolution: The Movement that Remade America* (New York: Free Press, 1999); Donald T. Critchlow, *The Conservative Ascendancy: The GOP Right Made Political History* (Cambridge: Harvard University Press, 2007); William C. Berman, *America's Right Turn: From Nixon to Bush* (Baltimore: Johns Hopkins Press, 1994); Brian J. Glenn and Steven M. Teles, *Conservatism and American Political Development* (New York: Oxford University Press, 2009); Kim Philips-Fein, *Invisible Hands: The Making of the Conservative Movement from the New Deal to Ronald Reagan* (New York: W.W. Norton, 2009); Matthew D. Lassiter, *The Silent Majority: Suburban Politics in the Sunbelt South* (Princeton: Princeton University Press, 2007).

44. Nicol C. Rae, *The Decline and Fall of the Liberal Republicans* (Cambridge: Oxford University Press, 1989); Stephen Hess and David Broder, *The Republican Establishment: The Present and Future of the GOP* (New York: Harper & Row, 1967); Donald B. Johnson, *The Republican Party and Wendell Willkie* (Urbana: University of Illinois Press, 1960); Fred I. Greenstein, *The Hidden Hand Presidency: Eisenhower as Leader* (New York: Basic Books, 1982); Chester J. Pach, Jr., and Elmo Richardson, *The Presidency of Dwight D. Eisenhower* (Lawrence: University of Kansas Press, 1991); Clyde P. Weed, *The Nemesis of Reform: The Republican Party During the New Deal* (New York: Columbia University Press, 1994); Richard N. Smith, *Thomas E. Dewey and His Times* (New York: Simon &

Schuster, 1982); Byron E. Shafer, *The Two Majorities and the Puzzle of Modern American Politics* (Lawrence: University of Kansas Press, 2003), 143–156; Cornelius P. Cotter, "Eisenhower as Party Leader," *Political Science Quarterly* 98 (1983).

45. Richard Welch, *George Frisbie Hoar and the Half-Breed Republicans* (Cambridge: Harvard University Press, 1971); Lewis L. Gould, *The Grand Old Party* (New York: Random House, 2003); Stanley P. Hirshson, *Farewell to the Bloody Shirt: Northern Republicans and the Southern Negro, 1877–1893* (Bloomington: Indiana University Press, 1962); Mark Wahlgren Summers, *Rum, Romanism & Rebellion: The Making of a President 1884* (Chapel Hill: University of North Carolina Press, 2000); Heather C. Richardson, *The Death of Reconstruction: Race, Labor, and Politics in the Post–Civil War North, 1865–1901* (Cambridge: Harvard University Press, 2001); David J. Rothman, *Politics and Power: The United States Senate, 1869–1901* (Cambridge: Harvard University Press, 1966); A. James Reichley, *The Life of the Parties: A History of American Political Parties* (Lanham, MD: Rowman & Littlefield, 1992).

46. Sharon Jarvis, *The Talk of the Party: Political Labels, Symbolic Capital, and American Life* (Lanham, MD: Rowman & Littlefield, 2005).

47. E.E. Schattschneider, "The United States: The Functional Approach to Party Government," in Sigmund Neumann, ed., *Modern Political Parties: Approaches to Comparative Politics* (Chicago: University of Chicago Press, 1965), 213.

48. Richard Bensel, *The Political Economy of American Industrialization, 1877–1900* (New York: Cambridge University Press, 2000), 529; Bensel, *Sectionalism and American Political Development, 1880–1980* (Madison: University of Wisconsin Press, 1984); Nicole Mellow, *The State of Disunion: The Regional Sources of Modern American Partisanship*, 4th ed. (Baltimore: Johns Hopkins University Press, 2008).

49. David R. Mayhew, "Wars and American Politics," *Perspectives on Politics* 3, no. 3 (Fall 2006); Robert P. Saldin, *War, the American State, and Politics since 1898* (New York: Cambridge University Press, 2010).

50. Nelson Polsby, "Coalition and Faction in American Politics: An Institutional View," in Seymour Martin Lipset, ed., *Emerging Coalitions in American Politics* (San Francisco: Institute for Contemporary Studies, 1978): 103–126.

51. Edmund Burke, "Thoughts on the Cause of the Present Discontents (1780)," in *Select Works of Edmund Burke*, ed. E.J. Payne (Indianapolis: Liberty Fund, 1999).

Chapter 2

1. James Madison, *Federalist No. 10*, in Clinton Rossiter ed., *The Federalist Papers*, intro. Charles Kesler (New York: Mentor Book, 1999); George Washington, "Farewell Address of 1796," http://avalon.law.yale.edu/18th_century/washing.asp (accessed July 21, 2011); Roberto Michels, *Political Parties: A Sociological Study of the Oligarchical Tendencies of Modern Democracy*, intro. Seymour Martin Lipset (New York: Free Press, 1998); Moisei Ostrogorski, *Democracy and the Organization of Political Parties* (New Brunswick, NJ: Transaction Publishers, 1981). The most recent statement of this sort of skepticism of political parties was made by Benjamin Barber, "The Undemocratic Party System: Citizenship in an Elite/Mass Society," in *Political Parties in the Eighties*, ed. Robert A. Goldwin (Washington, DC: AEI Press, 1980), 34–49.

2. James Bryce, *The American Commonwealth*, vol. 2, pt. 3 (Chicago: Sergel, 1891); Maurice Duverger, *Political Parties*, trans. Barbara and Robert North (New York: Wiley & Sons, 1954); Pendleton Herring, *The Politics of Democracy* (New York: W.W. Norton, 1940); Samuel J. Eldersveld, *Political Parties* (Chicago: Rand McNally, 1964); Robert Dahl, *Pluralist Democracy in the United States* (Chicago: Rand McNally, 1967).

3. Leon D. Epstein, *Political Parties in the American Mold* (Madison: University of Wisconsin Press, 1986), 19–30.

4. E.E. Schattschneider, *Party Government* (New York: Rinehart, 1942), 1.

5. Woodrow Wilson, *Congressional Government: A Study in American Government* (Boston: Houghton Mifflin, 1913, original, 1885); A. Lawrence Lowell, *The Government of England*, vol. 1 (New York: Macmillan, 1909), 467–468.

6. Henry Jones Ford, *The Rise and Growth of American Politics: A Sketch of Constitutional Development* (New York: Macmillan, 1898); Edward M. Sait, *American Parties and Elections* (New York: Century Co., 1927); Herbert Agar, *The Price of Union* (Boston: Houghton-Mifflin, 1950); Arthur N. Holcombe, *Political Parties of To-day* (New York: Harper & Bros., 1924); Edward C. Banfield, "In Defense of the American Party System," in *Political Parties, U.S.A.*, ed. Robert Goodwin (Chicago: Rand McNally, 1964), 21–39; Frank Sorauf, *Political Parties in the American System* (Boston: Little Brown, 1964).

7. Schattschneider, *Party Government*; Schattschneider, *The Struggle for Party Government* (Ann Arbor: University of Michigan Press, 1948); Committee on Political Parties, American Political Science Association, "Toward a Responsible Two-Party System," *American Political Science Review* 44, supplement (September 1950); Austin Ranney, *The Doctrine of Responsible Party Government* (Urbana: University of Illinois Press, 1954); Gerald Pomper, "Toward a Responsible Two-Party System? What, Again?" *Journal of Politics* 33 (November 1971): 916–940.

8. See, for example: David S. Broder, *The Party's Over: The Failure of Politics in America* (New York: Harper & Row, 1971); Gerald Pomper, ed., *Party Renewal in America: Theory and Practice* (New York: Praeger, 1980); Joel L. Fleishman, ed., *The Future of American Political Parties: The Challenge of Governance* (Englewood, NJ: Prentice-Hall, 1982); Walter Dean Burnham, *The Current Crisis in American Politics* (New York: Oxford University Press, 1982); William Crotty, *American Parties in Decline* (Boston: Little, Brown, 1984); Martin P. Wattenberg, *The Decline of American Political Parties, 1952–1980* (Cambridge: Harvard University Press, 1984); David E. Price, *Bringing Back the Parties* (Washington, DC: CQ Press, 1984); Xandra Kayden and Eddie Mahe, Jr., *The Party Goes On: The Persistence of the Two-Party System in the United States* (New York: Basic Books, 1985).

9. Norman Nie, Sidney Verba, and John Petrocik, *The Changing American Voter* (Cambridge: Harvard University Press, 1976), 346–347.

10. Donald Green, Bradley Palmquist, and Eric Schickler, *Partisan Hearts and Minds: Political Parties and the Social Identities of Voters* (New Haven: Yale University Press, 2002).

11. Geoffrey C. Layman, Thomas M. Carsey, and Juliana Menasce Horowitz, "Party Polarization in American Politics: Characteristics, Causes, and Consequences," *Annual Review Political Science* 9 (2006): 83–110; Geoffrey C. Layman, Thomas M. Carsey, John C. Green, Richard Herrera, Rosalyn Cooperman, "Activists and Conflict Extension in American Party Politics," *American Political Science Review* 104, no. 2 (May 2010).

12. Jon R. Bond and Richard Fleisher, eds. *Polarized Politics: Congress and the President in a Partisan Era* (Washington, DC: CQ Press, 2000); Jeffery M. Stonecash, Mark D. Brewer, and Mack D. Mariani, *Diverging Parties: Social Change, Realignment, and Party Polarization* (Boulder, CO: Westview Press, 2003); John C. Green and Paul S. Herrnson, eds. *Responsible Partisanship?* (Lawrence: University of Press Kansas, 2002); Fleisher and Bond, "The shrinking middle in the U.S. Congress," *British Journal of Political Science* 34 (2004): 429–451; John H. Aldrich and David W. Rohde, "Congressional Committees in a Partisan Era," in Lawrence C. Dodd and Bruce I. Oppenheimer, eds. *Congress Reconsidered* (8th ed., Washington, DC: CQ Press, 2005); Sean M. Theriault, *Party Polarization in Congress* (New York: Cambridge University Press, 2007); Nolan McCarty, Keith T. Poole, and Howard Rosenthal, *Polarized America: The Dance of Ideology and Unequal Riches* (Cambridge: MIT Press, 2002); Barbara Sinclair, *Party Wars: Polarization and the Politics of National Policymaking* (Norman: University of Oklahoma Press, 2006); Pietro Nivola and David Brady eds., *Red and Blue Nation? Consequences and Corrections of America's Polarized Politics* (Washington, DC: Brookings

Institution, 2007); Earl Black and Merle Black, *Divided America: The Ferocious Power Struggle in American Politics* (New York: Simon & Schuster, 2008); Marc Hetherington and Jonathan Weiler, *Authoritarianism and Political Polarization* (New York: Cambridge, 2009); Morris Fiorina, Samuel Abrams, and Jeremy Pope, *What Culture Wars? The Myth of Political Polarization in America* (New York: Longman, 2004); Morris Fiorina and Samuel Abrams, "Political Polarization in the American Public," *Annual Review of Political Science* 11 (2008): 563–588; Alan I. Abramowitz, *The Disappearing Center: Engaged Citizens, Polarization, and American Democracy* (New Haven: Yale University Press, 2010); Alan I. Abramowitz and Kyle Saunders, "Can't We All Just Get Along? The Reality of Polarized America," *The Forum: A Journal of Applied Research in Contemporary Politics* 3, no. 2 (2005).

13. Sarah Binder, *Stalemate: The Causes and Consequences of Legislative Gridlock* (Washington, DC: Brookings Institution, 2003); Gary Jacobson, *A Uniter, Not a Divider: George Bush and the American People* (New York: Pearson/Longman, 2007).

14. V.O. Key, *Politics, Parties, & Pressure Groups* (New York: Crowell, 1964).

15. Joseph Schumpeter, *Capitalism, Socialism, and Democracy* (New York: Harper & Bros. 1950); Anthony Downs, *An Economic Theory of Democracy* (New York: Harper & Row, 1957); John Aldrich, *Why Parties? The Origin and Transformation of Political Parties in America* (Chicago: University of Chicago Press, 1995); Joseph A. Schlesinger, "On the Theory of Party Organization," *Journal of Politics* 46, no. 2 (1984); Gary W. Cox and Mathew D. McCubbins, *Legislative Leviathan: Party Government in the House* (Berkeley: University of California Press, 1993); Cox and McCubbins, *Setting the Agenda: Responsible Party Government in the House of Representatives* (New York: Cambridge University Press, 2005); David W. Rohde, *Parties and Leaders in the Postreform House* (Chicago: University of Chicago Press, 1991); Keith T. Poole and Howard Rosenthal, *Congress: A Political-Economic History of Roll Call Voting* (New York: Oxford University Press, 1997).

16. Daniel Galvin, *Presidential Party Building: Dwight D. Eisenhower to George W. Bush* (Princeton: Princeton University Press, 2010); Gerald M. Pomper, *Voters, Elections, and Parties: The Practice of Democratic Theory* (New Brunswick, NJ: Transaction Publishers, 1988); Price, *Bringing Back the Parties*.

17. E.E. Schattschneider, *Party Government* (New York: Farrar and Rinehart, 1942); V.O. Key, *Parties and Pressure Groups*, 3rd ed. (New York: Thomas Crowell, 1952); Charles E. Merriam, *The American Party System* (New York: Macmillan, 1922); Marty Cohen, David Karol, Hans Noel, and John Zaller, *The Party Decides: Presidential Nominations Before and After Reform* (Chicago: University of Chicago Press, 2008).

18. Downs, *Economic Theory of Democracy*; Aldrich, *Why Parties?*; Gary W. Cox, *Making Votes Count: Strategic Coordination in the World's Electoral Systems* (New York: Cambridge University Press, 1997).

19. Cohen et al., *The Party Decides*. It is fair to call it the UCLA School because Cohen, Noel, and Karol were all graduate students at UCLA where Zaller is a professor.

20. Indeed, some members of the UCLA School have pursued the investigation of the idea of faction further than the original book. See Gregory Koger, Seth Masket, Hans Noel, "Cooperative Party Factions in American Politics," *American Politics Research* 38 (2010): 33–52.

21. David Plotke, *Building a Democratic Political Order: Reshaping Liberalism in the 1930s and 1940s* (New York: Cambridge University Press, 1996), 6–7, 11–46.

22. Louis Hartz, *The Liberal Tradition in America* (New York: Harcourt and Brace, 1955).

23. Stephen Skowronek, *Building a New American State: The Expansion of National Administrative Capacities* (New York: Cambridge University Press, 1982); Richard Bensel, *The Political Economy of American Industrialization, 1877–1900* (New York: Cambridge University Press, 2000); Elizabeth Sanders, *The Roots of Reform: Farmers, Workers, and the American State, 1877–1917* (Chicago: University of Chicago Press, 1999); Daniel

Carpenter, *Forging Bureaucratic Autonomy: Reputations, Networks, and Policy Innovation in Executive Agencies, 1862–1928* (Princeton: Princeton University Press, 2001).

24. Samuel Hays, *The Response to Industrialism, 1885–1914* (Chicago: University of Chicago Press, 1957); Robert Wiebe, *The Search for Order, 1877–1920* (New York: Hill and Wang, 1967); Richard McCormick, *The Party Period and Public Policy: American Politics from the Age of Jackson to the Progressive Era* (New York: Oxford University Press, 1976).

25. The classic statement of realignment's periodicity was made by Walter Dean Burnham, *Critical Elections and the Mainsprings of American Politics* (New York: Norton, 1970).

26. V.O. Key Jr., "A Theory of Critical Elections," *Journal of Politics* 17 (1955): 3–18.

27. Larry Bartels, "Electoral Continuity and Change: 1868–1996," *Electoral Studies* 17, no. 3 (1998), 301–326; David R. Mayhew, *Electoral Realignments: A Critique of an American Genre* (New Haven: Yale University Press, 2002).

28. Stephen Skowronek, *The Politics Presidents Make: Leadership from John Adams to Bill Clinton* (Cambridge: Harvard University Press, 1993), 17–58.

29. Jo Freeman, "The Political Culture of the Democratic and Republican Parties," *Political Science Quarterly* 101, no. 3 (1986); John Gerring, *Party Ideologies in America, 1828–1996* (New York: Cambridge University Press, 1998); Cornelius Cotter, James Gibson, John Bibby, and Robert Huckshorn, *Party Organizations in American Politics* (New York: Praeger, 1984); David R. Mayhew, *Placing Parties in America: Organization, Electoral Settings, and Government Activity in the Twentieth Century* (Princeton: Princeton University Press, 1986); Christopher Bruzios, "Democratic and Republican Party Activists and Followers: Interparty and Intraparty Differences," *Polity* 22, no. 4 (1990).

30. Edward G. Carmines and James A. Stimson, *Issue Evolution: Race and the Transformation of American Politics* (Princeton: Princeton University Press, 1989); Gary Miller and Norman Schofield, "Activists and Partisan Realignment in the United States," *American Political Science Review* 54, no. 7 (2003); 245–260; James L. Sundquist, *Dynamics of the Party System: Alignment and Realignment of Political Parties in the United States* (Washington, DC: Brookings Institution, 1983).

31. Sundquist, *Dynamics of the Party System*, 13.

32. Schattschneider, *Semisovereign People*, 63.

Chapter 3

1. James G. March and Johan P. Olsen, *Rediscovering Institutions: The Organizational Basis of Politics* (New York: Press, 1989); Ira Katznelson and Helen Milner, *Political Science: The State of the Art*, Centennial Edition (New York: W.W. Norton & Co., 2002); Karen Orren and Stephen Skowronek, *The Search for American Political Development* (New York: Cambridge University Press, 2004).

2. Samuel Beer, "In Search of a New Public Philosophy" in Anthony King, ed. *The New American Political System* (Washington, DC: AEI Press, 1978); James W. Ceaser, *What Is the Public Philosophy?: An Inaugural Lecture Delivered Before the University of Oxford* (Oxford: Cambridge University Press, 2000); Michael J. Sandel, *Democracy's Discontent: America in Search of a Public Philosophy* (Cambridge: Harvard University Press, 1998); Sandel, *Public Philosophy: Essays on Morality and Politics* (Cambridge: Harvard University Press, 2005); Walter Lippmann, *Essays in the Public Philosophy* (Boston: Little, Brown, 1955); John Gerring, "Ideology: A Definitional Analysis," *Political Research Quarterly* 50, no. 4 (December 1997): 657–694.

3. James W. Ceaser, *Nature and History in American Political Development* (Cambridge: Harvard University Press, 2006); Ceaser, "The Theory of Governance of the Reagan Administration," in Lester Salamon and Michael S. Lund, eds., *The Reagan Presidency and the Governing of America* (Washington, DC: Urban Institute Press, 1984).

4. Robert Erikson and Kent Tilden, *American Public Opinion*, 6th ed. (New York: Long-man, 2001); James A. Stimson, *Tides of Consent: How Public Opinion Shapes American Politics* (New York: Cambridge University Press, 2004); Benjamin I. Page and Robert Shapiro, *The Rational Public: Fifty Year Trends in Public Opinion* (Chicago: University of Chicago Press, 1992).

5. Edward G. Carmines and James A Stimson, "The Two Faces of Issue Voting," *American Political Science Review* 74, no. 1 (1980), 78–91; Carmines and Stimson, *Issue Evolution: Race and the Transformation of American Politics* (Princeton: Princeton University Press, 1989).

6. David Karol, *Party Position Change in American Politics: Coalition Management* (New York: Cambridge University Press, 2009).

7. J. David Greenstone, "Political Culture and Political Development," *Studies in American Political Development* 1 (1986).

8. Louis Hartz, *The Liberal Tradition in America* (New York: Harcourt and Brace, 1955).

9. J. David Greenstone, *The Lincoln Persuasion: Remaking American Liberalism* (Princeton: Princeton University Press, 1993).

10. For a discussion of this body of scholarship, see Skowronek and Orren, *Search for American Political Development*, 66–68.

11. Rogers Smith, "Beyond Tocqueville, Myrdal, and Hartz: The Multiple Traditions in America," *American Political Science Review* 87, no. 3 (1993); Smith, *Civic Ideals: Conflicting Visions of Citizenship in the United States* (New Haven: Yale University Press, 1997).

12. E. E. Schattschneider, *The Semisovereign People: A Realist's View of Democracy in America* (New York: Holt, Rinehart and Winston, 1960), 62.

13. Eric Foner, *Reconstruction, 1863–1877* (Harper & Row, 1988), 492.

14. It should be noted that "Liberalism" in the 1870s was something completely different from the varieties of twentieth-century liberalism. In the late nineteenth century, Liberals were elitists, indifferent to the fate of blacks—if not outright racists—and advocates of classical economics. Twentieth-century liberals have been populist, deeply concerned with the fortunes of African-Americans and other minorities, and economic statists. The only points of convergence are that both cast themselves as "reformers" concerned with "good" government and believed in the power of policy experts to improve society.

15. Henry Adams to Charles Francis Adams, Jr., November 21, 1864, in Worthington C. Ford, ed., *A Cycle of Adams Letters, 1861–1865*, 2 vols. (Boston: 1920), 211–212.

16. Geoffrey Blodgett, "Reform Thought and the Genteel Tradition," in H. Wayne Morgan, ed., *The Gilded Age*, rev. ed. (Syracuse, NY: Syracuse University Press, 1970), 67–68; Ari Hoogenboom, *Outlawing the Spoils: A History of the Civil Service Reform Movement 1865–1883* (Urbana: University of Illinois Press, 1961), 22, 89, 100, 137.

17. "The Business Side of Reform," *New York Times*, September 9, 1881, 4.

18. Carl Schurz, "Congress and the Spoils System," address to the National Civil Service Reform League, December 12, 1895.

19. Eric Foner, *Reconstruction, 1863–1877* (Harper & Row, 1988), 469–487.

20. Ingalls cited in *The Nation* 50 (May 22, 1890), 406.

21. Morton Keller, *Affairs of State: Public Life in Late Nineteenth-Century America* (Cambridge: Harvard University Press, Belknap Press, 1977).

22. Reichley, *The Life of the Parties*, 120–131; Rothman, *Politics and Power*, 26–36.

23. *Congressional Record*, December 4, 1882. Cited in Stephen Skowronek, *Building a New American State: The Expansion of National Administrative Capacities* (New York: Cambridge University Press, 1982), 47.

24. Conkling quoted in *New York Times*, March 22, 1873.

25. Allan Peskin, "Who Were the Stalwarts? Who Were Their Rivals? Republican Factions in the Gilded Age," *Political Science Quarterly* (Winter 1984–1985), 704–706, 715–716;

Matthew Josephson, *The Politicos* (New York: Harcourt, Brace & World, 1966), 179–180; William G. Eidson, "Who Were the Stalwarts?" *Mid-America* 52 (October 1970): 242, 247.

26. In general, scholars have placed the Half-Breeds between the Liberals and the Stalwarts. That is the approach taken here. Gould, *Grand Old Party*, 93–97; Mark D. Hirsch, "Election of 1884," in Schlesinger, ed., *History of American Presidential Elections*, vol. 2, p. 1562; Eidson, "Who Were the Stalwarts?" 242, 247; Peskin, "Who Were the Stalwarts?" 712; Norman E. Tutorow, *James Gillespie Blaine and the Presidency: A Documentary Study and Source Book* (New York: Peter Lang, 1989), 7–8; See also Justus D. Doenecke, *The Presidencies of James A. Garfield and Chester A. Arthur* (Lawrence: Regents Press of Kansas, 1981), 13–14.

27. Mark D. Hirsch, "Election of 1884," in Arthur J. Schlesinger, ed., *History of American Presidential Elections*, vol. 2, (New York: Chatham House, 1972), 1562.

28. Welch, *George Frisbie Hoar*, 2–3; see also 337.

29. Morgan, *From Hayes to McKinley*.

30. Richard Hofstadter, *Social Darwinism in American Thought*, reprint ed. (Boston: Beacon Press, 1992).

31. Andrew Carnegie, *The Gospel of Wealth* (New York: The Century Co., 1901). See also, Carnegie, "Wealth," *North American Review*, no. 391 (June 1889), http://www.swarthmore.edu/SocSci/rbannis1/AIH19th/Carnegie.html (accessed July 18, 2011).

32. Andrew Carnegie, "The Triumph of America" (1885), http://teachingamericanhistory.org/library/index.asp?document=1420 (Accessed July 18, 2011).

33. William H. Taft, *Four Aspects of Civic Duty* (New York: Charles Scribner's Sons, 1906), 18–19.

34. Nicholas Murray Butler, *True and False Democracy* (New York: Macmillan, 1907), 9, 14–15, 57.

35. Norman M. Wilensky, *Conservatives in the Progressive Era: The Taft Republicans of 1912* (Gainesville: University of Florida Press, 1965).

36. Taft quoted in Sidney M. Milkis, *Theodore Roosevelt, the Progressive Party, and the Transformation of American Politics* (Lawrence: University of Kansas Press, 2009), 89.

37. See also, Elihu Root, "Address of the Temporary Chairman," Republican National Convention, 1912.

38. Lewis L. Gould, *The Grand Old Party: A History of the Republicans* (New York: Random House, 2003), 91.

39. H. Wayne Morgan, *From Hayes to McKinley: National Party Politics, 1877–1896* (Syracuse, NY: Syracuse University Press, 1969), 365–395.

40. George E. Mowry, *The Era of Theodore Roosevelt: 1900–1912* (New York: Harper & Brothers, 1958), 38–45.

41. William H. Taft, *Popular Government: Its Essence, Its Permanence, and Its Perils* (New York, 1913), 35.

42. John Gerring, *Party Ideologies in America, 1828–1996* (New York: Cambridge University Press, 1998), 93–113.

43. William James to Sarah Wyman Whitman, June 7, 1899, in *The Letters of William James*, vol. 2 (Boston: Atlantic Monthly Press, 1920), 90.

44. Ceaser, *Nature and History*, 59–67.

45. Lester Frank Ward, "The Establishment of Sociology," Presidential Address to the American Sociological Association, Providence, RI, December 27, 1906.

46. Croly cited in William Schambra, "Obama and the Policy Approach," *National Affairs*, no. 1 (Fall 2009).

47. Walter Lippmann, *A Preface to Politics* (New York: Kennerley, 1913), 16.

48. Herbert Croly, *The Promise of American Life* (Cambridge: Harvard University Press, 1965; 1909), 400.

49. Leon Fink, *Progressive Intellectuals and the Dilemmas of Democratic Commitment* (Cambridge: Harvard University Press, 1999), 13–51; Charles Forcey, *The Crossroads of Liberalism: Croly, Weyl, Lippmann, and the Progressive Era, 1900–1925* (New York: Oxford University Press, 1971).

50. Sidney M. Milkis and Daniel J. Tichenor, "'Direct Democracy' and Social Justice: The Progressive Party Campaign of 1912," *Studies in American Political Development* 8, no. 2 (Fall 1994): 282–340.

51. Theodore Roosevelt, "The Right of the People to Rule," Speech delivered at Carnegie Hall, New York City, March 30, 1912.

52. Milkis, *Theodore Roosevelt, the Progressive Party, and the Transformation of American Politics*, 21–26.

53. Theodore Roosevelt, "The New Nationalism" (1910), http://teachingamericanhistory. org/library/index.asp?document=501 (last accessed July 18, 2011).

54. Ibid.

55. Herbert Croly, *Progressive Democracy* (New York: Macmillan, 1914), 347.

56. Roosevelt, "New Nationalism," 1910.

57. Milkis, *Theodore Roosevelt, the Progressive Party, and the Transformation of American Politics*, 15.

58. Croly, *Promise of American Life*, 278.

59. Albert Beveridge, "Keynote Address: Progressive Party National Convention," August 5–7, 1912.

60. David W. Reinhard, *The Republican Right Since 1945* (Lexington: University of Kentucky Press, 1983), 157–158.

61. Cited in Barry K. Breyer, *Thomas E. Dewey, 1937–1947: A Study in Political Leadership* (New York: Garland Publishers, 1979), 245.

62. Samuel Lubell, *The Revolt of the Moderates* (New York: Harper & Brothers, 1956), 89.

63. Jerome L. Himmelstein, *To The Right: The Transformation of American Conservatism* (Berkeley: University of California Press, 1990), 63–65, 84–94; George H. Nash, *The Conservative Intellectual Movement in America Since 1945* (New York: Basic Books, 1976).

64. "Prayer in School," Radio Address to the Nation, February 25, 1984, *Weekly Compilation of Presidential Documents* 20, no. 9 (March 5, 1984).

65. James W. Ceaser, "Creed Versus Culture: Alternative Foundations of American Conservatism," *Heritage Lectures*, no. 926, March 10, 2006; Ceaser, "True Blue Vs. Deep Red: The Ideas That Move American Politics," a discussion paper for the 2006 Bradley Symposium, May 2006; George H. Nash, "The Uneasy Future of American Conservatism," a paper presented at the Symposium in Honor of Ronald Reagan, Regent University (2006).

66. Ronald Reagan, "Remarks to Chief Executive Officers of National Organizations," March 14, 1982.

67. Leo Strauss, *Natural Right and History* (Chicago: University of Chicago Press, 1965).

68. Justin Vaisee, *Neoconservatism: The Biography of the Movement* (Cambridge: Harvard University Press, 2010).

69. Shafer, *Two Majorities*, 169–182. Michael Schaller, *Reckoning with Reagan: America and its President in the 1980s* (New York: Oxford University Press, 1992), 22–25; Robert Freedman, "The Religious Right and the Carter Administration," *Historical Journal* 48, no. 1 (2005).

70. Messe cited in Terry Eastland, "Teaching Morality in the Public School," *Wall Street Journal*, February 22, 1982.

71. Ronald Reagan, "State of the Union Address" (1984), http://www.presidency.ucsb. edu/ws/index.php?pid=40205#axzz1SkV17VHP (accessed July 18, 2011).

72. Nathan Glazer, "Towards an Imperial Judiciary?" *Public Interest* 41 (Fall 1975).

73. Daniel Galvin, *Presidential Party Building: Dwight D. Eisenhower to George W. Bush* (Princeton: Princeton University Press, 2009), 63–67.

74. Thomas Bryne Edsall and Mary D. Edsall, *Chain Reaction: The Impact of Race, Rights, and Taxes on American Politics* (New York: W.W. Norton & Co., 1992); Dan T. Carter, *From George Wallace to Newt Gingrich: Race and the Conservative Counterrevolution, 1963–1994* (Baton Rouge: Louisiana State University Press, 1999); Carter, *The Politics of Rage: George Wallace, the New Conservatism, and the Transformation of American Politics*, 2nd ed. (Baton Rouge: Louisiana State University Press, 2000); Joseph E. Lowndes, *From the New Deal to the New Right: Race and the Origins of Modern Conservatism* (New Haven: Yale University Press, 2009); Earl Black and Merle Black, *The Rise of the Southern Republicans* (Cambridge: Harvard University Press, 2003); Joseph A. Aistrup, *The Southern Strategy Revisited: Republican Top-Down Advancement in the South* (Lexington: University of Kentucky Press, 1996); Thomas Schaller, *Whistling Past Dixie: How Democrats Can Win Without the South* (New York: Simon and Schuster, 2006), 21–67.

75. Byron E. Shafer and Richard Johnston, *The End of Southern Exceptionalism: Class, Race, and Partisan Change in the Postwar South* (Cambridge: Harvard University Press, 2009); David Lublin, *The Republican South: Democratization and Partisan Change* (Princeton: Princeton University Press, 2004); Gerard Alexander, "The Myth of the Racist Republicans," *Claremont Review of Books* 4, no. 2 (Spring 2004); Alexander, "Conservatism does not equal racism," *Washington Post*, September 12, 2010, B1.

76. William Jennings Bryan, *The Commoner*, October 28, 1904. Cited in Kazin, *A Godly Hero*, 121.

77. Michael Kazin, "The Other Bryan," *American Prospect*, January 5, 2006. See also, Kazin, *A Godly Hero*, 123–127, 202–203.

78. Quoted in A. James Reichley, *Faith in Politics* (Washington, DC: Brookings Institution, 2002), 199.

79. Richard Franklin Bensel, *Passions and Preferences: William Jennings Bryan and the 1896 Democratic National Convention* (New York: Cambridge University Press, 2008).

80. Elizabeth Sanders, *The Roots of Reform: Farmers, Workers, and the American State, 1877–1917* (Chicago: University of Chicago Press, 1999), 389, 387–408; Sidney Milkis, "Progressivism, Then and Now," in Sidney Milkis and Jerome M. Mileur eds., *Progressivism and the New Democracy* (Amherst: University of Massachusetts Press, 1999).

81. "Will Soldiers Vote?" *Time*, February 14, 1944.

82. Smith quoted in *The Nation*, December 25, 1943, 748. See also, "Curtains for Cotton Ed," *Time*, August 7, 1944.

83. Bruce J. Dierenfield, *Keeper of the Rules: Howard W. Smith of Virginia* (Charlottesville: University of Virginia Press, 1987).

84. V.O. Key, Jr., *Southern Politics in State and Nation* (New York: Knopf, 1949), 5, 345, 367–368, 352.

85. *Congressional Record*, 78th Congress, 2nd session, January 31, 1944, 908, 911.

86. *Congressional Record*, 77th Congress, 2nd session, September 9, 1942, 7073–7074.

87. *Congressional Record*, 85th Congress, 1st session,

88. Russell cited in "Basic Democratic Divisions Examined," *Congressional Quarterly Weekly Report*, December 12, 1958.

89. Twelve Southerners, *I'll Take My Stand: The South and the Agrarian Tradition* (Baton Rouge: Louisiana State University Press, 1978).

90. Russell cited in "Basic Democratic Divisions Examined," *Congressional Quarterly Weekly Report*, December 12, 1958.

91. Ronald J. Pestritto, *Woodrow Wilson and the Origins of Modern Liberalism* (Lanham, MD: Rowman & Littlefield, 2005).

92. Arthur M. Schlesinger, Jr., *The Vital Center: The Politics of Freedom* (Boston: Houghton-Mifflin, 1949), 186.

93. Allen Matusow, *The Unraveling of America: A History of Liberalism in the 1960s* (New York: Harper & Row, 1984), 3–6; Steven M. Gillon, *Politics and Vision: The ADA and American Liberalism, 1947–1985* (New York: Oxford University Press, 1987), 9–10.

94. Reinhold Niebuhr, *The Children of Light and the Children of Darkness: A vindication of democracy and a critique of its traditional defense* (New York: Scribner, 1944); see also Niebuhr, "For Peace, We Must Risk War," *Life Magazine*, September 20, 1948, 38–39; Niebuhr, *The Irony of American History* (New York: Scribner, 1952); see also, Eyal Naveh, *Reinhold Niebuhr and Non-Utopian Liberalism: Beyond Illusion and Despair* (Brighton: Sussex Academic Press, 2002).

95. Schlesinger, *The Vital Center.*

96. Christopher Lasch, *The Agony of the American Left* (New York: Knof, 1969).

97. John Kenneth Galbraith, *American Capitalism* (New York: Houghton-Mifflin, 1952).

98. John T. Dunlap, Frederick H. Harbison, Clark Kerr, and Charles Myers, *Industrialism and Industrial Man: The Problems of Labor and Management in Economic Growth* (Cambridge: Harvard University Press, 1960), 10, 293.

99. Arthur M. Schlesinger, Jr., "Liberalism," *Saturday Review* 8 (June 1957), 11–12.

100. Lyndon B. Johnson, "Remarks at the University of Michigan," May 22, 1964.

101. Lyndon B. Johnson, "Remarks at the Civic Center Arena in Pittsburg," October 27, 1964.

102. Wilson W. Wyatt, "Address to Americans for Democratic Action national convention" ADA press release, February 21, 1948.

103. Karen Orren, "Union Politics and Postwar Liberalism in the United States, 1946–1979," *Studies in American Political Development* 1 (1986), 219–228.

104. For example, the 1964 platform declared: "[the] expansion of the American economy … will require continuation of flexible and innovative fiscal, monetary, and debt management policies, recognizing the importance of low interest rates." See Gerring, *Party Ideologies in America*, 232–253.

105. Arthur M Schlesinger, Jr., "The Perspective Now," *Partisan Review* (May–June 1947), 242.

106. Lyndon B. Johnson, "To Fulfill these Rights," Commencement Address at Howard University, June 4, 1965.

107. James L. Sundquist, *The Decline and Resurgence of Congress* (Washington, DC: Brookings Institution, 1981), 155–162.

108. Sundquist, *Decline and Resurgence of Congress*, 179; Farang and Katznelson, "Southern Imposition"; Katznelson, *When Affirmative Action Was White*, 29–50.

109. The reform program for strengthening Congress and the idea of responsible party government came from four sources: E.E. Schattschneider, *Party Government* (New York: Farrar & Reinhardt, 1942); Robert Heller, *Strengthening Congress* (Washington, DC: National Planning Association, 1945), 30–31; George Galloway, *The Reorganization of Congress: A Report to the Committee on Congress of the American Political Science Association* (New York: Public Affairs Press, 1945), 34, 37, 80; APSA Report, "Toward a More Responsible Two-Party System: A Report of the Committee on Political Parties" *American Political Science Review* 44, no. 3 (1950).

110. Sundquist, *Politics and Policy*, 415.

111. Port Huron Statement (1962), http://www.h-net.org/~hst306/documents/huron.html (acessed July 18, 2011); James Miller, *Democracy Is in the Streets: From the Port Huron Statement to the Siege of Chicago* (Cambridge: Harvard University Press, 1994).

112. Richard A. Harris and Sidney M. Milkis, *The Politics of Regulatory Change: A Tale of Two Agencies*, 2nd ed. (New York: Oxford University Press, 1996), 62, 3–22, 53–97.

113. Quoted in Dan Balz, "Democrats Chart the Way Back," *Washington Post*, November 19, 1984, A1.

114. Chiles quoted in *CQ Weekly Report*, March 9, 1985, 457.

115. Will Marshall, "A New Fighting Faith," *The New Democrat* (September–October 1996), 14.

116. David Osborne and Ted Gaebler, *Reinventing Government: How the Entrepreneurial Spirit Is Transforming the Public Sector* (New York: Plume Books, 1993).

Chapter 4

1. Austin Ranney, *Curing the Mischiefs of Faction: Party Reform in America* (Berkeley: University of California Press, 1975).

2. Marty Cohen, David Karol, Hans Noel, and John Zaller, *The Party Decides: Presidential Nominations Before and After Reform* (Chicago: University of Chicago Press, 2008), 81–89.

3. Ibid., 81.

4. For analysts stressing change in the system, see James W. Ceaser, *Presidential Selection: Theory and Development* (Princeton: Princeton University Press, 1979); Nelson Polsby and Aaron Wildavsky with David Hopkins, *Presidential Elections: Strategies and Structures of American Politics*, 12th ed. (Lanham, MD: Rowman and Littlefield Publishers, 2008);

5. Howard Reiter, *Selecting the President: The Nominating Process in Transition* (Philadelphia: University of Pennsylvania Press, 1985), 84–85; William G. Carelton, "The Revolution in the Presidential Nominating Convention," *Political Science Quarterly* 72 (June 1957): 224–240.

6. Aaron B. Wildavsky, "The Goldwater Phenomenon: Purists, Politicians, and the Two-Party System," *Review of Politics* 27 (1965): 387–413; James Q. Wilson, *The Amateur Democrat: Club Politics in Three Cities* (Chicago: University of Chicago Press, 1966); Everett Carll Ladd, Jr., *Transformations of the American Party System* (New York: W.W. Norton, 1975), 304–331.

7. Cohen et al., *Party Decides*, 107–118; David R. Mayhew, *Placing Parties in American Politics* (Princeton: Princeton University Press, 1986).

8. James I. Lengle, "Divisive Electoral Primaries and Party Electoral Prospects, 1932–1976," *American Politics Quarterly* 8 (1980): 261–277; Lengle, Diana Owen, and Molly W. Sonner, "Divisive Nominating Mechanisms and Democratic Party Electoral Prospects," *Journal of Politics* 75, no. 2 (1995): 370–383; Walter J. Stone, "The Carryover Effect in Presidential Nominations," *American Political Science Review* 80 (1986): 271–279; Patrick J. Kenney and Tom W. Rice, "The Relationship between Divisive Primaries and General Election Outcomes," *American Journal of Political Science* 31 (1987): 31–44; Martin P. Wattenberg, *The Rise of Candidate-Centered Politics: Presidential Elections of the 1980s* (Cambridge: Harvard University Press, 1991).

9. Lewis Gould, *Grand Old Party* (New York: Random House, 2004), 67, 72–74, 76–77; H. Wayne Morgan, "The Republican Party 1876–1893," in Schlesinger, ed., *History of U.S. Political Parties*, vol. 2, 1420.

10. Rutherford B. Hayes, *The Diary and Letters of Rutherford B. Hayes, Nineteenth President of the United States*, ed. Charles Richard Williams (Columbus: Ohio State Archeological and Historical Society, 1922), vol. 3, chap. 31, March 28, http://www.ohiohistory.org/onlinedoc/hayes/Volume03/Chapter31/March28.txt (accessed July 18, 2011).

11. Sidney I. Pomerantz, "Election of 1876," in *The History of American Presidential Elections* vol. 2, ed. Arthur M. Schlesinger Jr. (New York: Chelsea House Publishers, 1971); Vincent P. DeSantis, *Republicans Face the Southern Question: The New Departure Years, 1877–1897* (Baltimore: Johns Hopkins Press, 1959), 105–106, 112–113, 118–119; Ari Hoogenboom, *Outlawing the Spoils: A History of the Civil Service Reform Movement* (Urbana: University of Illinois Press, 1961); 155–178; Stanley P. Hirshson, *Farewell to the Bloody Shirt: Northern Republicans and the Southern Negro, 1877–1893* (Bloomington: Indiana University Press, 1962), 27–62, 123, 126–131, 132–135, 216, 244;

H. Wayne Morgan, *From Hayes to McKinley: National Party Politics, 1877–1896* (Syracuse, NY: Syracuse University Press, 1969), 26, 31–39; Morgan, "The Republican Party," in Schlesinger ed., *History of American Political Parties*, 1420–1422; Allan Peskin, "Was There a Compromise of 1877?" *Journal of American History* 60 (June 1973): 73–74; Keith Polakoff, *The Politics of Inertia* (Baton Rouge: Louisiana State University Press, 1973), 106–107, 157–163, 232–314, 317; Morton Keller, *Affairs of State: Public Life in Late Nineteenth-Century America* (Cambridge: Harvard University Press, Belknap Press, 1977), 264–265; Ari Hoogenboom, *The Presidency of Rutherford B. Hayes* (Lawrence: University of Kansas Press, 1988), 22–23, 32–33, 36, 56, 127–151; Hoogenboom, "Spoilsmen and Reformers: Civil Service Reform and Public Morality," in H. Wayne Morgan ed., *The Gilded Age: A Reappraisal* (Syracuse, NY: Syracuse University Press 1963), 69–90; and Hoogenboom, *Hayes: Warrior and President* (Lawrence: University of Kansas Press, 1995), 318–325, 350–356, 361–363, 370–377, 378–383, 407–413.

12. Herbert J. Clancy, *The Presidential Election of 1880* (Chicago: Loyola University Press, 1958), 22–51, 82–121; Richard C. Bain and Judith H. Harris, *Convention Decisions and Voting Records* 2nd ed. (Washington, DC: Brookings Institution, 1973), 109–116; Hoogenboom, *Outlawing the Spoils*, 179–183; Morgan, *From Hayes to McKinley*, 74, 84–96; Leonard Dinnerstein, "Election of 1880," in *The History of American Presidential Elections*, vol. 2, ed. Arthur M. Schlesinger Jr. (New York: Chelsea House Publishers, 1971); Justus D. Doenecke, *The Presidencies of James A. Garfield and Chester A. Arthur* (Lawrence: Regents Press of Kansas, 1981), 17–21; Allan Peskin, "Who Were the Stalwarts? Who Were Their Rivals? Republican Factions in the Gilded Age," *Political Science Quarterly* (Winter 1984–1985): 705–716; Hoogenboom, *Presidency of Rutherford B. Hayes*, 193–200; Norman E. Tutorow, *James Gillespie Blaine and the Presidency: A Documentary Study and Source Book* (New York: Peter Lang, 1989), 45–63.

13. Dinnerstein, "Election of 1880," 1492–1499.

14. Hayes, *Diary*, cited in Hoogenboom, *Presidency of Rutherford B. Hayes*, 198–199.

15. Cited in Sproat, *The Best Men*, 119.

16. Quoted in A. James Reichley, *The Life of the Parties* (Lanham, MD: Rowman & Littlefield, 1992), 160.

17. Rutherford B. Hayes, "Inaugural Address," March 5, 1877, http://avalon.law.yale.edu/19th_century/hayes.asp (accessed July 18, 2011).

18. Arthur S. Link, *Woodrow Wilson and the Progressive Era, 1910–1917* (New York: Harper & Row, 1963), 58.

19. James L. Holt, *Congressional Insurgents and the Party System* (Cambridge: Harvard University Press, 1967), 47–62. In the immediate aftermath of the elections, forty-seven progressive Republican members of Congress declared themselves unbound by the positions of the Republican Conference and thirteen Senators demanded recognition as a separate unit of the Republican Party entitled to their fair share of committee assignments. Steven J. Rosenstone, Roy L. Behr, Edward Lazarus, *Third Parties in America: Citizen Response to Major Party Failure* (Princeton: Princeton University Press, 1984).

20. Lewis Gould, *Grand Old Party* (New York: Random House, 2004), 185–192.

21. Quoted in Sindey M. Milkis, *Theodore Roosevelt, the Progressive Party, and the Transformation of American Politics* (Lawrence: University of Kansas Press, 2009), 86; see also, *San Francisco Examiner*, May 24, 1912.

22. Ibid., 62–69.

23. Ibid., 113–118.

24. Howard L. Reiter, "The Bases of Progressivism within the Major Parties: Evidence from the National Conventions," *Social Science History* 22, no. 2 (Spring 1998).

25. For the changes wrought by Bryan in Democratic Party ideology, see John Gerring, *Party Ideologies in America, 1828–2004* (New York: Cambridge University Press, 2004),

187–221; Michael Kazin, *A Godly Hero: The Life of Williams Jennings Bryan* (New York: Knof, 2006).

26. John M. Cooper, *The Warrior and the Priest* (Cambridge: Harvard University Press, 1983), 181; Link, *Woodrow Wilson and the Progressive Era,* 25–81; A. James Reichley, *The Life of the Parties: A History of American Political Parties* (Lanham, MD: Rowman & Littlefield, 1992), 189–190; David A. Sarasohn, *The Party of Reform: Democrats in the Progressive Era* (Jackson: University of Mississippi Press, 1989); James L. Sundquist, *The Decline and Resurgence of Congress* (Washington, DC: Brookings Institution, 1981), 168–176; Ralph M. Goldman, *Search for Consensus: The Story of the Democratic Party* (Philadelphia: Temple University Press, 1979), 81–85, 90–96; Milkis, *Theodore Roosevelt, the Progressive Party, and the Transformation of American Politics,* 129–42.

27. Gilbert C. Fite, "Election of 1896" in *The History of American Presidential Elections* vol. 2, ed. Arthur M. Schlesinger Jr. (New York: Chelsea House Publishers, 1971), 1787–1826.

28. Stanley L. Jones, *The Presidential Election of 1896* (Madison: University of Wisconsin Press, 1993).

29. Robert W. Cherny, *A Righteous Cause: The Life of William Jennings Bryan* (Boston: Little, Brown & Co., 1985), 38. Also, Louis W. Koenig, *Bryan: A Political Biography of William Jennings Bryan* (New York: Putnam, 1917), 3–17. Toward the end of the 53rd Congress, Bryan called upon silver supporters to "take charge of the party organization and make the Democratic Party an effective instrument in the accomplishment of needed reforms." Thirty-one Democratic congressmen signed his pamphlet. Alyn Brodsky, *Grover Cleveland: A Study in Character* (New York: Truman Talley Books, 2000), 321.

30. Cherny, *A Righteous Cause,* 40.

31. Bryan, "Cross of Gold Speech" (1896), http://www.pbs.org/wgbh/amex/1900/filmmore/reference/primary/crossofgold.html (accessed July 21, 2011). For a discussion of the power of this speech, see Richard Bensel, *Passions and Preferences: William Jennings Bryan and the Democratic National Convention* (New York: Cambridge University Press, 2007), 203–247. See also Bryan, "Speech," reprinted in *New York Times,* October 10, 1900. He was concerned with opening up government processes, so that that they could be understood and eventually controlled by the people. He supported a range of policy options to democratize the electoral system: direct primaries, initiatives, referenda, recall elections, and the direct election of senators. These measures would ensure that public interests trumped private ones. Bryan, "Acceptance Speech," Democratic National Convention, August 12, 1896; Bryan, "Acceptance Speech," Democratic National Convention, August 12, 1908. Paul W. Glad, *McKinley, Bryan, and the People* (New York: Ivan R. Dee, 1991), 52–69, 113–132; Gerring, *Party Ideologies in America,* 222–226.

32. Walter LaFeber, "Election of 1900," in Arthur M. Schlesinger, Jr., ed., *The History of American Presidential Elections, 1789–1968* vol. 3 (New York: Chelsea House Publishers, 1971), 1877–1918.

33. Cited in William H. Harbaugh, "Election of 1904," in *The History of American Presidential Elections,* vol. 3, ed. Arthur M. Schlesinger Jr. (New York: Chelsea House Publishers, 1971).

34. Lewis L. Gould, *Regulation and Reform: American Politics from Roosevelt to Wilson,* 3rd ed. (Prospect Heights, IL: Waveland Press, 1996), 95.

35. According to David Sarasohn, "The Democrats had been gaining strength steadily since 1904 and had dramatically improved their national image in the previous two sessions of Congress [before the 1912 election]. . . . Democrats fought the election of 1912 on same issues that had fueled their party's eight year surge." Sarasohn, *The Party of Reform: Democrats in the Progressive Era* (Jackson: University of Mississippi Press, 1989), xvi.

36. Cooper, *Warrior and the Priest,* 181.

37. Wilson quoted in Ibid.

38. Ibid.
39. Quoted in *New York Times*, January 31, 1912.
40. For the effects of the New Deal on the Republican Party, see Clyde Weed, *The Nemesis of Reform: The Republican Party During the New Deal* (New York: Columbia University Press, 1994); Nicol C. Rae, *The Decline and Fall of the Liberal Republicans* (New York: Oxford University Press, 1989).
41. Reiter, *Selecting the President*, 55.
42. Carelton, "Revolution in the Nominating Convention," 228.
43. Donald B. Johnson, *The Republican Party and Wendell Willkie* (Urbana: University of Illinois Press, 1960), 63–67; Steve Neal, *Dark Horse: A Biography of Wendell Willkie* (Garden City, NY: Doubleday, 1984), 66–121; Rae, *Decline and Fall of the Liberal Republicans*.
44. Richard N. Smith, *Thomas E. Dewey and His Times* (New York: Simon & Schuster, 1982).
45. Theodore H. White, *The Making of the President 1964* (New York: Signet Books, 1965); David S. Broder, "Election of 1964," in Arthur Schlesinger ed., *The History of American Presidential Elections*, vol. 4, (New York: Chelsea House Publishers, 1970).
46. William C. Berman, *America's Right Turn: From Nixon to Bush* (Baltimore: Johns Hopkins Press, 1994), 27.
47. Ronald Reagan, "A Time for Choosing," Speech at the Republican National Convention (1964), http://www.fordham.edu/halsall/mod/1964reagan1.html (accessed July 21, 2011).
48. Quoted in Craig Shirley, *Reagan's Revolution: The Untold Story of the Campaign That Started It All* (Nashville: Nelson Current, 2005), 339.
49. Andrew E. Busch, *Reagan's Victory: The Presidential Election of 1980 and the Rise of the Right* (Lawrence: Kansas University Press, 2005).
50. *WPNWE*, 9–5 June 1986, 12; NBC Nightly New, May 4, 1986.
51. Graham K. Wilson, *Unions in American National Politics* (New York: St. Martin's Press, 1979), 17–31.
52. J. David Greenstone, *Labor in American Politics* (Chicago: University of Chicago Press, 1968), 70.
53. Byron Shafer, *The Two Majorities and the Puzzle of American Politics* (Lawrence: Kansas University Press, 2004).
54. According to Theodore H. White, when President Lyndon Johnson asked Meany who his top three choices for vice president were, Meany responded that he had only one: Hubert Humphrey. Humphrey received the nomination. Theodore H. White, *The Making of the President 1964* (New York: New American Library, 1969), 327. Other labor leaders, including Walter Reuther and David Dubinsky, also urged Johnson to name Humphrey.
55. Taylor E. Dark, *Unions and the Democrats: An Enduring Alliance* (Ithaca, NY: ILR Press, 2001), 76–83. For a description of the decentralized properties of conventions, see Aaron Wildavsky, "What Can I Do? The Ohio Delegate's View of the Convention," in *Revolt Against the Masses and other Essays on Politics and Public Policy* (New York: Basic Books, 1971), 225–245.
56. David McDonald, *Union Man* (New York: E.P. Dutton, 1969), 283, 285.
57. Theodore S. Sorensen, "Election of 1960," in Arthur Schlesinger, Jr. ed., *The History of American Presidential Elections, 1789–1968* (New York: Chelsea House Publishers, 1972), 3449–3470
58. Dark, *Unions and the Democrats*, 92. Reuther and Meany operated in the same fashion at the convention, covertly supporting Kennedy among party leaders. Nelson Lichtenstein, *Most Dangerous Man in Detroit: Walter Reuther and the Fate of American Labor* (New York: Basic Books, 1995); Joseph Goulden, *Meany* (New York: Atheneum, 1972), 187.

59. Steven M. Gillon, *Politics and Vision: The ADA and American Liberalism, 1947–1985* (New York: Oxford University Press, 1987).

60. David Broder, "COPE Director Al Barkan Flexing Labor's Big Muscle," *Washington Post*, May 7, 1968; see also, Broder, "Election of 1968," in Arthur Schlesinger, Jr. ed., *The History of American Presidential Elections, 1789–1968* (New York: Chelsea House Publishers, 1972), 3705–3752.

61. Lewis Chester, Godfrey Hodgson, and Bruce Page, *An American Melodrama: The Presidential Campaign of 1968* (New York: Viking Press, 1969), 577–604.

62. Dark, *Unions and the Democrats*, 74–75.

63. Barkan quoted in James Singer, "Election Victories Mean Labor Can Come in from the Cold," *National Journal*, November 20, 1976, 1656.

64. Greenstone, *Labor in American Politics*, xxv.

65. Operative quoted in Norman Miller, "As Convention Opening Nears, All-Out Warfare Threatens to Rip Party," *Wall Street Journal*, July, 5, 1972.

66. Bruce Miroff, *The Liberals' Moment: The McGovern Insurgency and the Identity Crisis of the Democratic Party* (Lawrence: Kansas University Press, 2007).

67. Miroff, *Liberals' Moment*, 53–55.

68. Burton I. Kaufman and Scott Kaufman, *The Presidency of James Earl Carter*, 2nd ed. (Lawrence: University of Kansas Press, 2006), 11–16.

69. To stay competitive the other DLC-affiliated candidate Richard Gephardt was forced to modify his issue stances and become much more liberal. Gore's loss to Jackson on Super Tuesday also seemed to suggest that even the Southern state parties, especially with their large African-American constituencies, were becoming increasingly liberal.

70. Kenneth Baer, *Reinventing Democrats* (Lawrence: University of Kansas Press, 2000), 163–164.

71. Robin Toner, "Road to the Nomination," *New York Times*, July 12, 1992, A18.

72. James W. Ceaser and Andrew E. Busch, *Upside Down and Inside Out: The 1992 Elections and American Politics* (Lanham, MD: Rowman & Littlefield Publishers, 1993).

73. Steven M. Gillon, *The Pact: Bill Clinton, Newt Gingrich, and the Rivalry That Defined a Generation* (New York: Oxford University Press, 2008), 91–96.

74. Jerry Roberts, "Democratic Convention Ticket Stresses Shift in Ideas," *San Francisco Chronicle*, July 12, 1992, A9.

75. William Jefferson Clinton, "New Covenant Speech," Democratic National Convention (1992).

Chapter 5

1. James Q. Wilson and John J. DiIulio, Jr., *American Government: Institutions and Policies*, 10th ed. (Boston: Houghton Mifflin Co., 2006), 221.

2. V.O. Key, *Parties and Pressure Groups*, 3rd ed. (New York: Thomas Crowell, 1952), 294–295.

3. David J. Rothman, *Politics and Power: The United States Senate, 1869–1901* (Cambridge: Harvard University Press, 1966).

4. Hans L. Trefousse, *Carl Schurz* (Knoxville: University of Tennessee Press, 1982).

5. Earle Dudley Ross, *The Liberal Republican Movement*, intro. John Sproat (Seattle: University of Washington Press, 1917, 1970); John G. Sproat, *The "Best Men": Liberal Reformers in the Gilded Age* (New York: Oxford University Press, 1968).

6. Lewis L. Gould, *Grand Old Party: A History of the Republicans* (New York: Random House, 2003), 61–67; William Gillette, "Election of 1872," in Arthur Schlesinger, ed., *History of American Presidential Elections*, vol. 2 (New York: Chelsea House, McGraw-Hill, 1969), 1304, 1306; John M. Dobson, *Politics in the Gilded Age: A New Perspective on Reform* (New York: Praeger Publishers, 1972), 52, 57, 108–120; A. James Reichley, *The Life of the Parties* (Lanham, MD: Rowman & Littlefield, 1992), 146; Ralph M. Goldman,

The National Party Chairmen and Committees: Factionalism at the Top (Armonk, NY: M.E. Sharpe, 1990), 118.

7. Godkin to Schurz in Bancroft ed., *Speeches, Correspondence and Political Papers of Carl Schurz* (New York: Putnam, 1913), 363–364.

8. Frederic Bancroft ed., *Speeches, Correspondence and Political Papers of Carl Schurz*, vol. 2 (New York, 1913): 361–369, 377–378, 384. Thurlow Weed, a veteran politician, said: "Six weeks ago I did not suppose that any considerable number of men, outside of a Lunatic Asylum, would nominate Greeley for President."

9. After attacking slavery and the South, Greeley softened in the face of secession and argued that the North should let the South seceded peacefully. After the war began, he advised Lincoln to make peace with the South, largely on its terms. He then advocated vigorous prosecution of the war. Finally, he tacked again, and prematurely suggested the North open peace negotiations with the South, and tried to block Lincoln's renomination.

10. *Harper's Weekly*, May 24, 1884, 326.

11. *New York Times*, March 6, 1884, 5; April 1, 1884, 8; May 13, 1884, 2.

12. John A. Garraty, *The New Commonwealth, 1877–1890* (Harper & Row, 1968).

13. George E. Mowry, *The Era of Theodore Roosevelt: 1900–1912* (New York: Harper & Brothers, 1958), 38–45; Lewis L. Gould, "The Republicans Under Roosevelt and Taft," in Gould ed. *The Progressive Era* (Syracuse, NY: Syracuse University Press, 1974); Lewis L. Gould, *The Modern American Presidency* (Lawrence: University of Kansas Press, 2003), 35–38; Paolo E. Coletta, *The Presidency of William Howard Taft* (Lawrence: University of Kansas Press, 1973); Harlan Hahn, "President Taft and the Discipline of Patronage," *Journal of Politics* 28 (1966): 368–390; George E. Mowry, "Election of 1912," in Arthur M. Schlesinger, Jr. ed., *The History of American Presidential Elections, 1789–1968*, vol. 3 (New York: Chelsea House Publishers, 1971), 2135–2166.

14. Sidney M. Milkis, *Theodore Roosevelt, The Progressive Party, and the Transformation of American Democracy* (Lawrence: University of Kansas Press, 2009).

15. Rosenstone, et al., *Third Parties in America*, 81–88.

16. George E. Mowry, "The Election of 1912," in *History of American Presidential Elections*, ed. Arthur M. Schlesinger, Jr., vol. 3 (New York: Chelsea House Publishers, 1971), 2140–2141.

17. On progressive Republicans' attempts to increase the number of primaries as a delegate selection method to increase the chances of La Follete or Roosevelt's nomination, see Ceaser, *Presidential Selection*, 217–227.

18. Amos Pinchot, *History of the Progressive Party, 1912–1916* (New York: New York University Press, 1958), 172, 226–227.

19. Cited in William T. Leuchtenburg, *The White House Looks South: Franklin D. Roosevelt, Harry S. Truman, and Lyndon B. Johnson* (Baton Rouge: Louisiana State University Press, 2005), 75.

20. Sarah McCulloh Lemmon, "The Ideology of the 'Dixiecrat' Movement," *Social Forces*, 30, no. 2 (December 1951): 162–171; Dan T. Carter, *The Politics of Rage* (New York: Simon & Shuster, 1995); Richard S. Kirkendall, "Election of 1948," in Arthur Schlesinger ed., *The History of America Presidential Elections*, vol. 4 (New York: McGraw-Hill, 1976); David S. Broder, "Election of 1968," in Arthur Schlesinger ed., *The History of America Presidential Elections*, vol. IV (New York: McGraw-Hill, 1976); Kari Fredrickson, *The Dixiecrat Revolt and the End of the Solid South, 1932–1968* (Chapel Hill: University of North Carolina Press, 2001); Earl Black and Merle Black, *The Vital South: How Presidents Are Elected* (Cambridge: Harvard University Press, 1992).

21. Audio of Thurmand's speech can be heard at: http://www.npr.org/templates/story/story.php?storyId=865900 (accessed September 23, 2010).

22. David A. Horowitz, *Beyond Left & Right: Insurgency & the Establishment* (Urbana: University of Illinois Press, 1997), 291–293.

Chapter 6

1. "Toward a More Responsible Two-Party System: A Report of the Committee on Polit-ical Parties," *American Political Science Review* 3 (1950). For the vast literature written in response to the Schattschneider report, see the website created by the APSA's Orga-nized Section on Political Organizations and Parties: http://www.apsanet.org/~pop/APSA_Report.htm.

2. Gary W. Cox and Mathew D. McCubbins, *Legislative Leviathan: Party Government in the House* (Berkeley: University of California Press, 1993); *Setting the Agenda: Responsible Party Government in the U.S. House of Representatives* (New York: Cambridge University Press, 2005); David W. Rohde, *Parties and Leaders in the Postreform House* (Chicago: University of Chicago Press, 1991); Keith Krehbiel, "Where Is the Party?" *British Jour-nal of Political Science* 23, no. 2 (1993), 235–266; Krehbiel, *Pivotal Politics: A Theory of U.S. Lawmaking* (Chicago: University of Chicago Press, 1998); Steven S. Smith, *Party Influence in Congress* (New York: Cambridge University Press, 2007).

3. Walter Dean Burnham, *Critical Elections and the Mainsprings of American Politics* (New York: W.W. Norton & Co., 1970); Everett Carll Ladd and Charles D. Hadley, *Transfor-mations of the American Party System: Political Coalitions from the New Deal to the 1970s,* 2nd ed. (New York: W.W. Norton & Co., 1978); James L. Sundquist, *Dynamics of the Party System: Alignment and Realignment of Political Parties in the United States* (Wash-ington, DC: Brookings Institution, 1983); John Aldrich, *Why Parties? The Origin and Transformation of Political Parties in America* (Chicago: University of Chicago Press, 1995); Marc J. Hetherington and William J. Keefe, *Parties, Politics, and Public Policy in America,* 10th ed. (Washington, DC: CQ Press, 2007).

4. Howard Scarrow, "The Function of Political Parties: A Critique of the Literature and Approach," *Journal of Politics* 29, no. 4 (1967): 770–790.

5. Charles O. Jones, *The United States Congress: People, Place, and Policy* (Homewood, CA: Dorsey Press, 1982), 237.

6. James L. Sundquist, *Dynamics of the Party System: Alignment and Realignment of Polit-ical Parties in the United States* (Washington, DC: Brookings Institution, 1983); Nel-son W. Polsby, *How Congress Evolves: Social Bases of Institutional Change* (New York: Oxford University Press, 2004); Sarah Binder, *Minority Rights, Majority Rule: Parti-sanship and the Development of Congress* (New York: Cambridge University Press, 1997); Schickler, *Disjointed Pluralism*; Julian E. Zelizer, *On Capitol Hill: the Struggle to Reform Congress and its Consequences, 1948–2000* (New York: Cambridge Univer-sity Press, 2004); Thomas Mann and Norman Ornstein, *The Broken Branch: How Con-gress Is Failing America and How to Get it Back on Track* (New York: Oxford University Press, 2006).

7. John Gerring, "The Mechanismic Worldview: Thinking Inside the Box," *British Journal of Political Science* 37 (2007); "What Is a Case Study and What Is It Good for?" *American Political Science Review* 98, no. 2 (May 2004); *Social Science Methodology: A Critical Framework* (Cambridge: Cambridge University Press, 2001); Alexander L. George and Andrew Bennett, *Case Studies and Theory Development* (Cambridge: MIT Press, 2005).

8. Terry M. Moe, "Power and Political Institutions," *Perspectives on Politics* 3, no. 2 (June 2005): 215–233.

9. Gary W. Cox and Mathew D. McCubbins, *Legislative Leviathan: Party Government in the House* (Berkeley: University of California Press, 1993); Cox and McCubbins, *Legisla-tive Leviathan*; Cox and McCubbins, *Setting the Agenda: Responsible Party Government in the U.S. House* (New York: Cambridge University Press, 2005).

10. Ronald J. Peters, Jr., *The American Speakership: The Office in Historical Perspective,* 2nd ed. (Baltimore: Johns Hopkins University Press, 1997).

11. James L. Sundquist, *Decline and Resurgence of Congress* (Washington, DC: Brookings Institution, 1982), 164.

12. Claude G. Bowers, *Beveridge and the Progressive Era* (New York: Literary Guild, 1932), 321.

13. Eric Schickler, *Disjointed Pluralism: The Institutional Innovation and the Development of the U.S. Congress* (Princeton: Princeton University Press, 2001), 54; Robert Harrison, *Congress, Progressive Reform, and the New American State* (New York: Cambridge University Press, 2004), 156–191.

14. Evans C. Johnson, *Oscar W. Underwood: A Political Biography* (Baton Rouge: Louisiana State University Press, 1980).

15. Randall B. Ripley, *Party Leaders in the House of Representatives* (Washington, DC: Brookings Institution, 1967), 56.

16. Sundquist, *Decline and Resurgence of Congress*, 168–176.

17. James L. Sundquist, *Politics and Policy: The Eisenhower, Kennedy, and Johnson Years* (Washington, DC: Brookings Institution, 1968), 512–522; Sundquist, *Decline and Resurgence of Congress*, 157–162, 176–187; Julian E. Zelizer, *On Capitol Hill: The Struggle to Reform Congress and its Consequences, 1948–2000* (New York: Cambridge University Press, 2004), 33–65.

18. Michael Foley, *The New Senate: Liberal Influence on a Conservative Institution, 1959–1972*, (New Haven: Yale University Press, 1980).

19. Mark. F. Ferber, "The Formation of the Democratic Study Group," in *Congressional Behavior*, ed. Nelson Polsby (New York: Random House, 1971); Kenneth Kofmehl, "The Institutionalization of a Voting Bloc," *Western Political Quarterly* 17 (June 1964); Arthur G. Stevens, et al., "Mobilization of Liberal Strength in the House, 1955–1970: The Democratic Study Group," *American Political Science Review* 68 (June 1974): 667–681.

20. Zelizer, *On Capitol Hill*, 33–62.

21. Bruce J. Dierenfield, *Keeper of the Rules: Howard W. Smith of Virginia* (Charlottesville: University of Virginia Press, 1987).

22. Charles O. Jones, "Joseph Cannon and Howard Smith: An Essay on the Limits of Leadership in the House of Representatives," *Journal of Politics* 30 (August 1968); James A. Robinson, *The House Rules Committee* (Indianapolis: Bobbs-Merrill, 1963), 24–25; Robert V. Remini, *The House: The History of the House of Representatives* (Washington, DC: Smithsonian Books, 2006), 359–388; Sundquist, *Decline and Resurgence of Congress*, 183–185; Zelizer, *On Capitol Hill*, 3–32, 56–60.

23. Nelson Polsby, *How Congress Evolves: The Social Bases of Institutional Change* (New York: Oxford University Press, 2004), 20–36; Zelizer, *On Capitol Hill*, 28, 56–61, 234–236; Mark C. Shelley, *The Permanent Majority: The Conservative Coalition in the United States Congress* (Tuscaloosa: University of Alabama Press, 1983); John F. Manley, "The Conservative Coalition in Congress," *American Behavioral Scientist* 17 (1973).

24. "Deep Divisions Loom behind House GOP's Apparent Unity," *CQ Weekly Report*, March 23, 1985, 535–539.

25. William F. Connelly, Jr., and John J. Pitney, Jr., *Congress' Permanent Minority?: Republicans in the U.S. House* (Lanham, MD: Rowman & Littlefield Publishers, 1994) 7; Charles O. Jones, *The Minority Party in Congress* (Boston: Little & Brown, 1970), 5.

26. Dick Williams, *Newt! Leader of the Second American Revolution* (Marietta, GA: Longstreet Press, 1995), 98–110; John M. Barry, *The Ambition and the Power* (New York: Viking Press, 1989), 212–252, 362–372; Dan Balz and Ronald Brownstein, *Storming the Gates: Protest Politics and the Republican Revival* (Boston: Little, Brown, 1996), 113–130.

27. Nigel Ashford, "The Contract and Beyond: The Republican Policy Agenda," in Alan Grant ed., *American Politics: 2000 and Beyond* (London: Ashgate, 2000), 167–189. Armey also persuaded the House leadership to publish a follow-up book to the Contract called *Restoring the Dream*, and appointed his former assistant and Cato Institute economist Stephen Moore as editor. Armey's own book, *The Freedom Revolution*, was very

antigovernment, calling for cutting the size of government in half and ending mid-dle-class entitlements such as Social Security. On the Contract, see John B. Bader, *Taking the Initiative: Leadership Agendas in Congress and the "Contract with America"* (Washington, DC: Georgetown University Press, 1996); Nicol Rae, *Conservative Reformers: The Republican Freshman and the Lessons of the 104th Congress* (Armonk, NY: M.E. Sharpe, 1998), 37–44.

28. John E. Owen, "Taking Power? Institutional Change in the House and Senate," in Dean McSweeny and John E. Owen eds., *The Republican Takeover of Congress* (New York: St. Martin's Press, 1998), 57; Douglas L. Koopman, *Hostile Takeover: The House Republican Party, 1980–1995* (Lanham, MD: Rowman & Littlefield, 1996), 31–59; Rae, *Conservative Reformers*, 18–23.

29. Cited in Justus D. Doenecke, *The Presidencies of James A. Garfield & Chester A. Arthur* (Lawrence: Kansas University Press, 1981), 12.

30. William S. White, *The Citadel: U.S. Senators and Their World* (New York: Harper Bros., 1957).

31. *Congressional Record*, House of Representatives, January 10, 1940, 248.

32. Rae, *Southern Democrats*, 65–110; William S. White, *The Citadel: U.S. Senators and Their World* (New York: Harper Bros., 1957); Sean Farhang and Ira Katznelson, "The Southern Imposition: Congress and Labor in the New and Fair Deals," *Studies in American Political Development* 19 (2005): 1–30; Ira Katznelson, Kim Geiger, and Daniel Kryder, "Limiting Liberalism: The Southern Veto in Congress, 1933–1950," *Political Science Quarterly* 108 (Summer 1993): 296–297; Ira Katznelson, *When Affirmative Action Was White: An Untold History of Racial Inequality in Twentieth Century America* (New York: W.W. Norton & Co., 2005); Robert C. Lieberman, *Shifting the Color Line: Race and the American Welfare State* (Cambridge: Harvard University Press, 1998); Lieberman, *Shaping Race Policy: The United States in Comparative Perspective* (Princeton: Princeton University Press, 2005); Michael K. Brown, *Race Money, and the American Welfare State* (Ithaca, NY: Cornell University Press, 1999); Mary Poole, *The Segregated Origins of Social Security: African-Americans and the Welfare State* (Chapel Hill: University of North Carolina Press, 2006); Barbara Hinckley, *The Seniority System in Congress* (Bloomington: Indiana University Press, 1971); Nelson Polsby, Miriam Gallaher, and Barry Spencer Rundquist, "The Growth of the Seniority System in the U.S. House of Representatives," *American Political Science Review* 63 (September 1969): 787–807; George Goodwin, Jr., "The Seniority System in Congress," *American Political Science Review* 53 (June 1959): 418–420; Joseph Cooper, *Congress and Its Committees: A Historical Approach to the Role of Committees in the Legislative Process* (New York: Garland, 1988); Richard Fenno, *Congressmen in Committees* (Boston: Little, Brown, 1973).

33. Julian E. Zelizer, *On Capitol Hill: The Struggle to Reform Congress and Its Consequences, 1948–2000* (New York: Cambridge University Press, 2004), 33–38.

34. John F. Manley, "The Conservative Coalition in Congress," *American Behavioral Scientist* 17 (1973): 223–247; Mark C. Shelley, *The Permanent Majority: The Conservative Coalition in the United States Congress* (Tuscaloosa: University of Alabama Press, 1983), 104–107.

35. Manley, "The Conservative Coalition in Congress," 231–232.

36. Michael K. Brown, *Race, Money, and the American Welfare State* (Ithaca, NY: Cornell University Press, 1999), 110–131.

37. Kenneth W. Hechler, *Insurgency* (New York: Columbia University Press, 1940), 27–82; James L. Holt, *Congressional Insurgents and the Party System* (Cambridge: Harvard University Press, 1967); John D. Baker, "The Character of the Congressional Revolution of 1910," *Journal of American History* 60 (December 1973); Charles O. Jones, "Joseph Cannon and Howard Smith: An Essay on the Limits of Leadership in the House of Representatives," *Journal of Politics* 30 (August 1968).

38. David W. Rohde, *Parties and Leaders in the Postreform House,* (Chicago: University of Chicago Press, 1991), 4.
39. Eric Schickler, *Disjointed Pluralism: Institutional Innovation and the Development of the U.S. Congress* (Princeton: Princeton University Press, 2001), 75.
40. This development runs counter to the theory and practice of multiparty systems, where dominant subunits tend to expand by cooptation or pressure to increase the avenues of career advancement. See W.R. Schonfeld, "La Stabilité des Dirigeants des Parties Politiques," *Revue Française de Science Politique* 30, no. 4 (1980): 477–504. Rothman, *Politics and Power,* pp.15–28; Sarah Binder, *Minority Rights, Majority Rule: Partisanship and the Development of Congress* (New York: Cambridge University Press, 1997), 19–42, 167–201.
41. William G. Shade et al., "Partisanship in the United States Senate: 1869–1901," *Journal of Interdisciplinary History* 4 (Autumn 1973): 185–205; Jerome M. Clubb and Santa A. Traugott, "Partisan Cleavage and Cohesion in the House of Representatives, 1861–1974," *Journal of Interdisciplinary History* 7 (Winter 1977): 395–396; Carl V. Harris, "Right Fork or Left Fork? The Section-Party Alignments of Southern Democrats in Congress, 1873–1897," *Journal of Southern History* (November 1976): pp. 471–506. For an opposing view, see Keith T. Poole and Howard Rosenthal, *Congress: A Political-Economic History of Roll-Call Voting* (New York: Oxford University Press, 1997), 83.
42. Nicol C. Rae, *The Decline and Fall of the Liberal Republicans* (New York: Cambridge University Press, 1989), 167–168, 172–173.
43. David Hess and Stephen Broder, *The Republican Establishment: The Present and Future of the GOP* (New York: Harper & Row, 1967), 23.
44. Barbara Sinclair, *Congressional Realignment, 1932–1978* (Austin: University of Texas Press, 1982).
45. Mark Kady, "Party Unity," *CQ Weekly* (2005).

Chapter 7

1. Daniel Galvin, "The Dynamics of Presidential Policy Choice and Promotion," in Martin Levin, Daniel DiSalvo, and Martin Shapiro, eds., *Building Coalitions, Making Policy* (Baltimore: Johns Hopkins University Press, 2012).
2. David W. Brady and Craig Volden, *Revolving Gridlock* (Boulder, CO: Westview, 1998); Keith Krehbiel, *Pivotal Politics* (Chicago: University of Chicago Press, 1998); William Howell, *Power Without Persuasion: A Theory of Unilateral Action* (Princeton: Princeton University Press, 2003); Kenneth Mayer, *With the Stroke of a Pen: Executive Orders and Presidential Power* (Princeton: Princeton University Press, 2001); Terry Moe and William Howell, "A Theory of Unilateral Action," *Presidential Studies Quarterly* 29 (1999).
3. Paul E. Peterson, "The President's Dominance in Foreign Policy Making," *Political Science Quarterly* 109 (1994): 215–234; Steven Shull, ed., *The Two Presidencies: A Quarter Century Assessment* (Chicago: Nelson-Hall, 1991); Aaron Wildavsky, "The Two Presidencies," *Trans-Action* 4 (1966): 7–14.
4. Sidney M. Milkis, *The President and the Parties: The Transformation of the American Party System Since the New Deal* (New York: Oxford University Press, 1993); Daniel Galvin, *Presidential Party Building: Dwight D. Eisenhower to George W. Bush* (Princeton: Princeton University Press, 2010).
5. Paul Brace and Barbara Hinckley, *Follow the Leader: Opinion Polls and the Modern Presidents* (New York: Basic Books, 1992); Brandice Canes-Wrone and Scott de Marchi, "Presidential Approval and Legislative Success," *Journal of Politics* 64 (2002): 491–509; Charles W. Ostrom, Jr. and Dennis M. Simon, "Promise and Performance: A Dynamic Model of Presidential Popularity," *American Political Science Review* 79 (1985): 334–358; Brandice Canes-Wrone, *Who Leads Whom? Presidents, Policy, and the Public* (Chicago: University of Chicago Press, 2006).

6. The first group is headed by Richard Neustadt, *Presidential Power and the Modern Presidents* (New York: Free Press, 1990). The second group includes Samuel Kernell, *Going Public: New Strategies of Presidential Leadership*, 3rd ed. (Washington DC: CQ Press, 1997); Jeffrey K. Tulis, *The Rhetorical Presidency* (Princeton: Princeton University Press, 1988); Theodore Lowi, *The Personal Presidency: Power Invested, Promise Unfulfilled* (Ithaca, NY: Cornell University Press, 1985); Joseph M. Bessette, *The Mild Voice of Reason: Deliberative Democracy and American National Government* (Chicago: University of Chicago Press, 1994).

7. Kernell, *Going Public*; Canes-Wrone, *Who Leads Whom?*; Elvin T. Lim, *The Anti-Intellectual Presidency: The Decline of Presidential Rhetoric from George Washington to George W. Bush* (New York: Oxford University Press, 2008).

8. George C. Edwards III, *On Deaf Ears: The Limits of the Bully Pulpit* (New Haven: Yale University Press, 2003).

9. Tulis, *Rhetorical Presidency*; Bessette, *Mild Voice of Reason*.

10. Canes-Wrone, *Who Leads Whom?*

11. Neustadt, *Presidential Power and the Modern Presidents*; Charles O. Jones, *The Presidency in a Separated System* (Washington, DC: Brookings Institution, 1994).

12. There is some uncertainty in the scholarship on whether presidents' monitoring of public opinion induces them to follow it. Some scholars argue that the president is not very responsive to public opinion. Jeffrey E. Cohen, *Presidential Responsiveness and Public Policy-Making: The Public and the Policies Presidents Choose* (Ann Arbor: University of Michigan Press, 1997); Lawrence R. Jacobs and Robert Y. Shapiro, *Politicians Don't Pander: Political Manipulation and the Loss of Democratic Responsiveness* (Chicago: University of Chicago Press, 2000). Other scholars find that the president is responsive to public opinion. John G. Geer, *From Tea Leaves to Opinion Polls* (New York: Columbia University Press, 1996); Robert S. Erikson, Michael B. MacKuen, and James A. Stimson, *The Macro Polity* (Cambridge: Cambridge University Press, 2002); Canes-Wrone, *Who Leads Whom?*

13. George C. Edwards, *The Strategic President: Persuasion & Opportunity in Presidential Leadership* (Princeton: Princeton, 2009), 11–13.

14. Lyndon Johnson quoted in Doris Kearns, *Lyndon Johnson and the American Dream* (New York: Harper & Row, 1976), 226.

15. Neustadt, *Presidential Power*, x.

16. Byron Shafer, "The Partisan Legacy: Are there any New Democrats? (And by the way, was there a Republican Revolution?)," in C. Campbell and Bert Rockman, eds., *The Clinton Legacy* (New York: Chatham House), 1–32; John Ferejohn, "A Tale of Two Congresses: Social Policy in the Clinton Years," in Margaret Weir, ed., *The Social Divide: Political Parties and the Future of Activist Government* (Washington, DC: Brookings Institution Press, 1998), 49–82; Alex Waddan, *Clinton's Legacy? A New Democrat in Governance* (New York: Palgrave, 2002); Baer, *Reinventing Democrats*; William Galston, "Incomplete Victory: The Rise of the New Democrats," in Peter Berkowitz ed., *Varieties of Progressivism* (Stanford: Hoover Institution Press, 2004).

17. Stephen Skowronek, *The Politics Presidents Make: Leadership from John Adams to Bill Clinton* (Cambridge: Harvard University Press, 1993), 33–59; Jones, *Presidency in a Separated System*, 48–51.

18. George F. Hoar, *Autobiography of Seventy Years*, vol. 2 (New York: Scribner's, 1903), 46.

19. James Bryce, *The American Commonwealth*, vol. 3 (London: Macmillan, 1888), 533.

20. On Hayes's relationship with GOP machine politicians, see Vincent DeSantis, *Republicans Face the Southern Question: The New Departure Years, 1877–1897* (Baltimore: Johns Hopkins Press, 1959), 105–106, 112–113, 118–119; Ari Hoogenboom, *Outlawing the Spoils: A History of the Civil Service Reform Movement* (Urbana: University of Illinois Press, 1961); 155–178; Hirshson, *Farewell to the Bloody Shirt*, 27–62; H. Wayne Morgan, *From Hayes to McKinley: National Party Politics, 1877–1896* (Syracuse, NY: Syracuse

University Press, 1969), 26, 31–39; Morgan, "The Republican Party," in Schlesinger ed., *History of American Political Parties*, 1420–1422; Allan Peskin, "Was There a Compromise of 1877?" *Journal of American History* 60 (June 1973): 73–74; Keith Polakoff, *The Politics of Inertia* (Baton Rouge: Louisiana State University Press, 1973), 106–107, 157–163, 232–314, 317; Morton Keller, *Affairs of State: Public Life in Late Nineteenth-Century America* (Cambridge: Harvard University Press, Belknap Press, 1977), 264–265; Hoogenboom, *The Presidency of Rutherford B. Hayes* (Lawrence: University of Kansas Press, 1988), 22–23, 32–33, 36, 56, 127–151; Goldman, *The National Party Chairmen*, 123; Reichley, *The Life of the Parties*, 155–156; Hoogenboom, *Hayes: Warrior and President* (Lawrence: University of Kansas Press, 1995), 318–325, 350–356, 361–363, 370–377, 378–383, 407–413.

21. Roscoe Conkling, "Address to the New York State Republican Convention," Rochester, NY (1876).

22. Rutherford B. Hayes, *Diary and Letters*, July 14, 1880, Charles R. Williams, ed., 5 vols. (Columbus: Ohio State Historical Society, 1922–1926), 612–3.

23. *The Nation* (December 13–20, 1877): 357, 373.

24. "The President's Present Position as Described by Himself," *Nation* 6 (December 1877): 342.

25. Ari Hoogenboom, "Spoilsmen and Reformers: Civil Service Reform and Public Morality," in H. Wayne Morgan ed., *The Gilded Age: A Reappraisal* (Syracuse, NY: Syracuse University Press 1963), 69–90.

26. As one historian put it, "Guiteau's bullet killed more than a president." Morgan, *From Hayes to McKinley*, 142; Martin Shefter, *Political Parties and The State: The American Historical Experience* (Princeton: Princeton University Press, 1994); Leonard D. White, *The Republicans: A Study in Administrative History, 1869–1901* (New York: Macmillan, 1958); A.B. Sageser, *The First Two Decades of the Pendleton Act* (Lincoln: University of Nebraska Press, 1935).

27. On Arthur's relationship with the Stalwarts during his presidency, see Hoogenboom, *Outlawing the Spoils*, 215–238; Morgan, *From Hayes to McKinley*, 149–173; Doenecke, *Presidencies of Garfield and Arthur*, 75–76, 96–104.

28. Robert M. La Follette, *La Follette's Autobiography: A personal narrative of political experiences* (Wisconsin: The Robert M. La Follette Co., 1911).

29. Lewis L. Gould, *The Presidency of Theodore Roosevelt* (Lawrence: University of Kansas Press, 1991), 12.

30. Roosevelt cited in H.W. Brands, *TR: The Last Romantic* (New York: Basic Books, 1997), 424.

31. Theodore Roosevelt to William Howard Taft, March 19, 1903, *The Letters of Theodore Roosevelt*, vol. 3, ed. Elting Morison (Cambridge: Harvard University Press, 1953), 450.

32. Sindey M. Milkis, *Theodore Roosevelt, the Progressive Party, and the Transformation of American Politics* (Lawrence: University of Kansas Press, 2009), 29.

33. George E. Mowry, *The Era of Theodore Roosevelt: 1900–1912* (New York: Harper & Brothers, 1958), 38–45.

34. Gabriel Kolko, *The Triumph of Conservatism: A Reinterpretation of American History, 1900–1916* (New York: Free Press, 1963); James Weinstein, *The Corporate Ideal in the Liberal State, 1900–1918* (Boston: Beacon Press, 1968); Ari Hoogenboom and Olive Hoogenboom, *A History of the ICC* (New York: W.W. Norton, 1976), 12–17, 159–189.

35. Elizabeth Sanders, *The Roots of Reform: Farmers, Workers, and the American State, 1877–1917* (Chicago: University of Chicago Press, 1999), 199; Richard H.K. Vietor, "Businessmen and the Political Economy: The Railroad Rate Controversy of 1905," *Journal of American History* 64 (June 1977): 47–66.

36. Roosevelt to Lyman Abbott, July 1, 1906, Elting Morison ed., *Letters of Theodore Roosevelt*, vol. 5 (Cambridge: Harvard University Press, 1953), 328.

37. Dolliver quoted in Gould, *Modern American Presidency*, 37.

38. Arthur S. Link, *Woodrow Wilson and the Progressive Era* (New York: Harper & Row, 1963).

39. Gould, *Modern American Presidency*, 41.

40. Republican Party Platform (1908), http://www.presidency.ucsb.edu/ws/index.php?pid=29632#axzz1SkV17VHP (accessed July 21, 2011).

41. Taft's tilt toward the Old Guard faction began during the 1908 campaign, when he learned many Progressives had urged Roosevelt to run again. He feared that many might vote for Bryan as the heir to Roosevelt and that they would not support his administration. Therefore, Taft encouraged Elihu Root to work for the selection of conservative Senators. The Old Guard faction interpreted Taft's victory a signal to slow the pursuit of Roosevelt's agenda, if not an outright repudiation of the president. In addition, because Taft was forced to campaign against the progressive-sounding Bryan, he naturally appeared even more conservative. Paolo E. Coletta, "Election of 1908," in *History of American Presidential Elections*, vol. 3, ed. Arthur M. Schlesinger, Jr. (New York: Chelsea House Publishers, 1971); Taft to Elihu Root, August 15, 1908; Lewis L. Gould, "The Republicans Under Roosevelt and Taft," in Lewis L. Gould, ed. *The Progressive Era* (Syracuse, NY: Syracuse University Press, 1974), 76.

42. William H. Taft, *The President and His Powers: The United States and Peace*, edited with commentary by W. Carey McWilliams and Frank X. Gerrity (Athens: Ohio University Press, 2003); Mowry, *Era of Theodore Roosevelt*, 236; Paolo E. Coletta, *The Presidency of William Howard Taft* (Lawrence: University of Kansas Press, 1973).

43. Harlan Hahn, "President Taft and the Discipline of Patronage," *Journal of Politics* 28 (1966): 368–390. A provocative analysis that locates patronage parties at the centre of Progressive Era party reform initiatives (at least as regards the direct primary) is in Alan Ware, *The American Direct Primary: Party Institutionalization and Transformation in the North* (New York: Cambridge University Press, 2002).

44. Norman M. Wilensky, *Conservatives in the Progressive Era: The Taft Republicans of 1912* (Gainesville: University of Florida Press, 1965), 4–6.

45. Link, *Woodrow Wilson and the Progressive Era*, 26–29; A. James Reichley, *The Life of the Parties: A History of American Political Parties* (Lanham, MD: Rowman & Littlefield, 1992), 189–190.

46. Quoted in John Morton Blum, *The Progressive Presidents: Theodore Roosevelt, Woodrow Wilson, Franklin D. Roosevelt, Lyndon Johnson* (New York: W.W. Norton, 1980), 67.

47. Woodrow Wilson to W.G. McAdoo, November 17, 1914, printed in the *New York Times*.

48. Wilson's letter provoked a strong reaction from Herbert Croly in *The New Republic*. See Croly, "Presidential Complacency," *New Republic*, November 21, 1914.

49. William T. Leuchtenberg, *The White House Looks South: Franklin D. Roosevelt, Harry S. Truman, and Lyndon B. Johnson* (Baton Rouge: Louisiana State University Press, 2005), 2.

50. Brown, *Race, Money, and the American Welfare State*, 100–134; Schulman, *Cotton Belt to Sunbelt*, 116–117, 123–131.

51. Sundquist, *Politics and Policy*, 472

52. Theodore C. Sorensen, *Kennedy* (New York: Harper & Row, 1965), 346–340. For a list of successes and failures of Kennedy's program, see *Congressional Quarterly Almanac, 1962*, 82–91; Arthur M. Schlesinger, Jr., *A Thousand Days* (New York: Houghton Mifflin, 1965), 713.

53. John F. Kennedy to Anthony Celebrezze, Memo, May 6, 1963, copy, Health, Education, and Welfare, 1963 folder, JFK papers. For a detailed account of these legislative defeats, see James N. Giglio, *The Presidency of John F. Kennedy*, 2nd ed. (Lawrence: University of Kansas Press, 2006), 99–108.

54. *Congressional Quarterly Almanac*, 1962, 68.

55. Julian Zelizer, *Taxing America: Wilbur Mills, Congress, and the State, 1945–1975* (New York: Cambridge University Press, 1998), 212–218; Sundquist, *Politics and Policy*, 180–195 (elementary and secondary education), 254–265 (civil rights), 308–317 (Medicare), 471–481.

56. Eisenhower cited in Vaughn Davis Borney, *The Presidency of Lyndon B. Johnson* (Lawrence: University of Kansas Press, 1983), 95.

57. Lyndon B. Johnson, "State of the Union Address," January 8, 1964, http://www.pbs.org/wgbh/amex/presidents/36_l_johnson/psources/ps_union64.html (accessed July 21, 2011).

58. Borney, *Presidency of Lyndon B. Johnson*, 51–62, 94–100.

59. Joseph Califano, *A Presidential Nation* (New York: Norton, 1975), 215.

60. Borney, *Presidency of Lyndon B. Johnson*, 130.

61. Eric F. Goldman, *The Tragedy of Lyndon Johnson* (New York: Knopf, 1969), 332.

62. Taylor Dark, *Labor and the Democratic Party: An Enduring Alliance* (Ithaca, NY: Cornell University Press, 1999), 55.

63. Borney, *Presidency of Lyndon B. Johnson*, 222.

64. Borney, *The Presidency of Lyndon B. Johnson*, 118–121.

65. J. David Greenstone, *Labor in American Politics, Labor in American Politics* (Chicago: University of Chicago Press, 1969), chap. 10.

66. Congressional Quarterly, *Congress and the Nation*, vol. 2, *1965–1968* (Washington, DC: CQ Press, 1969), 601.

67. Transcript of President's remarks of November 7, 1956, in *Public Papers of the President: Dwight D. Eisenhower, 1956* (Washington, D.C: National Archives, 1958), 1090.

68. Quoted in Daniel J. Galvin, *Presidential Party Building: Dwight D. Eisenhower to George W. Bush* (Princeton: Princeton University Press, 2009), 62.

69. See Fred I. Greenstein, *The Hidden Hand Presidency: Eisenhower as Leader* (New York: Basic Books, 1982).

70. Cornelius Cotter, "Eisenhower as Party Leader," *Political Science Quarterly* 98 (1983), 256.

71. Nicol Rae, *The Decline and Fall of the Liberal Republicans* (Cambridge: Oxford University Press, 1989), 40–41.

72. Galvin, *Presidential Party Building*, 55–57, 63–67.

73. Ibid, 67.

74. Greenstein, *Hidden Hand Presidency: Eisenhower as Leader*, 58–72.

75. Samuel Lubell, *The Revolt of the Moderates* (New York: Harper & Brothers, 1956), 96.

76. James L. Sundquist, *Politics and Policy: The Eisenhower, Kennedy, and Johnson Years* (Washington, DC: Brookings Institution, 1968), 15–34.

77. Quoted in Lewis L. Gould, *The Grand Old Party* (New York: Random House, 2003), 342.

78. Chester J. Pach, Jr. and Elmo Richardson, *The Presidency of Dwight D. Eisenhower* (Lawrence: University of Kansas Press, 1991), 76–81, 82–104, 168–169.

79. Victor Lasky, *Jimmy Carter: The Man and the Myth* (New York: R. Marek, 1979); Burton I. Kaufman, *The Presidency of James Earl Carter Jr.* (Lawrence: Kansas University Press, 1993); Erwin Hargrove, *Jimmy Carter as President: Leadership and the Politics of the Public Good* (Baton Rouge: Louisiana State University Press, 1988).

80. Cited in Al Gordon, "Public Interest Lobbies: Nader and Common Cause Become Permanent Fixtures," *Congressional Quarterly Weekly Report*, May 15, 1976, 1197.

81. Sidney M. Milkis, *Political Parties and Constitutional Government: Remaking American Democracy* (Baltimore: Johns Hopkins University Press, 1999), 119.

82. Richard M. Scammon and Ben J. Wattenberg, "Jimmy Carter's Problem," *Public Opinion* (March/April 1978).

83. David Vogel, *Fluctuating Fortunes: The Political Power of Business in America* (New York: Basic Books, 1989), 148–149.

84. Juan Cameron, "Nader's Invaders Are Inside the Gates," *Fortune*, October 1977, 253.

85. Susan Hartmann, "Feminism and Public Policy," in *The Carter Presidency: Policy Choices in the Post-New Deal Era* (Lawrence: University of Kansas Press, 1998), 224–243.

86. Sean Wilentz, *The Age of Reagan: A History, 1974–2008* (New York: HarperCollins, 2008), 89.

87. Donald T. Critchlow, *The Conservative Ascendancy: How the Political Right Made History* (Cambridge: Harvard University Press, 2008), 162–166.
88. Galvin, *Presidential Party Building*, 120–142.
89. Critchlow, *Conservative Ascendancy*, 187.
90. Charles Kolb, *White House Daze: The Unmaking of Domestic Policy in the Bush Years* (New York: Free Press, 1994), 11.
91. John Podhoretz, *Hell of a Ride: Backstage at the White House Follies, 1989–1993* (New York: Simon & Schuster, 1993), 157.
92. John Micklethwait and Adrian Wooldridge, *The Right Nation: Conservative Power in America* (New York: Penguin Press, 2004), 98–99.
93. Quoted in Michael Duffy and Dan Goodgame, *Marching in Place: The Status Quo Presidency of George Bush* (New York: Simon & Schuster, 1992), 82.
94. For an analysis of the partisan logic of Clinton's governing strategy, see Sidney M. Milkis, *Political Parties and Constitutional Government* (Baltimore: Johns Hopkins University Press, 1999), 157–173.
95. Theda Skocpol, *Boomerang: Clinton's Health Security Effort and the Turn Against Government* (New York: W.W. Norton, 1996).
96. John Ferejohn, "A Tale of Two Congresses: Social Policy in the Clinton Years," in Margaret Weir, ed., *The Social Divide: Political Parties and the Future of Activist Government* (Washington, DC: Brookings Institution Press, 1998), 49–82.
97. Al From and Will Marshall, "The First 100 Days," *The New Democrat* (May 1993), 4–7.
98. For an excellent analysis of the politics of welfare reform, see R. Kent Weaver, *Ending Welfare as we Know it* (Washington DC: Brookings Institution, 2000), 206–207, 228–248, 274–289, 296–297, 300–303.
99. Cited in Jules Witcover, *Party of the People: A History of the Democrats* (New York: Random House, 2003), 683.
100. Alex Waddan, *Clinton's Legacy? A New Democrat in Governance* (New York: Palgrave, 2002).
101. James David Barber, *Presidential Character: Predicting Performance in the White House*, 4th ed. (New York: Pearson Logman, 2008).
102. Richard Neustadt, *Presidential Power*, 1990 ed. (New York: Wiley, 1960), 4.
103. Galvin, "The Dynamics of Presidential Policy Choice and Promotion," in Levin, DiSalvo, and Shaprio, eds., *Building Coalitions, Making Policy*.

Chapter 8

1. *State building* is the technical term used to describe this historical process in which new governing institutions are created or strengthened, existing institutions are expanded or reinforced, and the relationship between government and society is altered.
2. There is a rough consensus among scholars on the broad principles of state development. See Richard Bensel, *Yankee Leviathan: The Origins of Central State Authority, 1859–1877* (New York: Cambridge University Press, 1990), 106–114; Peter B. Evans, Dietrich Rueschemeyer, and Theda Skocpol, "On the Road toward a More Adequate Understanding of the State," in *Bringing the State Back In* (Cambridge; Cambridge University Press, 1985); Stephen Skowronek, *Building a New American State: The Expansion of National Administrative Capacities* (New York: Cambridge University Press, 1982), vii–x, 3–46; Theda Skocpol and Kenneth Finegold, "State Capacity and Economic Intervention in the Early New Deal," *Political Science Quarterly* 97 (Summer 1982): 255–278.
3. This analysis is similar to the scheme presented by Bensel in *Yankee Leviathan*, 114.
4. Scott C. James, *Presidents, Parties, and the State: A Party System Perspective on Democratic Regulatory Choice, 1884–1936* (New York: Cambridge University Press, 2000).

5. Elizabeth Sanders, *Roots of Reform: Framers, Workers, and the American State, 1877–1917* (Chicago: University of Chicago Press, 1998).

6. I thank Vince Boudreau for helping me develop this point.

7. For the state-centered position, see Theda Skocpol and Kenneth Finegold, "Explaining New Deal Labor Policy," *American Political Science Review* 84 (December 1990): 127–311. For the society-centered position, see Michael Goldfarb's rejoinder.

8. For a summary of this view, see Christopher Howard, *The Welfare State Nobody Knows* (Princeton: Princeton University Press, 2007), 13–25.

9. Peter Baldwin, *The Narcissism of Minor Differences: How America and Europe are Alike* (New York: Oxford University Press, 2009).

10. Martin Shefter, *Political Parties and the State: The American Historical Experience* (Princeton: Princeton University Press, 1994), 61.

11. H. Wayne Morgan, *From Hayes to McKinley: National Party Politics, 1877–1896* (Syracuse, NY: Syracuse University Press, 1968), 70; Morton Keller, *Affairs of State: Public Life in Late Nineteenth-Century America* (Cambridge: Harvard University Press, Belknap Press, 1977), 266–267; Justus D. Doenecke, *The Presidencies of James A. Garfield and Chester A. Arthur* (Lawrence: Regents Press of Kansas, 1981), 13–14; and Xi Wang, *Trial of Democracy: Black Suffrage and the Northern Republicans, 1860–1910* (Athens: University of Georgia Press 1996), 142.

12. Cited in John G. Sproat, *The Best Men: Liberal Reformers in the Gilded Age* (Oxford University Press, 1967), 45.

13. Theda Skocpol, *Protecting Soldiers and Mothers: The Political Origins of Social Policy in the United States* (Cambridge: Harvard University Press 1992), 83.

14. Ibid., 102–153.

15. A. James Reichley, *The Life of the Parties* (Lanham, MD: Rowman & Littlefield, 1999), 120–131; David J. Rothman, *Politics and Power: The United States Senate, 1869–1901*, 2nd ed. (Cambridge: Harvard University Press, 1965), 26–36.

16. Keller, *Affairs of State*.

17. Richard Bensel, *The Political Economy of Industrialization, 1877–1900* (New York: Cambridge University Press, 2000), 457–509.

18. Richard Bensel, *Sectionalism in American Political Development, 1880–1980* (Madison: University of Wisconsin Press), 62–73.

19. Bensel, *Political Economy of Industrialization*, 468.

20. Roscoe Conkling, "Speech at the New York State Republican Convention" in Alfred R. Conkling ed., *The Life and Letters of Roscoe Conkling: Orator, Statesman, Advocate* (New York: Charles L. Webster and Co., 1889), 540–542.

21. http://teachingamericanhistory.org/library/index.asp?document=607 (accessed, July 18, 2011).

22. Robert Harrison, *Congress, Progressive Reform, and the New American State* (New York: Cambridge University Press, 2003), 240–254.

23. Most historians conclude that this legislation enabled the ICC to finally bring the railroads under control by the outbreak of World War I. Sanders, *Roots of Reform*, 208; Ari Hoogenboom and Olive Hoogenboom, *History of the ICC: From Panacea to Palliative* (New York: W.W. Norton, 1976), 66, 73–80; Frank Dixon, *Railroads and Government: Their Relations in the United States, 1910–1921* (New York: Scribner's, 1922), 103.

24. William Jennings Bryan, "Speech Delivered at Notification Meeting," New York, August 12, 1896. Nebraska Historical Society, Box 2, Folder 5.

25. Elizabeth Sanders, "Industrial Concentration, Sectional Competition, and Antitrust Politics in America, 1880–1890," *Studies in American Political Development* 1 (1986): 142–214.

26. Seward Livermore, *Politics Is Adjourned: Woodrow Wilson and the War Congress: 1916–1918* (Middletown, CT: Wesleyan University Press, 1966).

27. Vaughn Davis Borney, *The Presidency of Lyndon B. Johnson* (Lawrence: University of Kansas Press, 1983), 233.
28. Ibid., 224.
29. Wilson, "New Politics, New Elites, Old Publics," 249–267.
30. David Vogel, *Fluctuating Fortunes: The Political Power of Business in America* (New York: Basic Books, 1989), 146.
31. Robert A. Kagan, *Adversarial Legalism: The American Way of Law* (Cambridge: Harvard University Press, 2003); Nathan Glazer, "Towards an Imperial Judiciary," *The Public Interest* 4 (Fall 1975): 104–123.
32. James Q. Wilson "New Politics, New Elites, Old Publics," in Marc K. Landy and Martin A. Levin, ed., *The New Politics of Public Policy* (Baltimore: Johns Hopkins University Press, 1995), 88–98 251.
33. Robert A. Kagan, "Adversarial Legalism and American Government," in Marc K. Landy and Martin A. Levin, eds., *The New Politics of Public Policy* (Baltimore: Johns Hopkins University Press, 1995), 88–98; Kagan, *Adversarial Legalism: The American Way of Law* (Cambridge: Harvard University Press, 2002), 34–60.
34. Kagan, *Adversarial Legalism*, 61–79, 159–228; Karen Orren, "Standing to Sue: Interest Group Conflict in the Federal Courts," *American Political Science Review* 70 (September 1976): 723–741.
35. For example, the Head Start program involved parents in day-to-day activities of the child care centers. Peter Skerry, "The Charmed Life of Head Start," *The Public Interest* 73 (Fall 1983). See also, R. Shep Melnick, *Regulation and the Courts: The Case of the Clean Air Act* (Washington, DC: Brookings Institution, 1983); Melnick, *Between the Lines: Welfare Rights in Court* (Washington, DC: Brookings Institution, 1994).
36. Joan B. Aron, "Citizen Participation at Public Expense," *Public Administration Review* 39, no. 5 (September/October 1979): 477–485; Heclo, "Issue Networks in the Executive Establishment"; Marc Landy, Marc Roberts, and Stephen Thomas, *The Environmental Protection Agency: Asking the Wrong Questions* (New York: Oxford University Press, 1990); Marc K. Landy, "The New Politics of Environmental Policy," in Marc K. Landy & Martin A. Levin, eds., *The New Politics of Public Policy* (Baltimore: Johns Hopkins University Press, 1995), 207–227.
37. Kagan, *Adversarial Legalism*, 34–60.
38. Sidney M. Milkis, *Political Parties and Constitutional Government: Remaking American Democracy* (Baltimore: Johns Hopkins University Press, 1999), 119.
39. David Stockman, "The Social Pork Barrel," *The Public Interest* 39 (Spring 1975): 3–30.
40. *Congressional Globe*, 39th Congress, 2nd Session, 1867, 838–839.
41. George Curtis, "The Evil and the Remedy," *Harper's Weekly*, October 7, 1871, 930.
42. Rutherford B. Hayes, "Inaugural Address," March 5, 1877.
43. James Garfield, "Inaugural Address," March 4, 1881.
44. Curtis quoted in Frank Stewart, *The National Civil Service Reform League* (Austin: University of Texas Press, 1929), 13; also cited in Skowronek, *Building a New American State*, 54.
45. Henry Adams, "Civil Service Reform," *North American Review* 190, 225 (October 1869), 456.
46. Ibid, 75.
47. Gabriel Kolko, *The Triumph of Conservatism: A Reinterpretation of American History, 1900–1916* (New York: Free Press, 1963); James Weinstein, *The Corporate Ideal in the Liberal State, 1900–1918* (Boston: Beacon Press, 1968).
48. Hoogenboom and Hoogenboom, *History of the ICC*, 12–17, 159–189.
49. Theodore Roosevelt, "Message to Congress," 1904, in *The Works of Theodore Roosevelt: State Papers as Governor and President, 1899–1909* (New York: Scribner's 1926), 226.
50. Skowronek, *Building a New American State*, 254.

51. Congressional Quarterly, *Congress and the Nation, 1945–1964* (Washington, DC: CQ Press, 1965), 1245.

52. Donald Howard, *The WPA and Federal Relief Policy* (New York, 1941), 162–163, 771; George Tindall, *The Emergence of the New South, 1938–1980* (Baton Rouge: Louisiana State University Press, 1967), 483–484.

53. Glass quoted in James T. Patterson, *Congressional Conservatism and the New Deal: The Growth of the Conservative Coalition in Congress, 1933–1939* (Lexington: University of Kentucky Press, 1967), 257.

54. Norman J. Ornstein, Thomas E. Mann, and Michael J. Malbin, *Vital Statistics on Congress, 1989–1990* (Washington, DC: American Enterprise Institute, 1990), 11–12, 15–16.

55. George Goodwin, Jr., "The Seniority System in Congress," *American Political Science Review* 52 (June 1959): 418–420.

56. Ira Katznelson, Kim Geiger, and Daniel Kryder, "Limiting Liberalism: The Southern Veto in Congress, 1933–1950," *Political Science Quarterly* 108 (Summer 1993): 296–297.

57. Barbara Hinckley, *The Seniority System in Congress* (Bloomington: Indiana University Press, 1971); Nelson Polsby, Miriam Gallaher, and Barry Spencer Rundquist, "The Growth of the Seniority System in the U.S. House of Representatives," *American Political Science Review* 63 (September 1969): 787–807; George Goodwin, Jr., "The Seniority System in Congress," *American Political Science Review* 53 (June 1959): 418–420; Joseph Cooper, *Congress and Its Committees: A Historical Approach to the Role of Committees in the Legislative Process* (New York: Garland, 1988); Richard Fenno, *Congressmen in Committees* (Boston: Little, Brown, 1973).

58. William S. White, *Citadel: The Story of the U.S. Senate* (New York: Harper Bros., 1957), 67–79; Donald R. Matthews, *U.S. Senators and Their World* (New York: Vintage Books, 1960), 92–117.

59. Michael Foley, *The New Senate: Liberal Influence on a Conservative Institution 1959–1972* (New Haven: Yale University Press, 1980), 2.

60. Morris P. Fiorina, *Representatives, Roll Calls, and Constituencies* (Lexington, KY: Lexington Books, 1974).

61. Edward L. Schapsmeier and Frederick H. Schapsmeier, "Farm Policy from FDR to Eisenhower: Southern Democrats and the Politics of Agriculture," *Agricultural History* 53 (1979): 352, 355.

62. Richard Fenno, *Homestyle* (Boston: Little Brown, 1978); John Kingdon, *Congressmen's Voting Decisions* (New York: Harper and Row, 1973); David Mayhew, *Congress: The Electoral Connection* (New Haven: Yale University Press, 1974).

63. Nelson Polsby, "Coalition and Faction in American Politics: An Institutional View," in Seymour Martin Lipset, ed., *Emerging Coalitions in American Politics* (San Francisco: Institute for Contemporary Studies, 1978): 103–126.

64. Southern Democrats were veto players in the sense identified by George Tsebelis in *Veto Players: How Political Institutions Work* (Princeton: Princeton University Press, 2002).

65. Daniel Berman, *In Congress Assembled: The Legislative Process in the National Government* (New York: Macmillan Co., 1964).

66. Cited in John F. Manley, "The Conservative Coalition in Congress," *American Behavioral Scientist* 17 (1973), 231–232.

67. Mark C. Shelley, *The Permanent Majority: The Conservative Coalition in the United States Congress* (Tuscaloosa: University of Alabama Press, 1983), 104–107. Shelley argues that the conservative coalition appeared more often and was more frequently successful in policy terms when Republicans controlled the White House, suggesting that Southern Democrats joined Republicans to take positive action, and not simply to block the initiatives of Democratic presidents.

68. Charles O. Jones, *The Minority Party in Congress* (Boston: Little, Brown, 1970).
69. Michael K. Brown, *Race, Money, and the American Welfare State* (Ithaca, NY: Cornell University Press, 1999), 100.
70. Ira Katznelson, *When Affirmative Action Was White: An Untold History of Racial Inequality in Twentieth Century America* (New York: W.W. Norton & Co., 2005). Southern Democrats also sought to circumscribe labor legislation so as to keep agricultural labor unregulated by the central state. In this, they were not alone: in the "marriage of corn and cotton," during the New Deal, "[t]he impact of the southern bloc in Congress was augmented considerably by the implementation of a strategic voting alliance with Midwesterners." Schapsmeier and Schapsmeier, "Farm Policy from FDR to Eisenhower," 352, 355. Robert Lieberman has argued that the occupational exclusions in the Social Security Act of 1935 were inserted at southern insistence, entwining racial considerations in the welfare state.
71. Robert C. Lieberman, *Shifting the Color Line: Race and the American Welfare State* (Cambridge: Harvard University Press, 1998). Gareth Davies and Martha Derthick have criticized this argument, arguing that there are other reasons why farm workers and domestic workers were excluded. See "Race and Social Welfare Policy: The Social Security Act of 1935," *Political Science Quarterly* 112 (1997).
72. Katznelson, *When Affirmative Action Was White*, 43.
73. Lieberman, *Shifting the Color Line*, 113–117. The expansion of Social Security to include agricultural workers and domestic servants—who were disproportionately black—occurred primarily with the 1954 amendment to the Social Security Act. This step was taken under unified Republican control of the national government, which briefly displaced Southern Democrats influence over the policy. See Brown, *Race, Money, and the American Welfare State*, 129–131; Lieberman, "Race and the Organization of Welfare Policy," in Paul Peterson, ed., *Classifying by Race* (Princeton: Princeton University Press, 1995), 171–176.
74. *New Republic* 102 (May 20, 1940): 664–666.
75. *Congressional Record*, 76th Congress, 1st session (1939), 84: 9582.
76. Ira Katznelson and Sean Farhang, "The Southern Imposition: Congress and Labor in the New and Fair Deals," *Studies in American Political Development* 19 (2005): 1–30.
77. Cited in Katznelson, *When Affirmative Action Was White*, 60.
78. In addition, the now-minority Democratic Party had grown more dependent on the fidelity of its southern members, who represented a greater proportion of the party in the 80th Congress than they had in a quarter century. Bensel, *Sectionalism and American Political Development*, 381–385.
79. Farhang and Katznelson, "The Southern Imposition," 15.
80. Barbara Griffith, *The Crisis of American Labor: Operation Dixie and the Defeat of the CIO* (Philadelphia: Temple University Press, 1988).
81. Bruce Bartlett, "'Starve the Beast': Origins and Development of a Budgetary Metaphor," *The Independent Review* (Summer 2007): 5–26.
82. Ronald Reagan, "First Inaugural Address," (January 1981).
83. Ronald Reagan, "Farewell Address," (January 1989).
84. Bryan D. Jones and Walter Williams, *The Politics of Bad Ideas* (New York: Pearson Longman, 2008), ix.
85. C. Eugene Steuerle, *The Tax Decade: How Taxes Came to Dominate the Public Agenda* (Washington, DC: The Urban Institute Press, 1992); see also C. Eugene Steuerle, *Contemporary U.S. Tax Policy* (Washington, DC: The Urban Institute Press, 2004).
86. Newt Gingrich, "The Battle Plan for Business in Politics: Stand Firm," *Nation's Business* (April, 1983), 30–32.
87. William Voegeli, *Never Enough: America's Limitless Welfare State* (New York: Encounter Books, 2010), 206.

88. Ronald Reagan, "State of the Union Address," January 26, 1982.

89. Paul Pierson, *Dismantling the Welfare State? Reagan, Thatcher, and the Politics of Retrenchment* (New York: Cambridge University Press, 1994), 120–122.

90. Juliet Eilperin, "Few Democrats Are Likely to Back House Tax Bill," *Washington Post*, March 6, 2001, A8.

91. On the founding of the COS, see Dick Williams, *Newt! Leader of the Second American Revolution* (Marietta, GA: Longstreet Press, 1995), 98–110.

92. Nigel Ashford, "The Contract and Beyond: The Republican Policy Agenda," in Alan Grant, ed., *American Politics: 2000 and Beyond* (London: Ashgate, 2000): 167–189. On the Contract, see John B. Bader, *Taking the Initiative: Leadership Agendas in Congress and the "Contract with America"* (Washington, DC: Georgetown University Press, 1996); Rae, *Conservative Reformers*, 37–44.

93. R. Kent Weaver, *Ending Welfare as we Know it* (Washington DC: Brookings Institution, 2000).

94. In general, scholars have placed the Half-Breeds between the Liberals and the Stalwarts. That is the approach taken here. Lewis L. Gould, *The Grand Old Party* (New York: Random House, 2003), 93–97; Eidson, "Who Were the Stalwarts?" 242, 247; Peskin, "Who Were the Stalwarts?" 712; Norman E. Tutorow, *James Gillespie Blaine and the Presidency: A Documentary Study and Source Book* (New York: Peter Lang, 1989), 7–8; Silbey, *The American Political Nation*, 231; See also Justus D. Doenecke, *The Presidencies of James A. Garfield and Chester A. Arthur* (Lawrence: Regents Press of Kansas, 1981),13–14.

95. Mark D. Hirsch, "Election of 1884," in Arthur J. Schlesinger, ed., *History of American Presidential Elections*, vol. 2 (New York: Chatham House, 1972), 1562.

96. Morgan, *From Hayes to McKinley*.

97. Quoted in Gould, *Grand Old Party*, 334–335.

98. Stephen Hess and David Broder, *The Republican Establishment: The Present and Future of the GOP* (New York: Harper & Row, 1967), 21.

99. William H. Whyte, *The Organization Man* (New York: Simon & Shuster, 1956).

100. Byron E. Shafer, *The Two Majorities and the Puzzle of Modern American Politics* (Lawrence: University of Kansas Press, 2003), 143–156.

101. Democratic Leadership Council, "The New Democrat Credo," January 1, 2001. See also, William Clinton, "The New Covenant: Responsibility and the Rebuilding of the American Community," Washington, DC, October 23, 1991.

102. Kenneth Baer, *Reinventing Democrats* (Lawrence: University of Kansas Press, 2000), 75–92, 94–109.

103. David R. Mayhew, "Much Huffing and Puffing, Little Change," in Martin A. Levin, Marc K. Landy, and Martin Shapiro, eds., *Seeking the Center: Politics and Policymaking at the New Century* (Washington, DC: Georgetown University Press, 2001), 339–349.

104. David Broder, "The Blue Dogs and the Block Party," *Washington Post*, August 6, 2009.

Chapter 9

1. Maurice Duverger, *Les Partis Politiques* (Paris: Colin, 1951).

2. The modification to Duverger's law proposed here is distinct from the critique offered by William Riker. See "The Number of Political Parties: A Reexamination of Duverger's Law," *Comparative Politics* 9, no. 1 (October 1976): 93–106; Riker, "The Two Party System and Duverger's Law: An Essay on the History of Political Science, *American Political Science Review* 76 (December, 1982): 753–766.

3. James L. Sundquist had this insight long ago but never fully developed it or drew out all of its implications. See Sundquist, *Dynamics of the Party System: Alignment and Realignment of Political Parties in the United States* (Washington, DC: Brookings Institution, 1973).

4. David R. Mayhew, *Electoral Realignments: A Critique of an American Genre* (New Haven: Yale University Press, 2002); Everett Carll Ladd, "Like Waiting for Godot: The Uselessness of 'Realignment' for Understanding Change in Contemporary American Politics," in Byron Shafer, ed., *The End of Realignment?* (Madison: University of Wisconsin Press, 1991).

5. For policy change driven by experts, judges, and bureaucrats, see R. Shep Melnick, *Between the Lines: Interpreting Welfare Rights* (Washington, DC: Brookings Institution Press, 1994); Melnick, *Regulation and the Courts: The Case of the Clean Air Act* (Washington, DC: Brookings Institution, 1983); See also Marc Landy, Marc Roberts, and Stephen Thomas, *The Environmental Protection Agency: Asking the Wrong Questions* (New York: Oxford University Press, 1990); Marc K. Landy, "The New Politics of Environmental Policy," in Marc K. Landy & Martin A. Levin, eds., *The New Politics of Public Policy* (Baltimore: Johns Hopkins University Press, 1995); Robert A. Kagan, *Adversarial Legalism: The American Way of Law* (Cambridge: Harvard University Press, 2002); Benjamin Ginsberg and Martin Shefter, *Politics By Other Means: The Declining Importance of Elections in America* (New York: Basic Books, 1990).

6. Edmund Burke, "Thoughts on the Cause of the Present Discontents (1780)," in *Select Works of Edmund Burke*, E.J. Payne ed., (Indianapolis: Liberty Fund, 1999).

7. APSA Report, "Toward a More Responsible Two-Party System: A Report of the Committee on Political Parties" *American Political Science Review* 44, no. 3, (1950). See also E.E. Schattschneider, *Party Government* (New York: Holt, 1942).

8. Paul S. Herrnson, "Why the United States does not have responsible parties," *Perspectives on Political Science* 21, no. 2 (Spring 1992): 91–98.

9. Geoffrey C. Layman, et al, "Party Polarization in American Politics: Characteristics, Causes, and Consequences," *Annual Review Political Science* 9 (2006), 83–110; Nolan McCarty, Keith T. Poole, and Howard Rosenthal, *Polarized America: The Dance of Ideology and Unequal Riches* (Cambridge: MIT Press, 2002); Jeffrey Stonecash, Mark Brewer, and Mack Mariani, *Diverging Parties: Social Change, Realignment, and Party Polarization* (Boulder, CO: Westview Press, 2003); Barbara Sinclair, *Party Wars: Polarization and the Politics of National Policymaking* (Norman: University of Oklahoma Press, 2006); Pietro Nivola and David Brady, eds., *Red and Blue Nation: Consequences and Corrections of America's Polarized Politics*, vols. 1 & 2 (Washington, DC: Brookings Institution, 2007).

10. Ronald Brownstein, *The Second Civil War: How Extreme Partisanship Has Paralyzed Washington and Polarized America* (New York: Penguin Press, 2007).

11. Analysts continue to debate the breadth and depth of these divisions. Two views have emerged on the issue. Morris Fiorina argues that the "Red-Blue" schema forced journalists and scholars into a binary mode of thought, encouraging them to see stark division where none really exists. Although polarization is a fact of life for the politically engaged, Fiorina insists that it doesn't touch average citizens. Polarization exists only among the political class, primarily inside the Washington Beltway, but not among "normal" Americans. Morris Fiorina, Samuel Abrams, and Jeremy Pope, *What Culture Wars? The Myth of Political Polarization in America* (New York: Longman, 2004); Morris Fiorina and Samuel J. Abrams, "Political Polarization in the American Public," *Annual Review of Political Science* 11 (2008): 563–588. The other view argues that polarization has penetrated deeply into the mass public; where it may well have emerged in the first place. James Q. Wilson, "How Divided Are We?" *Commentary* (February 2006); Alan Abramowitz and Kyle Saunders, "Can't We All Just Get Along? The Reality of Polarized America," *The Forum: A Journal of Applied Research in Contemporary Politics* 3, no. 2 (2005); Alan Abramowitz, *The Disappearing Center: Engaged Citizens, Polarization, and American Democracy* (New Haven: Yale University Press, 2010); James Q. Wilson, "How Divided Are We?" *Commentary* (February 2005); Gary Jacobson, *A Uniter, Not a*

Divider: George Bush and the American People (New York: Pearson/Longman, 2007). Scholars have now taken up the issue of polarization, bringing to bare all the sophisticated statistical tools of modern political science. But as attention has focused on efforts to model and measure the contemporary situation, an historical perspective has been lost. Two exceptions to this trend are Alan Abramowitz and Kyle Sanders, "Can't We All Just Get Along? The Reality of Polarized America," *Forum* 3, no. 2, 2005.

12. Keith T. Poole, "The Decline and Rise of Party Polarization in Congress in the Twentieth Century," *Extensions* (Fall 2005): 2; David Brady and Hahrie Han, "Polarization Then and Now: A Historical Perspective," in Nivola and Brady, eds., *Red and Blue Nation? Consequences and Corrections of America's Polarized Politics* (Washington, DC: Brookings Institution, 2007).

13. Doug Schoen and Scott Rasmussen, *Mad as Hell: How the Tea Party Is Fundamentally Remaking Our Two Party System* (New York: Harper, 2010).

14. James W. Ceaser and John York, "Blaming It All on the Tea Party," Contentions blog, *Commentary*, http://www.commentarymagazine.com/2011/07/15/blaming-it-all-on-the-tea-party/ (accessed July, 18, 2011). See also, Kate Zernike, *Boiling Mad: Inside Tea Party America* (New York: Times Books, 2010); Jill Lepore, *The Whites of Their Eyes: The Tea Party Revolution and the Battle Over American History* (Princeton: Princeton University Press 2010); Eugene Robinson, "What's Behind the Tea Party's Ire?" *Washington Post*, November 2, 2010; Kate Zernike and Megan Thee-Brenan, "Poll Finds Tea Party Backers Wealthier and More Educated," *New York Times*, April 14, 2010; Peter Berkowitz, "Why Liberals Don't Get the Tea Party Movement," *Wall Street Journal*, October 16, 2010; Theda Skocpol and Vanessa Williamson, *The Tea Party and the Remaking of Republican Conservatism* (New York: Oxford University Press, 2011).

15. James Q. Wilson, "Divided We Stand," *Wall Street Journal*, February 15, 2006.

16. James Q. Wilson, "New Politics, New Elites, Old Publics," in Marc K. Landy and Martin A. Levin, eds., *The New Politics of Public Policy* (Baltimore: Johns Hopkins University Press, 1995), 249–267.

17. Sidney Blumenthal, *The Rise of the Counter-Establishment: From Conservative Ideology to Political Power* (New York: Harper & Row, 1985); Nils Gilman, "What the Rise of the Republicans as America's First Ideological Party Means for Democrats," *The Forum*, 2, no. 1, (2004); Byron Shafer, *The Two Majorities and the Puzzle of Modern American Politics* (Lawrence: Kansas University Press, 2004), 156–169; Milkis, *Political Parties and Constitutional Government: Remaking American Democracy* (Baltimore: Johns Hopkins University Press, 1999), 107–121.

18. R. Kent Weaver, "The Politics of Blame Avoidance," *Journal of Public Policy* 6 (1986), 371–398.

INDEX

abortion, 46, 58, 112, 135, 138, 141

Adams, Henry, 35, 161

affirmative action, 46, 56, 58, 135, 176

African-Americans, 14, 36, 54, 103, 155, 167, 183. *See also* affirmative action; civil rights movement; Reconstruction; Southern Democrats

Aid to Families with Dependent Children (AFDC), 171–173

Aldrich, John, xiv, 5–6, 26

Aldrich, Nelson, 14, 70, 101, 122–126, 154, 163–164

Allison, William, 14, 101, 122, 124, 163

amateur activists, 28, 62, 68, 75

American Civil Liberties Union (ACLU), 15

American Federation of Labor (AFL), 15

American Federation of Labor and Congress of Industrial Organization (AFL-CIO), xi, 80–82

American Independent Party, 87, 94

Americans for Democratic Action (ADA), xi, 15, 53, 81, 130, 156

Armey, Dick, 172–173, 217n27

Arthur, Chester A., 68–69, 106, 116–121, 161

Bachmann, Michele, 185

Baker, Howard, 137

Baker, James, 137

Bakker, Jim, 46

Ballinger, Richard, 126

Barkan, Al, 81

Bayh, Evan, 112

Belmont, August, 89

Bensel, Richard, 20, 148–150

Beveridge, Albert, 43, 101

Blaine, James G.: 1876 election and, 67; 1880 election and, 68; 1884 election and, 64, 66–67, 69, 87, 90; Garfield administration and, 119–120; Half-Breed Republicans and, 37; Liberal Republicans and, 87, 90; Stalwarts and, 66–67, 69

Blue Dog Democrats, 98, 112

Brandeis, Louis D., 127

Bristow, Benjamin, 67

Brock, William, 137

Brown, Jerry, 83, 85, 94

Brown, Joseph E., 36

Bryan, William Jennings: 1912 election and 73–74; Populist Democrats and, 13, 20, 48–49, 72–73, 127, 154; presidential nominations of, 63, 72–73

Buchanan, Pat, 79

Burke, Edmund, 21, 182

Burleson, Albert, 127

Bush, George H.W.: 1992 election and, 85; Congress and, 139; New Right Republicans and, 79, 138–140; nonfactionalized party and, 65–66, 116; tax policy and, 139

Bush, George W.: New Right Republicans and, 171–172; nonfactionalized party and, 66, 116; tax policy and, 171–172

Byrd, Harry, 165

Cameron, Simon, 67

Cannon, Joseph, 97, 100–102, 108, 122, 124, 126, 152–153, 181

Carnegie, Andrew, 38

Carter, Jimmy: 1976 election and, 13, 65, 94; affirmative action and, 135; New Democrats and, 58; New Politics Democrats and, 83–84, 134–136, 158; New Right Republicans and, 46; nonfactionalized party and, 116

Changing American Voter, The, 23–24

Chiles, Lawton, 56

Church, Frank, 83

civil rights movement and legislation, xi, 47, 94, 103, 130–131, 156, 166, 183

civil service reform, 27, 35, 67, 69, 89–90, 118–121, 148–151, 160–162, 183. *See also* patronage